UNEXPECTED CONSEQUENCES

UNEXPECTED CONSEQUENCES

Why the Things We Trust Fail

James William Martin

 PRAEGER

AN IMPRINT OF ABC-CLIO, LLC
Santa Barbara, California • Denver, Colorado • Oxford, England

Library of Congress Cataloging-in-Publication Data

Martin, James W. (James William), 1949–
    Unexpected consequences : why the things we trust fail / James William Martin.
        p. cm.
    Includes index.
    ISBN 978-0-313-39311-2 (hardcopy : alk. paper) — ISBN 978-0-313-39312-9
(ebook)   1. Product design—Social aspects.   2. Industrial design—Social
aspects.   3. Organizational behavior.   I. Title.
    TS171.M377   2011
    745.2—dc23   2011013411

ISBN: 978-0-313-39311-2
EISBN: 978-0-313-39312-9

15   14   13   12   11   1   2   3   4   5

This book is also available on the World Wide Web as an eBook.
Visit www.abc-clio.com for details.

Praeger
An Imprint of ABC-CLIO, LLC

ABC-CLIO, LLC
130 Cremona Drive, P.O. Box 1911
Santa Barbara, California 93116-1911

This book is printed on acid-free paper ∞

Manufactured in the United States of America

TABLE OF CONTENTS

PREFACE

My great concern is not whether you have failed, but whether you are content with your failure.

—Abraham Lincoln

On the morning of September 11, 2001, I was quietly sitting in a parked car listening to the radio. It was a sunny and peaceful morning in Massachusetts. However, the peace abruptly ended when the announcer began to report a series of newscasts describing attacks on the Twin Towers of the World Trade Center in New York City. I had just returned from a trip to New Jersey the previous Friday afternoon from consulting with Merrill Lynch. The previous year it had been American Express in New York City, and several of their locations around the United States. The financial community was located in close proximity. In fact, the corporate headquarters for American Express and Merrill Lynch were near to the World Trade Center. After returning home, television news showed two airplanes crashing, each in turn, into the Twin Towers, and the subsequent catastrophic collapse of the buildings. Estimates are that approximately 3,000 people were killed and another 6,000 injured. The deaths were primarily American, but estimates showed these deaths included more than 70 other countries. I wondered, "Did I know anyone who was killed?" Other attacks occurred at the Pentagon in Arlington, Virginia, and a fourth plane crashed in rural Pennsylvania. The day was filled with grief and loss.

Prior to the event I flew weekly to New Jersey to work with Merrill Lynch. However, when I arrived at the airport the Sunday after the 9/11 attacks to continue the work in New Jersey, the airport security lines stretched outside the terminal. Passengers were missing flights because of the delays caused by security. After that day, I stopped flying for six months, not out of fear, but because of logistical issues at the airports. Instead, I rented an automobile and began weekly trips to New Jersey, traveling down Interstate 95 and the New Jersey turnpike. Once on the New Jersey turnpike, in the distance across the water toward Manhattan, I could see a smoldering heap of rubble that formerly was the World Trade Center. Smoke rose from the rubble for months as I traveled past it twice a week to and from Merrill Lynch.

Merrill Lynch was busy the week after the 9/11 attacks. The stock market had lost significant amounts of equity. As I consulted with employees on operational improvement methods, upstairs, margin calls were being made. People can purchase equities such as stocks and mutual funds on credit, that is, margin. If the value of these securities is less than what is owed, people must pay money to cover the difference or margin. If they cannot pay, the equity is sold at a loss. The person who purchased the equity must repay the difference either using money or other funds. The atmosphere was tense because of margin calls and the 9/11 attacks. Some of the people I consulted with had lost relatives and others had neighbors whose relatives were killed on 9/11. It was a close-knit community stretching from New Jersey into Manhattan.

The airplanes used in the 9/11 attacks were hijacked by 19 terrorists. These terrorists brutally killed pilots, airline attendants, and passengers before crashing into their targets. After the fact, the identities of the hijackers were determined by the Federal Bureau of Investigation (FBI). Information was found in luggage left off one of the planes. The luggage belonged to the leader of the attacks, Mohammed Atta, an Egyptian. Eventually, after an exhaustive investigation, the FBI determined the attacks were planned and organized by al-Qaeda and its leader, Osama bin Laden. In the aftermath of the attacks and subsequent investigation by the 9/11 Commission, 10 years of war have been fought in Iraq and Afghanistan. Currently, the war in Afghanistan continues. Fortunately, no major terrorist attacks have since occurred within the United States.

The 9/11 terrorist attacks are an example of how things go wrong if disparate events align to cause failure. Several events led to the attacks, but no one was able to see the relationships, to connect the dots. As early as 1998, the Central Intelligence Agency (CIA) reported potential attacks within the United States and specifically the hijacking of aircraft. Through several months of news reports after 9/11, we learned some of the hijackers had trained with flight simulators and attended flight schools in the United

States. Others were already pilots when admitted to the United States. There were continued lapses of security. In hindsight it is easy to see the weak signals or warning signs that something very tragic was going to happen. But this failure of foresight is a common characteristic of catastrophic events. It is difficult to anticipate them and although initial responses are strong, people begin to forget. Then another catastrophic event occurs. This book discusses how we can more effectively anticipate or prevent catastrophic events or at least mitigate their impact. More can be done.

Another tragic event occurred in August of 2005, when Hurricane Katrina breached New Orleans's protective levees to devastate the city and surrounding areas. Thousands of people were impacted by the disaster. Over the ensuing weeks, more than 1,800 people died and property damage exceeded $100 billion.[1] Unfortunately, only minimal precautionary measures had been taken at local, state, and national levels, despite the fact that it was widely known there was significant risk if such a powerful hurricane struck in the region. Even five years after the catastrophic event, only minimal actions have been taken to upgrade regional logistical systems to provide more effective disaster relief if similar disasters reoccur. Bridges are collapsing; airplane accidents continually occur, and regulatory, health care, political, and other systems are strained. We know how to fix many of our problems, but why can't we anticipate these disasters?

It is suggested that resource constraints, technical limitations, and political or economic dysfunctions are some of the major reasons. These may be true for systems heavily influenced by political and economic interests as well as different perspectives of how to do things. Different perspectives cause people to disagree regarding identification of potential problems and solutions. Even if there is general agreement regarding problems and solutions, there may also be differences of opinion regarding resource prioritization. These differences limit the abilities of organizations to prevent or mitigate the effects of catastrophic events. In upcoming chapters, we will show that even if prevention measures and solutions are not in dispute, there are other contributors to failures.

This book is not technical in its content, but it does present simple and useful tools and methods to show how products and services are designed and can sometimes fail. These discussions are based on research from social psychology, including cognitive factors and group dynamics as well as organizational culture. One goal of this book is to integrate concepts within a generalized discussion of failure analysis and prevention. A second goal is to find commonality between diverse events to identify ways for analyzing and even preventing their occurrence—to prevent deaths, injuries, and property damage across the world.

The events were chosen at random. However, many of them have been in the news within the past several years. At first glance, many of them appear isolated or unique, but on further examination are seen to be similar in relief response, causal factors, and solutions. The events have also been heavily researched and footnoted. Examples include construction, electromechanical products, and service systems. Service systems include process applications within finance, health care, government, and numerous other industries and their functions. Catastrophic failures can occur within these systems. As an example, there have been failures of the San Francisco Bay Bridge repairs.[2] Also note the August 1, 2007, collapse of the I-35W Mississippi River Bridge (Minnesota),[3] the Air France flight 447's breakup over the Atlantic on June 10, 2009,[4] and Continental Connection Flight 3407, which crashed near Buffalo, New York, on February 12, 2009.[5] These flight accidents both occurred in 2009 and there were many others! As a further example, regulatory failures within the financial industry contributed to the 2009 financial crisis in which the worlds' major economies were almost destroyed.

Another major goal of this book is to understand why these catastrophic events occurred. As we explain these failures, you may be surprised to learn that they have much in common. Important additions to this book are the 2010 Deepwater Horizon explosion and the 2010 Haiti earthquake, which occurred while the book was being written. They provide useful lessons for why these events occur. As an example, the Deepwater Horizon explosion and subsequent Gulf of Mexico oil spill was not simply a technical failure. It was a series of error conditions that aligned to cause the explosion and subsequent environmental damage. Prior decisions and actions set the stage for the catastrophic event. The former British Petroleum (now BP), its partners, and the oil industry failed to create effective control technologies to match production technologies involved in deep-water drilling. Also, a regulatory vacuum existed because the oil industry, like many other industries, influenced how it was regulated by outside agencies. However, human errors were the most immediate causes of the Deepwater Horizon explosion. Misreading test results and failing to follow industry best practices certainly contributed to the horrific event. Nor was BP alone in making decisions; Halliburton and Transocean were also players. However, each organization's relative contributions to the accident have not been sorted out as of 2011. In other words, the causes for failure were many. On that day, several error conditions aligned, causing an explosion, deaths, and injuries on the drilling platform. Although the exact location and timing of the event could not have been predicted, the event should not have been unexpected given the associated risks.

In contrast, the 2010 Haiti earthquake had different causal factors than the Deepwater Horizon event. First, it was an unavoidable natural disaster caused by an earthquake. Second, its resultant damage was exacerbated by a poor building infrastructure as well as the delay in relief responses caused by the massive damage to Haiti's infrastructure (ships and planes could not land at damaged ports and airfields). Although the timing of the earthquake could not be anticipated, its destructive aftermath could have been predicted in advance because of the poor quality of infrastructure. The damage caused by the earthquake should not have been unexpected.

Sudden and catastrophic failures are caused by a myriad of factors including technology, human error, and organizational dysfunctions. The story of why the things we trust fail begins with a discussion of how products and services are designed, built, distributed, and used. Once built, distributed, and in use, our focus changes to understand how products and services actually perform within their application environments. Sometimes these environments are not known with certainty. Some important key topics will be discussed within the context of effective designs. These include life cycle analysis, the project management of design activities, the translation of customer requirements into specifications, functions, and features, and the impact of social psychological factors (e.g., cognitive factors) on the design of products, services, and logistical systems.

These topics will be discussed using more than 40 recent catastrophic events. Some of these events include the I-35W Mississippi River Bridge (Minnesota); the April 25, 1986, Chernobyl Reactor 4 disaster; the Denver International Airport baggage system delays; the 2009 Air France Flight 447 disaster; the 2010 Toyota recall; the Ford cruise switch control fires in the late 1990s; the 2001 Ford/Firestone tire failures 2001; the Anderson Systems and Products in Data Processing (SAP) Enterprise Resource Planning (ERP) issues with Fox-Meyer; food contamination; the 2003 Severe Acute Respiratory Syndrome (SARS) outbreak in Asia; the production problems with the H1N1 swine flu vaccine; chronic infectious and parasitic diseases worldwide; and the 2005 Hurricane Katrina event. Also, as previously mentioned, the 2010 Haiti earthquake and the 2010 Deepwater Horizon explosion events will be discussed relative to other failures.

You will find that this book uses a unique approach for the application of failure analysis in that its focus is not only explaining the reasons for the failure of structures and machines, but also for failure of service processes and logistical systems with applications to information technology, health care systems, regulatory agencies, and security and political systems, as well as natural disasters. The goal is to understand similarities and differences between the events to help manage future events.

Originally this book was to be a technical discussion of how products failed. But as it was researched, services and logistical processes were incorporated into its seven chapters. Also, as stories appeared in the news week after week, some of them were incorporated into the book until the types of events became very diverse. Then I was left with the task of integrating the many different events into a coherent whole. I was intrigued with a simple question: "How are they related and can future events be predicted and their consequences mitigated?" In chapters 6 and 7, answers are provided. I hope the discussions and explanations contained in this book will help prevent future deaths and injuries as well as property and environmental damage. If even one life is saved, the effort will have been worth it to me.

Few authors write books in isolation. Although a book is filled with the author's words, other people's support helps turn an idea into something tangible such as a book. Over many years, I have been helped first to become an engineer, a teacher, and finally a consultant. The years have been filled with learning and experiences that have shaped the concepts discussed in this book. I have also created new products and services and used those of others with mixed results ranging between the good, the bad, and the ugly. I have been delighted and very disappointed through these experiences. I have also worked with numerous organizations through the many consulting engagements across the world. Some of them include Ford and BP prior the tragic 2010 Gulf of Mexico explosion. It was only a coincidence that some of them were discussed in this book. They happened to be newsworthy and associated with more catastrophic events. Along the journey, I helped thousands of people improve products. These experiences are, in part, the basis for this book.

A book requires a good editor because authors have poor habits of different kinds. Editors are like coaches, who help keep the pace and goal in mind. I thank Brian Romer, my senior editor from Praeger Press, for providing feedback and encouraging me to write this book. Also, I thank Stan Wakefield, an independent editor, for helping me find the right publisher. Finally, I thank my family, including my wife Marsha, an accountant, and my children Krysta, an Emory Law School graduate, and my son Paul, a PhD candidate in computer security at Johns Hopkins, as well as the many clients who provided the inspiration for this book.

NOTES

1. Do Something.Org, *11 Facts About Hurricane Katrina*, http://www.dosome thing.org/tipsandtools/11-facts-about-hurricane-katrina.

2. "Bridge Fix Awaits Further Tests," *Wall Street Journal*, October 29, 2009, http://online.wsj.com/article/SB125673037933212851.html.

3. The Minnesota Department of Transportation, *Interstate 35W Bridge in Minneapolis*, http://www.dot.state.mn.us/i35wbridge.

4. Mark Sappenfield, "Air France Crash: What Is Known so far," *The Christian Science Monitor*, June 14, 2009.

5. David Saltonstall and Richard Sisk, "Official: Pilots in Buffalo Crash of Continental Connection Flight 3407 May Have Been Distracted," *New York Daily News*, May 14, 2009, nydailynews.com.

INTRODUCTION

Truth is always a delusion.

—Friedrich Durrenmatt

On the night of March 13, 1964, a woman's screams were heard in Queens, New York, by more than 10 witnesses who remained in their apartments during the attack. As she cried for help, one of the witnesses shouted out a window for the attacker to leave her alone. The attacker left and the woman staggered into her apartment building's hallway. But the attacker soon returned and found her lying in the hallway. She was then raped and beaten. Eventually, police were called for help, but she died on the way to the hospital. The woman's name was Kitty Genovese and her attacker was Winston Mosley, who was eventually convicted of the murder. Psychologists have studied this violent incident for more than 40 years in an attempt to understand why the witnesses did not immediately help the woman.[1]

A phenomenon called *diffusion of responsibility* occurs in situations where there are many people present without clearly defined roles and responsibilities. In these situations, each person thinks someone else will take responsibility, but, no one does. This phenomenon is dependent on group size. Interestingly, people who witness such events would take action if by themselves or in the company of only a few people because in these situations, personal responsibility is known and is easily communicated between individuals. Diffusion of responsibility also occurs in organizations and work teams with poorly defined roles and responsibilities. It is one of several cognitive influences affecting how people work and make decisions.

With other cognitive factors such as group attitudes and behaviors, organizational culture, and ethics, diffusion of responsibility influences how things are designed and used, and how they fail, in the context of available technologies. Attitudes and behaviors have a significant influence when creating and using products and services. They are also often causal factors of catastrophic failures.

People also directly and indirectly influence the complexity of products, services, and the systems used for design, production, and distribution. Complexity is caused by combinations of cognitive, group, and organizational influences in association with technologies and their use. Albert Einstein said, "Common sense is the collection of prejudices acquired by age eighteen." People accumulate prejudices (that is, biases) that distort the information they perceive, remember, and use. Some of the things we think are true are not.

Complexity creates a fog that makes it difficult to see risks and consequences. This increases the likelihood of failure. The Microsoft *Encarta Dictionary* defines it as "the condition of being difficult to analyze, understand, or solve . . . the condition of being made up of many interrelated parts."[2] It occurs when people, machines, equipment, and management systems are brought together and coordinated for work or other activities. Complexity is also exacerbated by great distance, unfamiliar cultures, different languages, the use of leading-edge technologies, the types of work performed, the machines and equipment employed, and the application environments in which these things are used by people, machines, and systems. Depending on the alignment of risks such as failure recurrence for each component of the scenario, the resultant failures may be catastrophic and deadly when these error conditions align.

The effects of complexity are commonly seen as undocumented work activities, poorly trained workers, little or no performance measurements, dangerous working environments that incur such problems as fatigue, near misses almost causing failure, frequent changes to work procedures, and complicated instructions and controls. There are many others. Complexity overwhelms people, creating conditions in which even the easiest activities become difficult to do for lack of time and resources. Energy levels alternate between low levels if overwhelmed to high levels because of uncontrolled stress. Poor prioritization of work activities is another characteristic of complex work environments. Nothing seems to get done or the wrong things get done. However, an obvious sign that complexity has overwhelmed a system is catastrophic failure.

What are some solutions? An easy answer would be to say, "Simplify, standardize, and mistake proof everything and all the time." These are important activities. They are effective preventive strategies, but they may not be enough. There are also other effective tools and methods for helping reduce complexity. But, depending on the system, catastrophic failures may still occur. These methods provide partial solutions. A clear sign they are not enough is repeated failure.

One major reason for high complexity is an over-reliance on technologies rather than social psychological influences. Important details can also be lost when translating customer and stakeholder requirements to design products, services, buildings, infrastructure, and other systems including logistics. These systems can fail for purely nontechnical reasons; an example would be airplane accidents caused by the pilot's perceptual errors, fatigue, or poor maintenance. A higher number of deaths, injuries, and damage to property and the environment are caused by human and organizational errors and mistakes than technology. This book attempts to answer an important question: "Why do things fail?" The answer would be difficult if failures were considered in isolation. However, supposedly isolated and other types of failures such as project failures, chronic failures, and natural or man-made events have much in common. Considering them together will help identify commonality of cause and effective solutions.

It is interesting that the United States does not have a coordinated policy to ensure dependable and cost-effective sources of energy over the next several decades. There are several energy options such as oil and gas, ethanol blends, coal, solar, wind, nuclear energy, and geothermal energy. Each option has advantages and disadvantages, relative to efficiency and cost, depending on the application. However, most experts agree that combinations of energy sources are likely to be the best long-term policy. Conservation is also an important consideration and one that is often neglected. Arguments can be made regarding assumptions and solutions; but an indisputable fact is that a sole reliance on oil will result in scarcity and higher cost under current consumption rates. However, converting to solar or wind energy will be more costly in the short term and limited to certain regions of the world. There must be an optimum combination of energy sources for various geographies to supply energy over the next several decades.

An examination of per capita energy usage would find that countries in very cold or hot climates use more energy than other countries. An exception is the United States, which is on par with countries in more extreme environments. Other major industrial countries are near the 75th quartile. China is near the 50th quartile and India is near the 25th quartile. Of course there are other relevant factors such as number of people, level of industrialism, and geography that affect per capita usage. Complicating a solution are the enormous infrastructure costs associated with making changes in percentages and amounts of alternative energy sources as well as the systems necessary to migrate to them. These costs include laws and regulations to change behaviors, identification of specific delivery systems, and specific solutions, such as cogeneration of power, changes in building design, increasing public awareness, promoting green vehicles, retrofitting buildings to reduce energy losses, and employing unique ways to reduce energy (e.g., telecommuting). It's a very complicated list of options. However, a solution begins with gathering facts, rather than opinions, and creating a long-range plan that integrates all available options. Other than the logistics and planning challenges, why is this difficult? The answer lies principally with individuals and organizations whose influences, for good and bad, create the unnecessary complexity preventing a holistic solution.

Why can't people and organizations objectively determine a best energy policy? Attitudes and behaviors at individual and group levels are part of the problem. Another part is special interests that fight for their constituents' use of different sources of energy. A third element is high absolute consumption patterns in major industrialized countries such as the United States and Europe, and now China and India, to increase living standards. The effects are becoming apparent via higher prices and scarcity of supply as economies around the world recover from the recent recession. People are oblivious to the consequences of their individual and group behaviors in the context of the world's competition for energy.

A recurring theme in this book will be how people perceive risk relative to its magnitude (or payout) and likelihood of occurrence (probability). People consider risk from different perspectives. Some avoid risk while others enjoy taking it. Those who take risk often prefer high risk and higher payouts. This fact has been repeatedly proven to be true in the gaming industry. These attitudes and behaviors have consequences. People also have difficulty evaluating very low probabilities. If you ask a person if he prefers a 10 percent chance of winning $10,000 or a 1 percent chance of winning $100,000, he would chose the $100,000 payout option. However both expected payouts are the same: $1,000. Unfortunately, the same thinking is applied to other risks and consequences in the real world. In later chapters we will show that people relate more to immediate rather than long-term risks and consequences. This makes it difficult to get them to plan for the distant future in matters such as energy policies. Finally, if a low-risk event is combined with a long-range prediction of occurrence, little action is taken. This is why pressing issues often remained unresolved until their effects become urgent. Energy planning, climate change, pandemics, reinforcing buildings, and similar actions are delayed until after catastrophic events are imminent or occur.

People also continually fool themselves. They tend to distort reality in more optimistic directions. Interestingly, an exception is depressed people. Their negative view of reality has been shown to become more accurate. In the past few months, Massachusetts temperatures appeared (to me) moderate. There was little snow on the ground in early January. I began to think we would have a mild winter. It has turned out January temperatures are 3 degrees Fahrenheit lower than average and significant amounts of snow lie on the ground. I fool myself every year being too optimistic because I like warm weather. In contrast, a person who likes cold weather would likely be biased in the opposite direction. Biased perspectives affect the ways people interact, receive and interpret information, make decisions, and behave. Friedrich Durrenmatt was correct when he said, "Truth is always a delusion." Whose truth? Unfortunately, not seeing reality or acting appropriately to risk has consequences that can be a matter of life or death.

This winter, I noticed the frequency and price per gallon of oil delivered to my home increased. The cost of purchasing gasoline for my automobile is also increasing. The world's commodity market determines pricing based on supply, demand, and supply risk. In the future, oil supplies will decrease while demand increases, which will push prices higher. Wealth will be transferred between nations and conflicts may occur because of competition. A change of direction requires a very long-term energy strategy to maintain stable and predictable pricing. Infrastructure must also be built; but it must be based on science, not politics. Energy shortages shouldn't be unexpected if actions are not taken to reverse these trends. However, there has been little action taken around the world.

Creating an effective long-range energy policy for the United States and other countries is an example where complexities at first appear overwhelming. They are overwhelming unless a dialogue is properly facilitated to ensure facts and transparent debate of issues, policies, and available options. Sorting these things out will help simplify debates. There must also be analyses of relevant constraints and goals. Stakeholders must be engaged and participate. There will likely be unpopular actions and remedies. People will not voluntarily give up a perceived right to recklessly use energy. Imposition of arbitrary laws and regulations is also a poor option because they create disincentives and additional complications.

Higher complexity is guaranteed when politically divergent interests compete. While such behaviors may exist within an isolated country, consequences for poor decision making eventually become unavoidable. External groups will force a solution if they can. This fact should influence debates and resultant decisions of energy usage within the United States and other countries; otherwise the effects will be catastrophic in terms of higher national debt and lower living standards. The confusion and complexities of these debates need to be reduced.

In addition to complexity based on social psychological and technical influences, higher population densities in certain regions of the world will continue to exacerbate the effects of major catastrophic events. The effects from these events will likely become worse. In the late 1960s I was in high school. At that time the world's population was approximately 3 billion people. There were major campaigns to reduce population growth rates because it was widely recognized that higher numbers of people, especially in poorer regions of the world, would only make worse conditions of poverty, disease, and conflict. However, little was done because of competing philosophies, religions, cultures, and similar factors. The result is that 40 years later the world's population is more than 6 billion people and it is growing. Forecasts are the world's population will be more than 9 billion people in 40 years. This is not good news. In latter chapters we will discuss one example where 10 megacities containing more than a million inhabitants live on earthquake-prone areas. The likelihood of catastrophic loss of life, injuries, and damage is very high in these densely populated areas.

Society is complicated and so are the things we use. This is one explanation for failure. But, as we shall see, there are other explanations of which people are unaware. Not a day passes without reports of catastrophic failures. We see a relentless series of failures such as automobiles and airplane accidents, food contamination and shortages, ineffective or deadly medicines, poorly constructed buildings we live and work in, failures of logistical systems as well as the equipment and machines we use for work, and other activities. Additional failures are caused by natural disasters or poor responses to disasters, that is, logistical failures.

Failures are more likely to occur if risk recurrence factors exist and error conditions align to cause mistakes. Recurrence risks are influenced by high complexity; personal and group attitudes and behaviors, organizational culture, structures, and ethics, a history of prior catastrophic failures, a lack of risk analyses or contingency planning, the application of production technologies far ahead of control technologies, dependencies on complicated logistical systems, constrained resources, and a history of poor root cause analyses and problem resolution. It is made worse when using dangerous machines and equipment, when people work in dangerous places, when work activities rely on people, when there is a potential for significant loss of life, injuries, and property damage, when many people are potentially affected across large geographical regions, and when failures are politically sensitive. Risk recurrence factors will be used to explain why man-made and natural disasters sometimes become worse than they should.

There are other types of risks. Some are beyond our control, including natural disasters such as earthquakes, tornados, and hurricanes. Others occur if we take direct action or fail to do so. There are also specific types of risks (e.g., project risks) that are incurred when creating new products and services. Examples include project risks associated with scheduling, technology, supply and demand, product performance, cost, laws, and regulations. Project risks affect how things are designed and used. Failures also occur if people do not understand how to use something, or intentionally misuse it for other reasons.

However, much of the time, things go well. Products, services, and other things like the extensive infrastructure and systems supporting major civilizations around the world perform as expected. Societies depend on this expected performance. But if failures occur, it is important to identify causal factors and solutions to prevent or mitigate failures, their effects, and their frequency of occurrence. We can do much better. With the right strategies, analyses, and dialogue, the world will be safer. Attitudes and behaviors will need to be modified because difficult choices are likely. It is essential we understand the underlying reasons why the things we trust sometimes fail. This requires consideration of human, organizational, and technological influences that contribute to the likelihood of catastrophic events by increasing risks.

The first chapter is titled, "Designing Products and Services Is a Process." The process for designing products, services, and other systems consists of an integrated set of activities that bring them through several design steps or phases. These include identifying customer requirements, translating them into specifications, creating the products and services including their functions and features, and integrating and optimizing subsystems to ensure they meet requirements under expected usage conditions. Other considerations include ease of use, reliability, maintainability, reusability, disposability, and cost. The chapter ends with a discussion of several common issues negatively affecting the design of products and services. Some of these include the effects of various types of human errors, degrading effects of application environments, technology constraints, performance issues, various types of project risks, and resource scarcity. Design failures are inevitable if these are not properly managed.

Key topics include systems, marketing, life cycles, project management, basic design steps, requirements translation, and 12 best design practices. Systems consist of customers and requirements that are identified by market segment, internal stakeholder requirements that reflect the needs of a business regarding cost, performance, and scheduling, project activities and risks, design attributes, and feedback of performance in use (e.g., failure analysis and continuous improvement). Market intelligence is focused on how, where, when, and why products and services are used, and who uses them. This is the external application environment. Stakeholder analyses identify business needs and project management design activities. Important considerations for this work are individual perceptions, group dynamics, project management activities, team dynamics, and organizational culture and ethics. These comprise the internal design environment. This combined information enables designers to create needed functions, features, and attributes for customers and organizations. The result will be a balance between external and internal requirements. Throughout these projects there are project risks and those risks associated with usage. At the end of a design process the proper functions, features, structural form, and aesthetics are created to ensure it is easy to produce, distribute, maintain, upgrade, dispose of, and recycle a new design.

Several books have been written describing the catastrophic failure of bridges, buildings, and similar works. Other books describe failures of commercial aircraft and electromechanical systems. Technology is often not a major cause of failure even if the effects are horrific and sudden. People blame technology because they do not understand it. An examination of the deeper causal factors, that is, root causes, will show that many catastrophic failures have human and organizational contributions.

This first chapter also describes some of the underlying attitudes and behaviors of individuals and groups and their effects on design teams from a social psychological perspective. Designers bring attitudes and images of self to teams. This influences interpersonal relationships both within and outside their group with customers and key stakeholders. Sometimes behaviors are constructive, but they may also become destructive. Attitudes and behaviors must be well managed. Good design practices must also be used to reduce the likelihood of unexpected failure.

On April 25, 1986, Chernobyl's Reactor 4 was being shut down for routine maintenance. A complication of the shutdown was a planned experiment of the cooling system for the safety emergency core. The necessary approvals to conduct this test were not obtained by plant personnel according to established policies and written procedures. In fact, the maintenance team and engineers disabled several of the reactor's key safety systems. These errors and contributing factors caused a massive explosion of Reactor 4 in the early morning hours of April 26, 1986. The explosion destroyed the reactor. Radiation levels within the reactor building skyrocketed. This event caused an explosion and widespread environmental contamination as well as the deaths of the team within weeks of exposure to high radiation levels within the reactor building. In fact, according to the International Atomic Energy Agency (IAEA) and World Health Organization (WHO), there were 56 direct deaths and 4,000 indirect cancer deaths associated with the Chernobyl incident.[3]

It was later found that the Chernobyl disaster was caused by several factors including a poor reactor design and human error. Complicating the situation were inaccurate measurement systems preventing detection of increasing radiation levels. The Chernobyl disaster is a classic example of how human error contributes to catastrophic failure.

In the second chapter, we will discuss key topics such as individual attitudes, persuasion, social cognition, self-concept, cognitive dissonance, the social psychology of formal groups, social influence, group dynamics including interpersonal relationships and attraction, and their effects on the design process including failures of products and services. The Chernobyl disaster provides justification for wanting to understand social psychological factors that affect people who create or use new products, services, and other systems because these things often fail through human error rather than technology.

These social psychological influences have significant effects on how things are designed both from a technical perspective as well as a project management one. If people have poor attitudes, in the absence of facilitation, incorrect work activities will be selected, prioritization will be ineffective, and required information may not be acquired or analyzed correctly. Persuasion is also always active for good or bad. Correct persuasive methods will move a team to a high performance stage; otherwise it may become dysfunctional and fail to achieve its goals in a timely and efficient manner. If a team operates by groupthink or selectively filters information, incorrect design goals or targets may be selected or critical information may be incorrectly interpreted, resulting in wrong conclusions. Goals and targets may also not be effectively prioritized. Also, to the extent that members of a team have not been persuaded to agree with the group's goals and work activities, they may not support the team. Confidential information may be leaked, work activities may not be completed, or interpersonal conflict may erupt, causing people to leave a team. There are many other potential issues caused by individual, group, and organizational dysfunctions.

The third chapter discusses the application of design principles from perspectives of perception and learning (e.g., cognition and mental models). Its focus is how people design and use products and services. Some products and services are easier to use than others. The consequence of poor designs (e.g., ones that do not consider the impact of cognitive influences) is that misuse often occurs to cause failures. Flipping the wrong switch or pushing the wrong button may cause explosions in some systems because of misinterpretation, information filtering, or other cognitive issues such as mental models.

The chapter also discusses error conditions and mistake proofing to help prevent failures. This discussion is broken into red flag and error conditions and mistake proofing. Red flag conditions include high complexity, poor design, an inability to measure performance, poor documentation and procedures, using the wrong tools and methods, little training, poor environmental conditions, stressful working relationships between people and groups, and utilizing capacity beyond stable levels. If these conditions exist, the likelihood of error conditions is higher. Error conditions may or may not cause failure if they are found early. As an example, if an inaccurate customer requirement is translated into a specification, little harm is done if it is caught before a drawing is released to production. Several red flag conditions may have contributed to the error conditions (poor training, poor documentation, poor procedures, little training, etc.).

Another example would be poorly calibrated test equipment found early before being used to measure. Red flag conditions would have set up the error condition.

In these examples, an error condition was found before mistakes were made. There are also mistake proofing strategies that can be taken if errors occur. One is to shut down an operation or stop an activity until the causes for the error are found. This prevents the creation of additional mistakes. The third chapter discusses these topics in the context of human error.

Mental models sometimes cause people to make incorrect decisions based on prior experience. As an example, some people do not believe wolves attack people or children. However, history shows otherwise. There have been wolf attacks both in the wild and in captivity. The causes are wolves being rabid, hungry, or too familiar with people. As an example, recently, a 13-year-old boy walking home from a school bus stop in Rakkestdad, Norway, saw a pack of four wolves in the distance. He was listening to a song by Creed called "Overcome." Creed was a popular rock band in the late 1990s.[4] Unable to run to safety, the boy turned up the volume and flapped his arms to scare the wolves away. This event ended well, but, it could have easily been otherwise. Prior to the incident there was little fear of the wolves.

People may also not realize coyotes can also be dangerous. A recent article in the *Huffington Post* described coyote attacks on small children in Rye, New York.[5] The children were bitten while playing in their backyards. Coyotes have moved across the United States and many live near residential neighborhoods to look for food. This proximity increases the likelihood they may attack people. In the past several years there have been more than 40 coyote attacks on people. The danger is real. People need to change their mental models regarding wolves and coyotes, as is also true for other potentially dangerous situations.

Understanding the effects of cognitive influences on the creation and use of design functions, features, and other attributes is important when attempting to understand the source of failures. It is also a basis for creating strategies to prevent them. Taken together, the technological and cognitive aspects of design activities and customer usage can help organizations improve design safety and reliability. In this context, simple systems are usually preferable to more complex ones, automation of work is often better than reliance on manual work tasks, and certain shapes, colors, and patterns are preferable to others. These are only a few of the many cognitive influences discussed in the third chapter. This information is both interesting and critical for creating easy-to-use, safe, and reliable products, services, and other things.

Organizational structure and culture also directly affect the design of products and services. First organizations create procedures and policies for project management activities. Some organizations have well-defined policies and procedures for creating and producing new products and services whereas others may not. There may also be interference with design activities by customers or key stakeholders. These people control resources and the employees supporting a design project. This is why it is important that design activities be aligned with an organization's strategic goals and integrated into other key processes. Important contributing factors affecting how effectively design activities are managed include organizational structure, strategy, culture, policies and procedures, communications, and enforcement of ethical standards. These topics are discussed relative to creating error conditions or making wrong decisions that degrade safety.

The fourth chapter shows there are often serious and deadly consequences for not creating a vigilant organizational culture and supporting structure to ensure that employees ethically adhere to established policies and procedures. Organizations are complicated systems containing fragmented processes. Fragmentation occurs over many years because of process modifications. Eventually, no one person understands or can manage the many interacting parts of these systems. In addition to process complexity, dysfunctions occur if informal and formal groups compete because of goal misalignment. Misalignment causes miscommunication and haphazard hand-offs from one group to another. These situations also contribute to process breakdowns. Unfortunately, these types of organizational dysfunctions are common. In fact, management consultants make billions of dollars each year helping organizations unravel outdated management policies, create new ones, and restructure work processes to make them more effective, efficient, and safe. Competing groups and key stakeholders may also interfere with design activities, production and safety systems, or the ways an organization reacts to catastrophic events. Policies, procedures, and similar controls are usually in place, but, they can be easily ignored.

On March 23, 2005, a major explosion occurred at BP's Texas City oil refining facility. Fifteen workers were killed and more than 100 others injured.[6] The cause of the accident was later found to be a widespread disregard for worker safety by local management and workers. The investigation also found safety systems were routinely ignored or disabled. In its report, the United States Chemical and Safety Hazard Investigation Board (CSB) cited a long list of contributing factors that caused the accident. These included a deliberate failure by AMOCO or BP (BP merged with AMOCO in 1998) between 1991 and 2004 to implement numerous safety recommendations. In response to the original accident report, BP initiated many of the needed reforms. However, in October 2009, BP was fined $87.4 million by the United States government for failing to fix all the original hazardous conditions.[7] In this chapter we will discuss organizational structure, culture, and ethics, and their contribution to catastrophic failure.

Unethical or incompetent leadership will exacerbate the likelihood of failures. The Chernobyl explosion and the BP Texas City accident are just a few examples of the types of catastrophic failures that result from organizational breakdowns contributing to error conditions and mistakes. Interestingly, the 2009 global financial crisis provides additional examples showing potentially negative effects of organizational dysfunction. The crisis was caused, in part, by organizational fraud and misconduct as well as a failure by regulatory agencies (themselves organizations) to effectively regulate financial markets across the world. Although there are several underlying reasons for these events, they can be summarized as a general inability of the respective organizations to follow their own policies and procedures. The lesson is that despite established policies and procedures, errors occur if higher-level executives or trusted professionals in positions of authority take short-cuts or cheat. We will show that unethical conduct is very common.

In the fifth chapter, we integrate the information from several previous chapters and introduce several important failure analysis principles. The chapter describes major historical failures across diverse industries including construction, electronics, electromechanical and other products, as well as information technology, health care, regulatory, and political systems. Sometimes the causes for failures are similar, even across diverse industries, systems, and applications. The focus of the failure analysis discussion is not only with technical failures usually ascribed as the cause for bridges and building collapse, or electromechanical accidents such as commercial aircraft and automobile disasters, but also human and organizational failures. This is a different approach for understanding why things fail. It provides a unique perspective of causes and solutions. We are not only harmed by a collapsing bridge or building, but also by vaccines that are not available, or by laws and regulations fail to protect us. These topics will be integrated to describe a generic strategy for failure analysis to help understand similarities and differences between the different failure types.

Computerworld published a list of the top 10 corporate information technology failures in the United States based on financial losses from lawsuits. The combined losses exceeded hundreds of millions of dollars.[8] The underlying issues were usually poor project management. Software viruses are also a major problem. According to a September 2002 issue of

Computerworld, in the prior decades, software viruses had caused more than $10 billion of damage worldwide because security or safety had been compromised by poorly designed software.[9] In addition to software, people across the world experience failures in very different industries and organizations. Our goal will be to explain the causes for unexpected catastrophic events from different perspectives.

The sixth chapter discusses ways to prevent catastrophic failures. As an example, although the automotive industry's average number of defects per 100 vehicles declined from 118 to 108 in 2008 (8.4% improvement), vehicle recalls and accidents occur. Recent examples include the Ford/Firestone tire failures, which accounted for at least 174 deaths, and Ford's recall of millions of vehicles having a faulty cruise-control switch, which was thought to have caused deaths and vehicle fires.[10] Of course these safety issues were eventually resolved, but not without having caused deaths, personal injuries, and property damage.

Learning why the things we trust sometimes fail is useful, but it is also important, from a practical perspective, to prevent failures. This is not always easy. But if analyses are expanded from a historical focus on isolated events, patterns emerge. These provide guidelines for preventive efforts. In this sixth chapter, we differentiate between four types of events. These include isolated technical failures, isolated project failures, chronic issues, and major events and natural disasters. Understanding the different approaches for identifying causal factors and implementing solutions for each event type will help create strategies for preventing or mitigating the effects of future events.

An analysis of risk recurrence factors is another important topic in this chapter. To the extent they exist, the likelihood of failure will be higher than otherwise. Risk recurrence factors include: organizational and cultural issues that have resulted in previous failures; a chronic absence of risk analysis and contingency planning; regulatory laxness; the use of dangerous equipment; operating within dangerous work environments; using complex systems; a high degree of dependency on manual work tasks (which involves cognition issues); a significant potential for financial loss or loss of life if failures occur; many people likely to be impacted across large geographical regions if failures occur; failures that would be politically sensitive; production or application technologies that are ahead of required control technologies; and relief efforts that are dependent on complicated logistical systems in which there is a history of poor root cause analysis and mitigation. The chapter provides an integrative approach to failure analysis using this approach to risk identification.

The last chapter shows the value of creating scenarios to help prevent and manage catastrophic events. Forecasts of timing, location, or magnitude of catastrophic events can seldom be made because the quantitative information necessary to create predictive models rarely exists. However, scenarios can be created to explore potential outcomes of hypothetical catastrophic events. Although outcomes may never occur, creating scenarios enables contingency plans to be constructed in advance of these potential events. Preplanning associated with a scenario may also help. As an example, although the exact time of a major earthquake cannot be predicted with certainty, plans can be made to reinforce buildings and other infrastructure and create logistical systems that can be quickly activated if an earthquake occurs.

Once scenarios have been created, outcomes and threats are mapped to coordination infrastructure and emergency response planning activities. Typical outcomes and threats include earthquakes, diseases, terrorism acts, wars and conflicts, extreme weather conditions, fire and flooding, shortages of food and water, as well as environmental and technology accidents. Coordination infrastructure coordinates relief efforts related to establishing situational control and communications, assessing damage and needs, activating logistical support systems, activating operations teams for stabilization and recovery, and reassessing damage and needs as well as restoration of infrastructure and normalcy. The chapter discusses ways to prevent or mitigate the effects of potential outcomes. Finally, it concludes with a reexamination of the risk recurrence factors as applied to several recent catastrophic events to show the likelihood of catastrophic events can be reduced.

The discussions throughout the book are reinforced by examination of diverse recent events: I-35W Mississippi River Bridge (Minnesota); April 25, 1986, Chernobyl Reactor 4 disaster; Denver International Airport baggage system delay; 2009 Air France Flight 447 disaster; 2010 Toyota recall; Ford cruise switch control fires (late 1990s); 2001 Ford/Firestone tire failures; Anderson SAP ERP issues for Fox-Meyer; food contamination; 2003 SARS in Asia; production problems with the H1N1 swine flu virus vaccine; infectious and parasitic diseases worldwide; 2005 Hurricane Katrina (New Orleans); 2010 Haiti earthquake; and the 2010 Deepwater Horizon explosion and Gulf of Mexico oil spill, as well as others. The goal is to identify similarities and differences between these diverse catastrophic events to help prevent or better manage future ones.

In summary, this book discusses more than 40 unexpected and catastrophic events. The goal is to show interrelationships between events. One conclusion is that consequences of catastrophic events are not always unexpected. In many situations, failures can be prevented or the aftermath of an event could be better managed. But to become better, we need to expand our failure analysis methods past a technological focus into areas of cognition, group dynamics, and organizational culture.

NOTES

1. Rachel Manning, "The Kitty Genovese Murder and the Social Psychology of Helping: The Parable of the 38 Witnesses," *American Psychologist* 62 no. 6, Sep. 2007: 555–62.

2. Encarta Dictionary, http://encarta.msn.com/encnet/features/dictionary/DictionaryResults.aspx?lextype=3&search=complexity; Encarta World English Dictionary [North American Edition] 2009. Microsoft Corporation. All rights reserved. Developed for Microsoft by Bloomsbury Publishing Plc.

3. International Atomic Energy Agency,(IAEA) report, "Chernobyl's Legacy: Health, Environmental and Socio-Economic Impacts and Recommendations to the Governments of Belarus, the Russian Federation and Ukraine," *The Chernobyl Forum: 2003–2005*, 2nd rev. Vienna, Austria: Vienna International Centre.

4. Tim Grierson, *Creed*, About.com Guide, http://rock.about.com/od/creed/p/creed.htm.

5. Jim Fitzgerald, "Coyote Attacks: Rye Parents Told to Keep Children Indoors after Animal Attacks," *Huffington Post*, June 30, 2010, http://www.huffingtonpost.com/2010/06/30/coyote-attacks-3-year-old_n_630451.html.

6. "What Went Wrong: Oil Refinery Disaster," *Popular Mechanics*, September 14, 2005, http://www.popularmechanics.com/technology/gadgets/news/1758242.

7. "BP Disappointed with Texas City Fine," Associated Press, October 30, 2009.

8. "The Best and the Worst: A Look at the Projects that Bombed the Viruses that Bugged Us and Other Facts from the World of IT," *Computerworld*, September 30, 2002.

9. "Most Costly Computer Viruses," *Computerworld*, September 30, 2002 http://www.computerworld.com/s/article/74620/The_best_and_the_worst.

10. Michelle Krebs, "Vehicle Quality Improves Despite Bumpy Financial Ride," *Auto Observer*, June 22, 2009, http://www.autoobserver.com/2009/06/vehicle-quality-improves-despite-bumpy-financial-ride.html; John Greenwald, "Inside the Ford/Firestone Fight," *Time*, May 29, 2001, http://www.time.com/time/business/article/0,8599,128198,00.html; "Ford's Recall Leaves Public at Risk," August 3, 2007, http://www.safetyfo rum.com/fordcruisecontrol/.

Chapter 1

DESIGNING PRODUCTS AND SERVICES IS A PROCESS

Design is the method of putting form and content together. Design, just as art, has multiple definitions; there is no single definition. Design can be art. Design can be aesthetics. Design is so simple, that's why it is so complicated.

—Paul Rand

On the evening of April 14, 1912, in the cold north Atlantic, the *Titanic* struck an iceberg and sank into the ocean.[1] The ship was designed and constructed using a double-bottomed hull divided into 16 compartments. These compartments were considered watertight, but the ship had an unknown design flaw in that the tops of the compartments were not sealed. As a result, after the *Titanic* hit an iceberg that evening, water moved from the top of the ruptured compartment to undamaged compartments. This caused the ship to lean and eventually sink with a heavy loss of life. The design weakness was not foreseen by the ship's designers. This is often the situation when catastrophic failures occur. Designers fail to anticipate failures for a variety of reasons. Some are technical, some are cognitive, and others are unavoidable.

Service and logistics systems also fail. A noteworthy example is the failure of a new baggage handling system at the new Denver International Airport in 1994.[2] The Denver airport baggage handling system was scheduled for completion in March of 1994, but in tests the system damaged and misrouted luggage bags. These issues delayed the opening of the airport until February 1995. The financial impact was estimated at approximately

$1 million each day consisting of interest payments on bonds and operational expenses. Complex service systems fail for a variety of reasons including poor identification of customer requirements, human errors caused by poor design, and poor use of technology as well as other factors. Service and logistical failures cause simple disappointments as well as widespread loss of life, injuries, and property damage. As an example, they were recently seen during the federal, state, and local relief responses to victims of Hurricane Katrina as well as the production and distribution problems of the swine flu H1N1 strain vaccine.[3] In the aftermath of Katrina, it became apparent that logistical systems were not designed to effectively manage communications or provide a rapid relief response. In the H1N1 vaccine event, demand for the vaccine exceeded worldwide manufacturing and distribution capacity.

This chapter introduces some basic methods used to design products and services. Unfortunately, because design and production processes are complex and the impact of application environments on designs cannot always be predicted, failures can appear in various forms. Complicating the design of products and services are the effects of personal and organizational behavior. For this reason, we will discuss the design of products and services from the three perspectives of technology, social psychology, and organizational culture. Regardless of how well products or services are designed from a technical perspective, if people cannot easily understand features and functions, or correctly interpret how to safely and efficiently use them, catastrophic failure may occur.

To understand why the things we trust fail, let's start at the beginning of a typical design process. The ideas for creating products and services are obtained from a variety of sources including internal and external marketing research, major customers, and competitive analyses as well as other sources. In contrast, minor modifications of designs require the limited involvement of a few designers, salespeople, and customers. This implies that a first step when designing is to determine if requested features and functions are an extension of those existing in current products or services or entirely different.

A cross-functional design team is formed to manage the activities necessary to ensure successful commercialization of a product or service. These work activities are well defined and organized into sequential steps. Tollgates are also inserted at critical points of the design process. A tollgate is reached after a team completes several related activities. Each activity consists of standardized work tasks, work products, and deliverables, and each activity requires resources. Resources include such things as people, testing facilities, materials, and equipment.

The basic approach for designing is similar across different industries, although specific design methods and tools may vary. As an example, an organization designing automobiles will use computer aided design (CAD), tolerance models, reliability modeling, vehicle testing, and other specialized design tools; whereas an insurance organization, designing an actuarial model, would employ Excel-based annuity tables and might simulate changing modeling assumptions. Other diverse design applications include civil engineering projects, hospital systems processes, and a variety of other applications. However, the generalized approach to design that is discussed in this chapter is useful and will enable us to understand why things fail from perspectives of technical design as well as project management.

A structured approach toward project management, as it applies to the design of new products and services, reduces the likelihood of unexpected failures. Project management ensures roles and responsibilities are clearly defined and work activities are done in the right order, on schedule, and that they deliver functions and features in their proper sequence. Although any approach for creating new designs is never perfect, a structured and transparent design process will help reduce the likelihood of product and service failures because issues will be identified up front rather than hidden. Let's discuss an example: medical devices designed to be implanted in patients.

The design and manufacturing of medical devices is a demanding set of activities impacting millions of people. Although these devices have excellent safety records, given their demanding applications, they do fail within patients. As an example, although heart pacemakers are modern engineering miracles that save many lives and mortality statistics show them to be relatively safe, there are occasional failures. In fact, according to a Federal Drug Administration news release dated September 16, 2005, "From 1990 to 2002, there were approximately 2.25 million pacemakers (PMs) and 416,000 ICD (implantable cardioverter defibrillators) implanted in the United States. During the same time period, 17,323 devices (8,834 PMs and 8,489 ICDs) were removed from patients due to confirmed device malfunction. . . . PM or ICD malfunctions were directly responsible for 61 confirmed deaths out of nearly three million devices implanted during the same time period."[4]

A pacemaker is an electromechanical device designed to regulate a patient's heartbeat. Its key components include a generator and leads. The generator is a computer that is hermetically sealed with a battery. The battery has an expected life of between five and eight years. The leads are inserted into the heart's right atrium and ventricles. The electrical feedback from the heart to the computer is used to regulate the timing of the heart's muscle. Sometimes there are serious issues.

Common failures include ineffective pacing of the heartbeat or pacing it at an abnormal rate. Ineffective pacing is caused by one of several defective conditions. These include cardiac depolarization, disconnected leads, and battery depletion. An abnormal pacemaker rate is caused by over-sensing of the device. These and similar pacemaker defects result in a degradation of its ability is to pace the heart's rate. The practical implication of device failure or performance degradation is that it must be replaced or a patient's life will be jeopardized.

Common pacemaker failures include mechanical and electrical defects, material or chemical incompatibilities, deterioration and leakage of materials into a patient, and nonfunctioning or error-prone software. These failures are caused by poor product design, manufacturing errors, surgical mistakes, or stresses caused by a patient's body after implantation. Design errors occur when functions, features, and other requirements have not been properly identified, translated, or tested to create a reliable product. Manufacturing errors occur if accelerated life testing is improperly conducted, quality assurance testing is faulty, or a pacemaker's packaging is compromised through careless handling that results in unsterile conditions or a compromised shelf life. Errors also occur if a surgical implantation procedure is faulty, if there is severe electromagnetic interference around a patient, or if there are biological environments that degrade a device or its ability to function.

Pacemakers may also fail for other causes. As an example, their metal enclosure could rupture through heat buildup, resulting in chemical leakage into a patient's body. Metal fatigue could cause in-case fracture, resulting in leakage of chemicals within a patient or scarring and damage to surrounding tissue. The battery could also unexpectedly fail. Design and manufacturing engineers work hard to prevent these types of failures by working through multidisciplinary design teams. But, although risks are reduced, unexpected failures and deaths occur. Unfortunately, many products and services are not designed as well as pacemakers and their failure rates are higher.

The products and services we use every day are created by multidisciplinary design teams that translate needs and requirements of customers into product and service features, functions, and other attributes. A design process may be relatively simple and require only a few people, or they may be very complex and require managing thousands of people working in many different organizations across the world. Complicating the situation is that the cycle time required to design new products and services may range between a few weeks and several years. Regardless of its specific form, design activities follow a carefully structured roadmap. As an example, I recall my first design review meeting almost 30 years ago. I represented quality assurance. Several major functions from the organization were in attendance. The new product was requested by a major customer and forecasted by marketing to have an important impact on future sales. Design engineers had already been working with the customer and created drawings and samples (prototypes) of the new product for review and discussion. Based on this initial work, preliminary specifications had been created and purchasing had contacted key suppliers to obtain cost estimates for several major components that were to be included in the new product. In parallel, manufacturing engineers had contacted machine suppliers and calculated preliminary manufacturing costs. It was my responsibility to review the design specifications and performance testing to ensure they could meet original customer requirements and to also create the product's quality assurance plan.

As the product moved toward its manufacturing release date, limited production quantities (a pilot run) were manufactured, under very controlled conditions, to verify the product met customer requirements (at least on a short-term basis) as specified by its quality assurance plan. Information from the pilot runs was also used to resolve outstanding design or manufacturing issues and finalize the product's costing.

Although this organization manufactured simple and disposable consumer products, its project management process is similar to most manufacturing organizations. A similar approach is used when designing service and logistical systems. Customer requirements are translated into features and functions and eventually a new process is created. The work is routinely conducted in diverse organizations including those in private, non-profit, and governmental applications.

Organizations ensure their products and services will not unexpectedly fail by using proven design methods.[5] In this chapter we will discuss the basic tools and methods used for designing products and services. So what are the common activities that designers use to create products and services? First, there is always a translation process. New products and services must meet the requirements of their customers and end users. This information must be converted into workable internal specifications controlling features, functions, esthetics, and similar attributes. Designers obtain requirements using different tools and methods. These include marketing research, team meetings, competitive analysis and reverse engineering, target costing, and other methods to help gather information.

Once requirements have been gathered, the information is reviewed, analyzed, and integrated to create internal specifications. Then, depending on the industry, various design tools, methods, and systems may be used to improve efficiencies of the design process. Some examples include computer aided design (CAD), prototyping, computer aided manufacturing (CAM), and periodic reviews of a project's status. Analytical methods include statistical analyses, tolerance estimates, finite element analysis

(FEA), simulations, and similar methods that help gather, organize, and analyze the information required to understand the interrelationships between specification and performance (these specialized terms are defined in this book's glossary).

The Microsoft *Encarta Dictionary* defines a system as "a complex whole formed from related parts . . . a combination of related parts organized into a complex whole."[6] The concept of system is important because a product or service is not used in isolation. Figure 1.1 provides a perspective of this concept, that is, a generic system that can be used to discuss product and service failures. A system consists of internal and external environments and their combined effects on a product or service. An external environment is defined in terms of how, where, when, why, and by whom a product or service is used, as well as the environmental factors causing system degradation and failure. Designers, through experience, know many of the most important factors for their industries firsthand from products previously designed for similar applications.

Internal environments can be considered from two perspectives. First, how is the product design or development process managed? Second, what is the impact of production operations on quality and reliability of newly designed products and services? In this context, quality implies a product or service meets customer requirements after it is manufactured or produced. Reliability implies it continues to meet requirements, over time. Product and service failures are caused by the stresses of various types within external environments, design weaknesses, production problems that introduce defects, and combinations of these factors. It should be noted that production operations are also affected by suppliers of materials, people, methods, machines, measurements, and other relevant factors. The overall result is that there are many ways in which products and services can fail.

The basic purpose for designing is to create product or service attributes corresponding to customer needs and requirements. These include functions (how it works), features (distinct ways it is used), aesthetics (how it looks), the structural form (distinctive character), its ability to be easily manufactured, how it is distributed for sale, its ease of maintenance, how easy it is to upgrade, and its ease of disposal or recyclability. These design characteristics directly depend on the effectiveness of a design team and how it works. In addition to the issues faced by a product or service design and its environment, the design process for creating products and services can also lead to issues because it is dependent on individual, group, and organizational behavior. Good designs are difficult to create when the process for creating them is poorly managed.

Environmental stresses degrade products and services once they begin to be used by customers. This is true for consumer products, large machines,

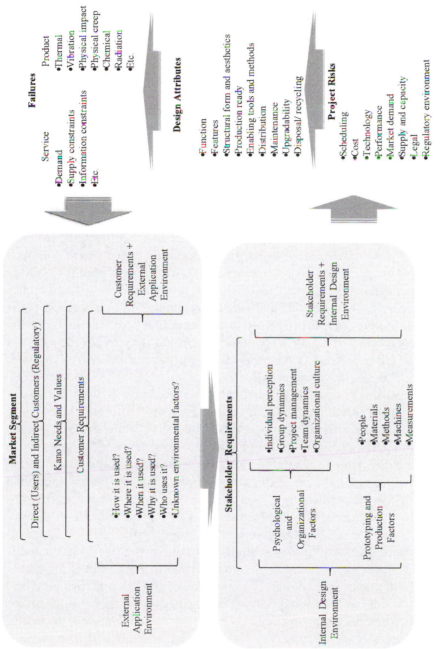

Figure 1.1 What is a system?

construction works, and service systems as well as designs. Stresses on physical products, depending on the application, include heat, vibration, physical impact or creep, radiation, and other factors. Stress may also be magnified depending on a product's structural form or geometry, its materials, and how it is constructed. As an example, it is a fact that the increased stress caused by a circular geometry is magnified by a factor of three whereas a sharp geometry may multiply the same initial stress by a factor of one hundred. Mechanical and civil engineering designers know this fact. As a result, they avoid designing sharp geometries to maintain strength when subjected to mechanical stress. Also, certain designs containing deep recesses, voids, and high surface areas accelerate corrosion rates. A product or service's functions, structure and form, aesthetics, and other attributes may also increase the likelihood of failure. The unintentional or intentional misuse of product or service functions and features also leads to failure.

Service systems are also subject to stresses that are different from those affecting products. As an example, many are subject to demand fluctuations and constraints of supply or capacity and information availability. Service system degradation is usually detectable by lower service levels and higher costs as well as lower quality and satisfaction ratings by employees and customers. Employee safety may also be an issue. Our goal will be to use the concepts shown in Figure 1.1, in the next several chapters, to identify and analyze failures across different industries, products, and services to look for the reasons they unexpectedly fail.

The process of designing is defined by the *Merriam-Webster Dictionary* as "to create, fashion, execute, or construct according to plan." Designing includes the elements that support its production, transport, and usage.[7] Designing has specific objectives. Figure 1.1 shows that designing products and services requires accurately reflecting external customer and internal stakeholder requirements. External customer requirements are identified using a market segmenting strategy. The methodology classifies customers in various ways. One classification is by direct and indirect customers. Direct customers use a product or service. Indirect customers include regulators and other stakeholders, who have an interest in but do not actually use a product or service. Accurate requirements translation is important because if one or more design objectives have not been met, products and services will be considered failures by their users. Costly modifications may become necessary in the field. Examples include automobile recalls, which are very common and costly. Also, even when a product or service has been well designed, it may be misused or its application environment may change. These types of situations also cause issues.

A good marketing plan consists, in part, of estimates of future demand and the identification of the critical characteristics that products and services need to satisfy potential customers. Ideas for new products and services come from a variety of sources. Typical examples include direct requests from external customers to satisfy unmet needs, supplier requests to lower costs by making design modifications, internal requests to improve manufacturability, requests from senior management to lower costs or improve performance, and competitive analyses of industry trends.

This information is analyzed and prioritized using specialized tools and methods, some of which are proprietary to an organization. Unfortunately, sometimes effective marketing research does not exist, is poorly executed, or is ignored. There are several reasons for these situations. There may be a lack of necessary quantitative skills, constraints of resources or schedule, or other reasons. Poor marketing research usually results in designing the wrong products, poor cost estimates, poor performance, and failure to meet other important customer requirements. The result is often product and service failure. The effects are seen as reduced market share as well as lower sales revenue and profitability over their life cycle.[8] Poor marketing research can also be exacerbated by fragmented or culturally diverse markets.

The failure rates of new products are staggering even when marketing research is well done. Depending on where relevant information is obtained, failure rates of newly introduced products and services typically range between 20 and 90 percent.[9] Just as a new house must have a good foundation, so a new product or service must have a good marketing analysis and plan. If not, there will be a difference between customer expectations and the functions and features a new product or service actually delivers. The result will be a perception of failure.

Market research identifies and classifies, by market segment, customer and stakeholder requirements using satisfaction models and value analysis. One way to identify market segments is to ask questions such as how, where, when, and why a customer uses a product or service. This helps to differentiate design attributes to understand how products and services should be designed, modified, or improved. Although there are several types of satisfaction models, the Kano model is one of the more popular ones. It is also a useful approach for organizing a product or services' design attributes based on an evaluation of customer needs.

A Kano analysis requires identifying and classifying design attributes through information gathered by interviewing customers within market segments. As an example, Figure 1.2 breaks customer needs into basic (required), performance (differentiated), or excitement (new and unique) categories. Value analysis is a second useful method for identifying and prioritizing customer and stakeholder requirements relative to cost, time, utility, or perceived usefulness, function, or performance and relative importance. Kano and value analysis are done for each market segment.

Once customer requirements have been identified, they are translated into internal specifications to clearly describe functions, features, structural form, and aesthetic properties of a product or service. Additional requirements that must also be considered by designers include product and service distribution, packaging, maintenance, upgradability, disposal, and recyclability.

In summary, marketing uses information gathered from customers to identify critical design requirements by market segment. It uses this information to estimate annual demand by market segment and plans advertising campaigns to increase product awareness among potential customers to achieve sales, usage, and price targets. It is the responsibility of designers, production, and other organizational functions to keep marketing promises

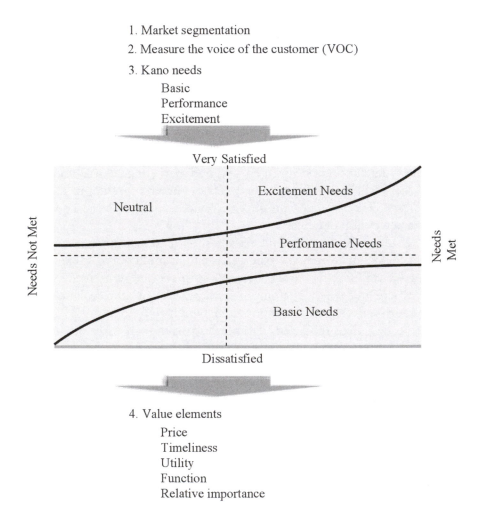

Figure 1.2 **What are key marketing activities?**

made to customers. This is done by accurately translating requirements into internal specifications and designing products and services to meet them.

Figure 1.3 shows that a marketing life cycle consists of several stages. These include introduction to the market (introduction stage), accelerated sales growth (growth stage), level sales (maturity stage), decreasing sales (decline stage), and the disposal or recyclability stages. There are differing life cycle patterns that reflect lengths of time within and between stages. These life cycle patterns vary from weeks to several decades depending on a specific product or service. As an example, seasonal consumer disposable products are sold for a few months each year whereas commercial aircraft, when properly maintained, may remain in service for several decades. Also, some bridges in Europe have been used for several hundred years. There are many such examples.

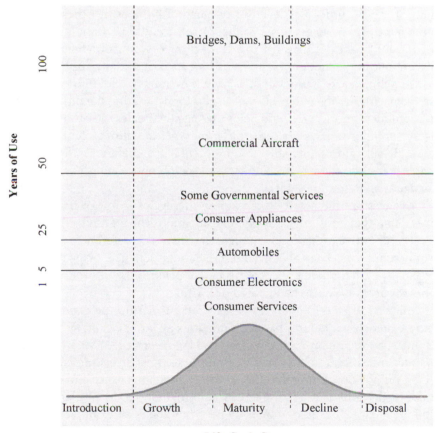

Figure 1.3 Life cycles of different products and services

In the introduction stage, sales of most products and services start off slowly. However, depending on consumer demand and available supply, sales may rapidly increase. In the introduction phase of the life cycle, products are undifferentiated and have an initial high price. Distribution is focused on select areas and marketing efforts are targeted toward early adopter customers. However, this is not true for all products. Products and services sold by contract may have very brief introduction phases and rapidly move through their growth and maturity phases. Examples include commercial and military aircraft, shipping, construction projects, and the distribution of vaccines.

In the growth stage sales increase assuming there is sufficient supply of a new product or service and there are no available capacity constraints. In this stage, product features and options increase, distribution is expanded, and advertising is used to build consumer demand. Pricing may be maintained at its current level or reduced to meet competitive pressures. In the maturity stage, unit sales level off because of competitive pressures that often force price concessions. Product or service differentiation may begin to increase. In the decline stage of a life cycle an organization may choose to discontinue a product or service or reduce its cost. Finally, in the disposal and recycling stages a product or service is no longer sold. Life cycle analysis, from a marketing perspective, is useful for estimating potential sales for new products and services and helps manage their sales over time. It is also useful for failure analysis because different types of failures occur over a life cycle. Repair and maintenance requirements also change. A common example is automobile service. The types of maintenance and their frequency change as an automobile ages.

Designers are impacted by marketing life cycles from several perspectives. First, they must make design modifications throughout a life cycle to meet competitive pressures or changes in consumer preferences and to correct design flaws. They also need to create maintenance, disposal, and recyclability systems, and polices as necessary prior to the introduction stage. These systems may also be updated over time.

Designers also use life cycle analysis for estimating the expected types and frequencies of failures based on previous experience and testing. As an example, because commercial aircraft will be in service for several decades, maintenance requirements over many decades must be estimated to ensure a continuing source of replacement parts. These life cycle estimates can be more easily done if warranty, return, failure analysis, or similar information is available. An automobile's owner's manual is an example. It usually recommends required maintenance at periodic intervals because designers know a vehicle's mileage is directly related to the types of components that will fail. They have already done the testing. If a vehicle's maintenance schedule is followed, the likelihood of an unexpected failure is very low. If a failure does occur, it can usually be attributed to an undetected design flaw, a manufacturing defect, an unanticipated environmental stress, or a combination of these factors. Vehicle failure information is used to make design, manufacturing, and maintenance schedule modifications. Commercial products and services are continually improved using life cycle analyses to reduce the likelihood of future failures. If properly done, failures should not be unexpected or catastrophic.

Failure types and frequencies are specific for different products and services. As an example, leading-edge electromechanical products such as computers, phones, cameras, and automobiles have initially high failure rates just prior to their introduction stages. These are called infant mortalities or marginal units. Manufactured units are tested under accelerated conditions known as stress testing. This is done to identify units with marginal strength when exposed to a specific types of stresses (e.g. thermal, vibrational, physical, chemical, electrical, or others). It is less expensive to find failures prior to shipment because of higher warranty or return goods and related service expenses. They exist because of design and manufacturing technological limitations. Units passing accelerated stress testing exhibit normal wear-out patterns and predictable failure rates if they are properly maintained according to recommendations. Toward the end of their useful life, electromechanical products fail at a higher rate and eventually are disposed or recycled.

Different products have different failure rates and types within their life cycle stages. As an example, durable goods are designed for longer usage periods. They also contain varying amounts of design redundancy. Examples include commercial aircraft and large machines. Redundancy is also used for other types of products and services. Construction works such as bridges, dams, and buildings are designed using redundancy principles for strength to prevent catastrophic failure. Regardless of the product, life cycle analysis helps estimate when maintenance and upgrades should be scheduled to prevent unexpected failures.

Services also have life cycles. They are usually easier to modify or upgrade unless they are heavily dependent on fixed assets such as buildings, information technology (IT) systems, consumer preferences, legal and regulatory constraints, or highly skilled workers. Changes to any of these assets or systems will have dramatic effects on the design and efficiency of service systems based on their dependencies. Service systems also become obsolete when they move through their life cycles. Eventually, they will not meet customer and stakeholder requirements. As an example, a hospital emergency room is designed to move patients through its process based on required care with economic efficiency and quality. This service system is flexible to a degree. If process inefficiencies are found, its design can be modified to increase operational efficiency while meeting external customer, stakeholder, and regulatory requirements for quality care. Although process designs also have life cycles depending on technology, regulations, and other factors, design modifications extend their useful life.

In the consumer electronics industry, the first company to commercialize a product will gain a major and permanent market share. This ensures higher profitability over the product's life cycle. Unfortunately, organizations often fail to meet product launch dates despite the fact that getting products and services to market, ahead of competitors, is critical for long-term market share and profitability. In fact, estimates of on-time launches for new products are that they succeed only 45 percent of the time.[10]

Boeing's new 787 Dreamliner had already incurred more than $4 billion in development cost overruns as of October 15, 2009, and it was more than two years behind its original release schedule.[11] There were several reasons for the delay, including new technologies incorporated into its original design. Some were related to the airplane's leading-edge design functions and features. These needed to be carefully tested under actual flight conditions. These and other design modifications and new requirements delayed the plane's commercial release.[12] Schedule delays are also common for very different products such as civil engineering works. As an example, in late 2004, California State Auditor Elaine Howle released a report stating cost increases for a new span on the San Francisco Bay Bridge exceeded $1 billion because of a failure to manage and report cost overruns.[13] Project issues and risks are common across diverse industries, products, and services. There are also several types of project risks other than the application of new technologies.

However, the use of good project management methods can prevent or mitigate the effects of technological and other types of project risks associated with commercialization of new products and services. In fact, without effective project management the incidence rate of unexpected failures significantly increases. Different industries may also use modified project management methods and technologies to commercialize products and services. As an example, although there are similarities, the methods used to coordinate the design and commercialization of a consumer product would be different than those used for building commercial aircraft or bridges.

A generic approach toward project management includes identifying customer and stakeholder requirements and translating them into a new design's features and functions (e.g., internal specifications). This requires breaking a project's work activities into lower-level work tasks. Each work task has a starting and ending date, requires resources, and must meet deliverables aligned with requirements. A Gantt chart is used to schedule work tasks and higher-level activities over time to manage projects. Design teams control project activities using this methodology. The design team is composed of people from different organizational functions who contribute expertise and represent their stakeholder groups. As an example, purchasing members represent suppliers and related business interests relative to the purchase of materials, services, and other project resources. The human resources department helps staff production and other functions if capacity must be increased. There are also manufacturing, safety, quality, sales, marketing, and other team members. In addition to different roles and responsibilities, a team also follows a structured approach for identifying, prioritizing, and completing its work activities. Although different industries may use modified approaches for managing their design process, they require periodic reviews and approvals prior to proceeding to subsequent steps or tollgates.

Figure 1.4 describes five key project management steps known as tollgates having deliverables. These project steps have a work breakdown structure based on project work tasks. These lower-level work tasks are combined into higher-level activities. Effective project management requires identifying critical activities and work tasks, scheduling their completion dates, tracking actual to scheduled performance, meeting budgeting constraints, tracking key project metrics, and periodically communicating a project's status to customers and stakeholders. The efficiency and effectiveness of project management is important for ensuring that products and services perform as designed without failing.

A generic Gantt chart is also shown in Figure 1.4 with common deliverables. The activities and subordinate work tasks shown on the Gantt chart are scheduled depending on their sequential relationships. This implies that some activities must be completed before others can begin. Notice that the numbering of the first deliverable begins at 5. These deliverables are a continuation of the four marketing deliverables shown in Figure 1.2. In combination, Figures 1.2 and 1.4 describe a generic process for designing products and services. Table 1.1 describes, in more detail, basic methods used for each of the five design steps. The specific tools and methods used to achieve project deliverables vary for different types of products and services. But the approaches for designing across different industries and organizations are similar.

Once marketing estimates potential sales for a new product or service, a multidisciplinary design team is formed to gather and analyze customer and stakeholder requirements. This information is used to create preliminary cost, performance, and other design goals or targets. As a team begins its work there will usually be various issues regarding one or more project risks. These issues must be resolved during the project. There may also

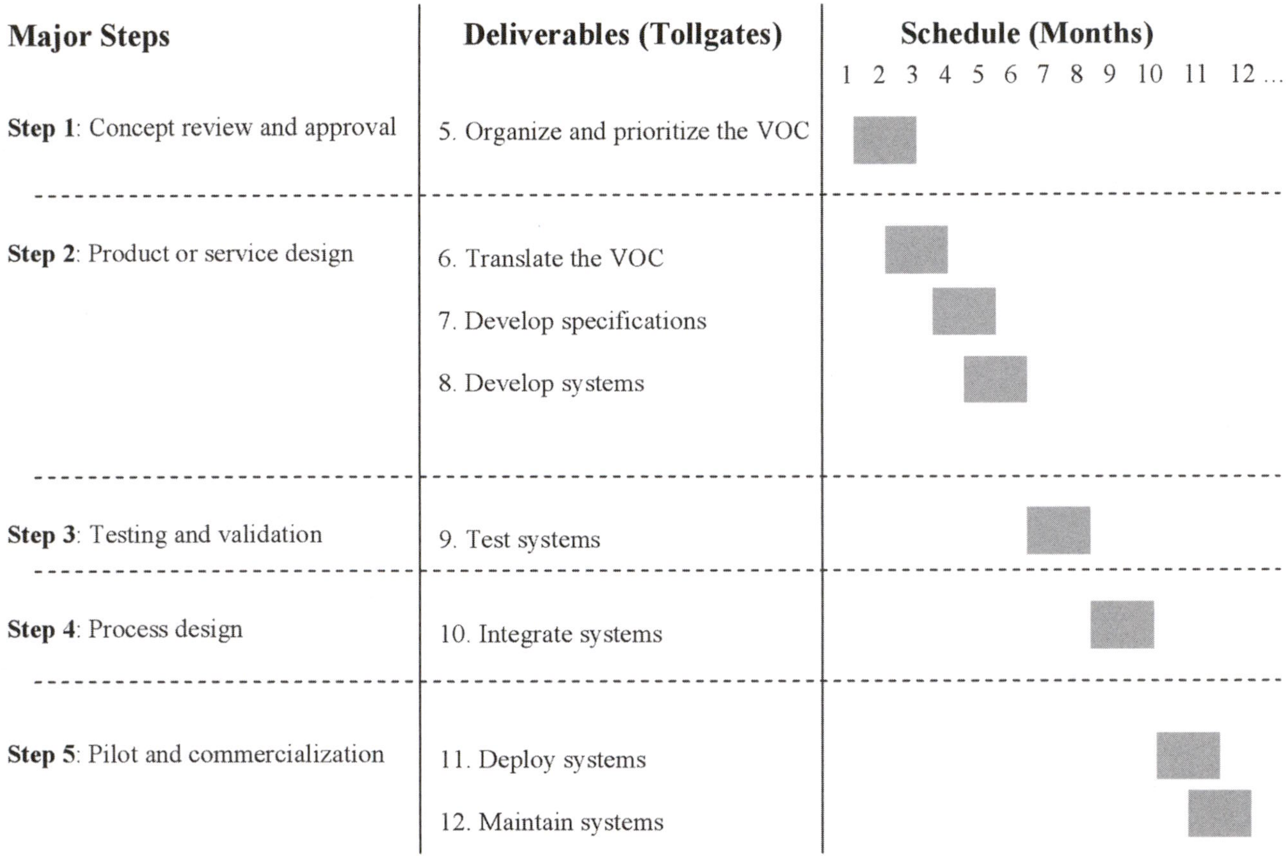

Figure 1.4 Key elements of project management

Table 1.1
Five basic design steps

1. Concept Review and Approval
   Create cross-functional team, define customer requirements, identify key design requirements and goals, preliminary process flow charts and basic sequence of production or construction, draft of quality assurance plan.
2. Product and Service System Design
   Design failure modes and effects analysis (DFMEA), design for manufacturability, design verification, design reviews, prototype build, control plan, engineering drawings, engineering specifications, new equipment, tooling and facilities requirements, special product and process characteristics, prototype control plan, gauges/testing equipment requirements, team feasibility.
3. Testing and Validation
   Laboratory and field testing of prototypes, reliability testing and modeling, tolerance design, design capability analysis, updated design FMEA.
4. Process Design
   Packaging standards, product/process quality systems review, process flow chart, floor plan layout, process failure mode and effects analysis (PFMEA), prelaunch control plan, process instructions, measurements systems analysis, preliminary process capability study plan, packaging specifications.
5. Pilot and Commercialization
   Trial runs of new design, initial capability analyses, measurement systems analysis, manufacturing control plan, approval of quality plan.

be customers and key stakeholders involved at critical reviews of a project's status. The overall goal is to bring a product or service from a concept through to its full commercialization. A critical goal is that all information and activities are well integrated with respect to current sales, the proposed design, and technologies that will be used, as well as requirements of manufacturing, distribution, and other functions and systems.

A decision may also be made, very early at this point of the marketing review, to purchase the product or service from outside the organization, that is, outsource it or manufacture it internally. Considerations for outsourcing may include unexpected higher costs, an inability to meet performance targets, lack of technology, lack of capacity, lower than expected sales revenues, external competitive threats, and regulatory or other issues. Regardless if a product or service is outsourced or produced internally, at the end of the marketing review, all customer and internal stakeholder requirements must be identified. At the end of this first design step, a team should have confidence its product or service has a high likelihood of being efficiently designed, produced, distributed, sold, maintained, and disposed or recycled.

Customers have needs that are represented as the voice of the customer (VOC) and an organization's internal stakeholders have their needs represented as voice of the business (VOB). This implies a balance must be achieved between customer and stakeholder needs or requirements relative to functions, features, and other design attributes. Although a new product or service must meet customer requirements, it must also be cost effectively produced. It must also have high reliability to ensure customer's requirements are consistently met over its useful life. To ensure a proper balance between VOC and VOB, it is important that new products and services be aligned with an organization's long-term strategic goals and objectives regarding markets, market share, and other strategic goals. Customers and stakeholders also have different perspectives of a project's benefits, risks, and the resources that are necessary for success. Frequent design reviews are a good way to capture this information and to quickly review and resolve issues.

Creating useful designs begins with translating customer requirements into very detailed specifications. Specifications describe required functions, features, form or structure, aesthetics, and other relevant requirements necessary to satisfy customers and stakeholders. Requirements translation is important because customers qualitatively communicate needs, values, and expectations. For this reason, an effective translation process is critical for ensuring the right features and functions are identified and quantified prior to investing significant amounts of time and other resources designing and producing a product or service. Key considerations important for creating internal specifications are that they are quantitative and measurable, consistent, customer-focused, balanced, and simple. *Quantitative* implies specifications can be efficiently analyzed using small samples. *Measurable* implies specifications can be tested with the required accuracy and precision. *Consistent* implies one specification does not contradict another. *Customer-focused* implies specifications represent real customer requirements. *Balanced* implies specifications also meet stakeholder requirements. *Simple* implies that specifications are easy to understand when people have been properly trained to measure and interpret them.

This is not an easy process. As an example, consider a situation where one customer wants a car to quickly accelerate after a traffic light changes from red to green. The problem is that different customers perceive acceleration differently. This implies a design team will need to discuss the acceleration needs of many customers. Before creating an acceleration specification they must evaluate the impact of the specification on different customers as well as other product attributes.

Very different types of products require a similar approach. As an example, when software is being created, user requirements must be understood prior to creating software code and other attributes. Customers may say they want their software to be very visual, intuitive to use, free from errors, and low in cost. Qualitative statements such as these reflect how customers often describe needs and wants. Software designers have created tools to translate subjective customer requirements into quantifiable and testable software code. As an example, some useful requirements translation strategies for customers include screen shots, prototypes, and demonstration software with visual and highly interactive communication styles to help the requirements translation process.

Requirements translation activities also occur in different forms in very different industries. Examples include the construction of bridges, dams, and buildings as opposed to the design of service systems. Construction projects usually begin with a visual representation or model of the work structure within its future geography. These types of prototypes represent analytical work represented as quantitative specifications (the model). Superimposed on the model are physical constraints. Simulations are also made to understand how the system functions under various types of stress. These stresses vary by product and service application. Examples include evaluations of maximum traffic flow across bridges, the flow of water across dams, and occupancy and aesthetic requirements for occupied buildings. Of course there are also physical evaluations of structural strength for these systems. Service systems are also evaluated under stress, but, relevant for their application environments.

Regardless of the specific tools and methods used, each industry meets the challenge of efficiently translating customer requirements in ways that make sense, to its customers, key stakeholders, designers, and other groups. A new product or service design will fail if customer requirements are inaccurately translated into internal specifications or if internal specifications have not been properly balanced against the competing priorities of an organization's key stakeholders. Poor translation results in incomplete, non-testable, and inconsistent specifications. In turn, poor specifications result in higher project cost, lower performance, and inferior quality as well as a longer time to bring products and services to market.

Table 1.2 provides a simple example of a SIPOC diagram (supply, inputs, process, outputs, customer) to show how customer requirements are translated into internal specifications suitable for designing a simple service process. The acronym SIPOC captures information related to suppliers (S), their inputs (supplier specifications, or I), the process steps (P), the outputs (internal specifications tied to customer requirements, or O), and the original customer (and stakeholder) requirements (C). Customer requirements are usually obtained through customer interviews, surveys, or other methods. In the current example the requirements are that customers do not want coffee if it is too cold, too hot, or poor-tasting. The table service should also be fast, the silverware clean, and the bill correct. Currently, these requirements are qualitative. A service system cannot be directly

Table 1.2
Requirements translation using a SIPOC—coffee example

Supplies	Inputs	Process	Outputs	Customers
• Coffee	• Thermometer to measure temperature, procedure and training	• Customer walks in and sits down at a table.	• >110⁰ F	• Not too cold
• Water		• Within 3 minutes customer order is taken.	• Target = 145⁰ F	• Not too hot
• Cups	• Coffee is brewed according to procedure and tasted prior to serving	• If coffee is requested, the cup is checked for cleanliness and coffee poured.	• <180⁰ F	• Tastes good
• Coffee brewer			• Within 3 minutes for order and 3 minutes for coffee	• Fast Service
• Servers (people)	• Timer to measure time, procedure, and training	• Its temperature is automatically measured at a target of 145⁰ F to ensure it is within the allowed temperature range.		• Clean cup and silverware
• Thermometer	• Visual procedure and training		• No dirt, grease, or spots	• Accurate bill
• Timer		• Coffee is brought to table within 3 minutes.	• Item charged	• Self seating
• Invoice (bills)	• Procedure and training	• Bill is calculated, checked, and presented to customer.	• Amount charged	
• Money (change)		• Customer checks bill; if correct, bill is paid; otherwise a complaint is made to server.	• Self seating	

designed using qualitative information because it will either fail to meet customer expectations or it will be too costly. Lacking quantitative requirements, most likely, it will fail on both counts. As a result more information will be needed by a design team before proceeding with its work.

These customer requirements must be translated into quantified and measurable specifications to design and manage this new process. As an example, a quantified temperature specification would be that coffee should be served at a temperature between 110° F and 180° F. Other quantitative specifications would be that coffee is served within three minutes from taking an order, the silverware should be free of visible dirt, grease, or spots, and the bill should be accurate with no errors. Of course, there would be other specifications regarding food and other service system attributes. This example shows a simple strategy for creating a service system: understanding what customers need and creating a process to satisfy those needs.

Column P in Table 1.2 describes sequential operations that align to customer specifications. If these activities are well done, customer specifications will be met. The sequence begins when a customer walks in and sits down at a table (self-seating), then within three minutes the customer's order is taken. If coffee is requested, a cup is selected and checked for cleanliness. The coffee is poured and measured to be a target temperature of 145°F. The coffee is brought to the table within three minutes. There are also other processes such as ordering and serving food and related activities. After the customer has been served, a bill is calculated, checked, and presented to the customer. The customer also checks the bill for accuracy and pays if it is correct.

There would also be several supporting activities necessary to create this simple process. Examples include creating floor layouts describing the locations of tables, chairs, cooking equipment, and materials, creating procedures and policies, training employees, scheduling work, and so forth. Specifications would also be created to control incoming materials, equipment, labor, information, and items purchased from suppliers.

These are the basic activities necessary to design a simple service system that reflects customer and stakeholder requirements. To the extent design goals are successfully achieved, the likelihood of unexpected failures will be reduced. Of course, some specifications are common sense. An example is the cleanliness specification. However, other specifications, such as coffee temperature, require systematically asking customers their opinions prior to creating it. Let's discuss a few common methods for translating customer requirements into useful specifications.

After suppliers, input specifications, the basic process steps, output specifications, and customers have been identified using a SIPOC diagram, an input/output matrix that is sometimes called a quality function deployment

(QFD) matrix is used to map specifications to the systems and subsystems that provide functions and features necessary to meet them. Figure 1.5 shows how this is done. The goal is to ensure alignment of functions and features with customer requirements. Although different industries use modified versions of this type of input and output matrix, its basic purpose does not change. It is always used to link specifications and the subsystems providing functions, features, form or structure, and aesthetic properties. If performance gaps are identified between specifications and actual performance, modifications are made or new functions and features created to ensure all specifications are finally met. Incorrect translation will result in product and service failures. These will eventually be seen as breakdowns of usability, maintainability, upgradability, recyclability, and disposability.

Prioritizing tools and methods are used to help make tradeoff decisions between the functions, features, and other attributes. Models are also

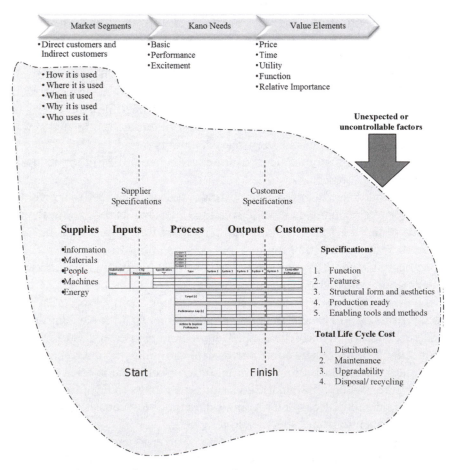

Figure 1.5   Overview of requirements translation

created to understand and explain the combined effects of subsystem inputs on outputs (specifications). Some of these models are very quantitative and based on advanced statistical methods such as design of experiments, regression analysis, Monte Carlo simulation, and reliability models. To the extent performance gaps exist between specifications and subsystem performance, design modifications will be necessary.

There are accepted principles for good design. However, specific tools, methods, and technologies vary between industries. An integrative philosophy for designing products and services, across all industries, is concurrent engineering. *Concurrent* implies that all the relevant design activities are integrated throughout a project in ways that enable rapid sharing of information across functional groups. A concurrent engineering approach for design improves communication between a design team as well as its customers and stakeholders. Its proven benefits include reduced cycle times for commercialization of new products and services, higher productivity and quality, and lower tooling and capital expenditures because there are fewer design and production errors.

Design for manufacturability (DFM) is a set of design principles that ensure efficient manufacturing of products and services.[14] Table 1.3 shows 12 of these principles relative to manufacturing and service applications. These best practices have proven useful for ensuring that new products and services are economically designed with high quality and reliability. These 12 principles also depend on and integrate well with other important design activities such as creating a balanced team, using a structured project management approach, and a employing correct application of tools, methods, and technologies.

The first principle requires understanding customer and stakeholder requirements. A correlating principle to requirement translation is there should also be effective communication with stakeholders. Communication helps ensure that design teams, customers, and stakeholders coordinate information and activities in ways that help enhance design activities. Effective translation of requirements is the foundation on which products and services should be designed to reduce the likelihood of failure.

The second principle is simplicity. Simplicity encourages designers to create simplified designs by eliminating unnecessary materials, components, and processes that are hazardous or require specialized training and maintenance. Additional useful strategies include identifying and eliminating unnecessary components, operations, or substituting safer materials for more dangerous ones. There are many other ways to simplify products and services. To the extent simplifications can be achieved, the likelihood of unexpected failure will decrease. This is because simple designs usually have fewer subcomponents to purchase, handle, assemble, and test. Fewer

Table 1.3
Twelve common design principles

Principle	Manufacturing Examples	Service Examples
1. Understand customer and stakeholder requirements.	Market research, design reviews.	Market research, design reviews.
2. Eliminate materials, components, and processes that are unnecessary or hazardous, or require specialized training and maintenance.	Identify and eliminate useless components; substitute safer materials for dangerous ones.	Identify and eliminate useless operations; substitute safer materials for dangerous ones.
3. Use standardized rather than customized materials, components, and procedures.	Insist designers use purchasing approved suppliers and currently available products.	Train employees and insist they provide services the same way every time according to procedure.
4. Combine several functions and consolidate materials into one component or operation.	Combine features and functions into fewer components.	Eliminate process steps and operations; automate where possible.
5. Eliminate secondary operations where practical (screws, fasteners, adhesives).	Create snap fits and combine components into fewer ones.	Combine operations into the same process step where practical, and present to customers at same time.
6. Ensure easy alignment of components to ensure visibility to enable vertical assembly and inspection (by machines).	Taper mating surfaces and design alignment vertically top to bottom (90 degrees).	Ensure the status of operations are visible and aberrations are easy to see.
7. Integrate mistake proofing strategies into the design to prevent errors.	Ensure mating components are asymmetrical and can be assembled only one way.	Ensure departures from standards are detected immediately; use automated systems to check functions, features, or process outputs.
8. Ensure the design is easy to test and analyze.	Ensure specifications are testable, and configurable for automatic testing and analysis.	Ensure designs, requirements, and testing are simple so operators know when a departure from standard occurs.

(continued)

Principle	Manufacturing Examples	Service Examples
9. Understand the dynamic relationships between materials, components, and subsystems to create tolerances that help achieve high capability.	Test design parameters as systems using statistical models to evaluate parameter interactions against specifications.	Create system models and test them under all expected usage conditions. Validate models in actual situations.
10. Design components, subsystems, and products based on machine and tooling (production) capability and to reduce production operations	Pilot a new product under controlled conditions to ensure it can be economically manufactured with high quality.	Pilot a new service under controlled conditions to ensure it can be economically manufactured with high quality
11. Design to enable production to delay final product customization based on actual customer demand.	Ensure design commonality across several products to reduce their production costs.	Design services using a basic design, with differentiation used only as necessary.
12. Ensure designs are easy to disassemble, service, maintain, and dispose.	Ensure designs are easy to break down and reassemble for maintenance. Ensure materials can be safely disposed or recycled at the end of their lives.	Ensure workers are cross-trained and information technology systems reconfigurable to ensure modifications to services are easy to make.

subcomponents also help reduce development costs, cycle times, and failure rates. In contrast, complexity increases the likelihood of failures because errors increase with the number of subcomponents. In summary, simplicity is an essential strategy for designing products, services, and logistical systems to make them easier to assemble, learn, use, repair, and eventually dispose and recycle.

The third design principle promotes standardized tools, methods, materials, machines, measurements, and people who are well trained. In contrast, using customized components and methods requires having to train people to use them, creating new procedures, and sometimes purchasing new equipment. A lack of standardization increases complexity. In turn, complexity increases the likelihood of errors.

Product and service functions should also be combined or modularized for easy assembly, testing, and servicing, as well as disposal and recycling. Ideally, subcomponents should also be combined and modularized where practical. The result will be a simpler design having fewer components that fail.

Once several functions and features are combined, specification tolerances must be analyzed and rationalized. A tolerance is the amount of deviation allowed from a specification. Wider tolerances result in fewer internal failures, but the tolerances must be carefully calculated to ensure required functions and features are not adversely impacted when products and services are used. In other words, they must be generous where practical, but also be set to ensure function and feature specifications are met under all conditions of expected usage. Ideally, they should be calculated using statistical models to ensure they are wide enough: they do not interfere with other specifications and are also compatible with production capabilities.

Some other important design principles include eliminating different materials and secondary operations, mistake proofing, and ensuring subcomponents are visible and easy to align. Designs should also be easy to test, analyze, disassemble for service, maintain, dispose, and recycle. This integrated approach to design helps reduce unexpected failures.

There are many examples showing how these best practices have been implemented. As an example, eliminating secondary operations may require creating snap fits and combining several subcomponents. The same principle for a service process may be seen when several similar operations are combined into only one. Examples of easy alignment include tapering mating surfaces to ensure easy subcomponent alignment or using a simple vertical top-to-bottom (90 degrees) assembly process. In a service process, creating visual operations where the output of one operation clearly becomes the input for the next one is a similar application of the concept. Abnormal processing conditions are easier to see when using these simplification and standardization methods.

There are also numerous examples where mistake proofing has been successfully used both in product design and use as well as service processes to prevent the occurrence of errors and mistakes. As an example, assembly operations can be mistake proofed by ensuring mating components are asymmetrical so they can be assembled only one way. From a service perspective, systems can be created to immediately detect departures from standards. Table 1.3 provides examples for the remaining 12 principles. This information will become very useful in latter chapters to help understand why the things we trust fail.

When new products or services are designed by global teams, new and unique challenges occur. As an example, if they will be used in several countries and regions or within a single country having different customer preferences, laws, or regulations, they may have to be reconfigured for use. Examples include designing computer power systems so they automatically adjust to operate at electrical voltages of 120 or 240 volts. The 120 voltage is common within the United States while the 240 voltage is used throughout most of the rest of the world. There are also many different types of power sources and receptacles across the world. This fact needs to also be considered by a team that must design such products. Another example is an automotive steering wheel. Automobiles in different countries have steering wheels located on the left or right side. There are similar considerations for products and services used in different countries.

Global designs should also incorporate intuitive symbols and use the simplest language possible to ensure their functions and features are easy to use. This helps prevent misinterpretation and misuse. They should also be free of jargon and acronyms that are difficult to understand. As an example, when I travel to Asia, many of the instructions are visual: restaurant menus have pictures rather than words only, and there are other images that guide me when using basic services and products. It is also important that products, services, and subsystems be designed in ways that enable them to be transferable from one country to another without expensive and time-consuming requalification.

The 12 design principles are also useful for global design teams. Using modular design principles and common interfaces helps simplify and standardize designs, even if higher-level systems are designed differently from one country to another. This makes them easier to use from one country to another. Products and service technology should also be flexible and scalable if customer preferences or customer demand should change. The design of products and services for use across the world requires thoughtful planning by cross-cultural design teams. Common reasons for product and service failures are global design teams that do not understand cultural issues or good design principles.

Outsourcing the design or production of products and services will also affect design activities. Prior to beginning its design work, a team will need to analyze customer requirements as well as internal design and production capabilities. In some situations, minor modifications to a current product or service may be all that is necessary to meet a customer's needs. Or a different organization may already be offering a similar product or service, but at lower cost and higher quality. It may be prudent to simply contract this organization to directly supply the product or service. Either strategy will save an organization significant time and money. It may also be useful to outsource design activities if comparable internal capabilities do not exist within an organization. Outsourcing may also be a good strategy if projected demand is less than forecast, if needed technologies or patents are owned by other organizations, when there are high internal development costs and risks, if internal knowledge and skills are lacking, if there is insufficient internal capacity, or when investment capital is limited.

In most situations, outsourcing results in lower cost and development time as well as higher quality and reliability, but not always. Organizations can make major mistakes when they outsource to organizations that do not have the required design or productive capabilities. Outsourcing also increases the complexity of design and production activities. Recall that complexity increases the likelihood of errors and mistakes.

There are also many different types of tools and methods that are used to design, test, and commercialize new products and services. Because the focus of this book is on describing how products and services fail, one method in particular is especially important for evaluating the likelihood of product or service failure. It is called design failure mode and effects analysis (DFMEA). An example, of a DFMEA applied to coffee is shown in Table 1.4. The method is used by engineers to identify all the known ways in which their product or service designs could fail: the mode or type of failure, the causes of failure, the effects of failures on external customers, and the ability to detect a failure before a customer is negatively impacted. The purpose for using a DFMEA is to identify the causes of failure and prevent or reduce the likelihood they actually occur. In other words, once the types of failures and their causes are known, solutions and controls can be identified to prevent or manage them. A design and its production process will usually be modified because of a DFMEA analysis. In summary, the method enables designers to create more reliable products and services having a lower likelihood of failure. Once designers identify important functions, features, and other attributes by showing how and why they may fail, operations people use this information to create a process failure mode and effects analysis (PFMEA) to identify operational weaknesses.

Manufacturing an automobile tire is an example showing how design and process FMEAs are useful. A tire is actually a composite of several subcomponents of rubber (polymer) glued and molded together using heat and pressure. The process results in a crosslinking of polymer molecules known as curing, which increases the strength of a tire's material. One important requirement is that a tire's sidewall not unexpectedly fail because a driver may be harmed if a tire suddenly loses its pressure and vehicle control is lost. In an analysis of this failure mode, this information will be noted by designers. The designers will also identify potential causes for a sidewall bursting. These may include improper assembly of the tire's components through insufficient gluing, poor molding, or insufficient curing, and external damage, such as punctures or other failures. There may be several potential causes for these failure modes such as low tire pressure, which heats a vehicle's tire when driven at high speeds. High heat degrades a tire's polymeric materials and can lead to sudden failure.

Table 1.4 applies the DFMEA concept to the coffee example, which was shown in Table 1.2. Let's examine the method in more detail. There are several useful features of a DFMEA. First, potential failures modes or types are described in detail using the DFMEA. Second, the effect of each failure

Table 1.4
Design Failure Mode and Effects Analysis (DFMEA)—coffee example

Process Step	Potential Failure Mode	Potential Failure Effects	S E V	Potential Causes	O C C	Current Controls	D E T
1. Customer walks in and sits down at a table.	Customer cannot sit down	Customer waits	5	Not enough tables	2	None	10
2. Within 3 minutes customer order is taken.	Customer not greeted in 3 minutes	Customer waits	5	Customer arrives too quickly	1	Manager helps greet customers	10
3. If coffee is requested, the cup is checked for cleanliness and coffee poured.	Customer received dirty cup	Customer dissatisfied, returns coffee resulting in longer waiting time	7	Failure to inspect cup	2	Training, procedure, customer feedback	2
4. Its temperature is automatically measured at a target of 145°F to ensure it is within the allowed temperature range.	Coffee too cold	If too cold, customer returns coffee	5	Failure to follow procedure, incorrect thermometer, etc.	4	Training, procedure, customer feedback	2
	Coffee too hot	If too hot, customer must wait to drink coffee	5	Failure to follow procedure, incorrect thermometer, etc.	5	Training, procedure, customer feedback	2
5. Coffee is brought to table within 3 minutes.	Customer not served in 3 minutes	Customer waits	5	Kitchen backed up	1	None	10
6. Bill is calculated, checked and presented to customer.	Inaccurate bill	Customer is dissatisfied and must wait	8	Not checking calculations	1	Training, procedure, customer feedback	2
7. Customer checks bill; if correct, bill is paid, otherwise a complaint is made to server.	Inaccurate bill	Customer is dissatisfied and must wait	9	Not checking calculations	2	Training, procedure, customer feedback	3

mode on external customers (e.g., severity, or SEV) is described. The list can become very long, but descriptive details are essential for this analysis. The severity of each failure effect on external customers is rated between 1 and 10. A rating of 1 is a minor annoyance and a rating of 10 is very severe. In some industries, a rating of 10 or severe implies loss of life. The cause of each failure mode is then identified. A failure mode may have several potential causes. This example has several possible causes for tire wall bursting including a puncture and low tire pressure leading to overheating. An occurrence probability (OCC) is also estimated for each cause of failure using a rating between 1 and 10 with a 1 implying failures are infrequent and 10 implying failures occur frequently. In some industries a rating of 1 implies one in a million failure frequency and a 10 implies a one in two failure frequency.

Designers use the information from a DFMEA to eliminate failure causes or reduce their occurrence. A third analysis, detection probability, is made to determine if an internal failure can be detected using currently available control methods (DET). The detection probability rating is also between 1 and 10 with a 1 implying robust control methods are available and a 10 implying it is very difficult to identify an internal failure event prior to shipment to customers. Finally, an overall risk prioritization number (RPN) is calculated by multiplying the three ratings. The RPN range is between 1 and 1,000. The higher the RPN number, the higher the priority for elimination, detection, or control of potential failure causes.

It is obvious DFMEAs are essential useful tools for helping prevent failures. Every new product and service design should have both a DFMEA and PFMEA. However, they are not always used with the result that design flaws are often missed. From a different perspective, the likelihood of unexpected failures can be reduced using standardized materials, procedures, and technologies because their failure modes, causes, and effects are known from experience. The coffee example shown in Table 1.4 is a much simplified and summarized version of a DFMEA. It encourages a designer to think about the many ways in which coffee service could fail. This type of detailed analysis provides useful information for making modifications to a process to prevent failures from occurring, or if prevention is not feasible, it is helpful for designing process controls to manage failures when they occur.

New products and services must also be tested and validated under conditions of expected usage at several steps of their development process to ensure they meet customer requirements. After testing has been successfully completed, a pilot evaluation using limited production quantities is conducted under controlled conditions. A pilot should always be done before full-scale commercialization of a new product or service. Pilot evaluations are discussed in more detail later in this chapter because they may occur several times during a project. After a successful pilot evaluation, a ramp-up occurs in which products or services are made available in larger quantity, that is, more people are exposed to a new product or service process and over longer periods of time.

This generalized strategy for testing and validation of features, functions, and other attributes is used to commercialize most new products or services, but of course specific methods vary greatly across industries. Consumer electronics, large machinery such as automobiles and aircraft, construction products, and service systems are tested at several points within their development cycle. They are retested just prior to commercialization and their performance is monitored over their useful life cycle. In contrast, low-cost seasonal and disposable consumer products may not be tested at all. Also, large construction projects require continual proof testing of materials and intermediate construction work. Even service processes are tested using modified methods.

There are also commonly accepted standards for testing and validation, although specific methods vary across industries. Testing and validations are often controlled by industry organizations such as ASTM International and the International Standards Organization (ISO).[15] Industry standards are also used to ensure customers receive products and services meeting minimum industry requirements for economical and safe use. The testing itself is as diverse as the products and services being tested. Products are exposed to mechanical, electrical, chemical, and visual and other types of stress. There are also nondestructive testing methods employed when a product must be later sold. Alternatively, destructive testing will be used if alternative testing methods do not exist. Design teams often use combinations of several testing methods in which less costly internal testing is applied to materials, subcomponents, and subsystems prior to more realistic field testing of finished products or services. Field testing is an excellent way to verify that products and services meet customer requirements under actual usage conditions.

There are three basic analyses associated with testing and validation activities. The first are focused on tolerance design, which was briefly discussed earlier in this chapter. Recall, a tolerance is the amount by which a specification can change. Whereas a new design may be perfectly acceptable in the mid-range of its specification or over its entire range when it is evaluated in isolation, tolerance analyses are useful for evaluating the combined effects of specification changes on several functions and features. Tolerance interrelationships are analyzed using statistical models that show the combinations of specification levels that optimize feature and function performance and overall expected usage conditions. The second type of analysis is focused on capability modeling. Capability modeling helps ensure a new design meets original customer requirements with a high confidence. The third analysis is reliability testing. Reliability testing is used to verify a new product or service will meet specifications under a variety of usage conditions over time when used by customers.

Let's review a simple call center that handles millions of incoming telephone calls in a year. Customer expectations are that their calls are answered relatively quickly, they are provided with correct information, and appropriate actions are taken if necessary to meet their service request. These expectations are translated into specification or service metrics. In this service system, there are several different work activities that must be integrated, balanced, and optimized to ensure customer service metrics are met cost effectively and with high quality. How is this type of service system designed? First, anticipated incoming call volumes by type of customer and service request are forecast, over a year, by day and hour throughout the system. Incidentally, a call system usually consists of several integrated facilities across the world using advanced information and communication technologies. This infrastructure enables an organization to create work schedules and optimally route incoming and outgoing calls to ensure agents are not overloaded. To help manage these systems, operational statistics are visually displayed for everyone to see. These statistics typically show, by customer segment and type of service request, how long customers wait and the number of dropped calls, as well as similar information useful for managing customer requirements and maintaining operational efficiencies.

Models are also used to manage and improve service systems. As an example, queuing and simulation models are useful for balancing demand with available capacity to ensure call centers meet service levels. They also show the effects of varying the number of agents, routing strategies, and other variables relative to effects on operational costs, response times, and other service statistics when the systems are exposed to a variety of conditions such as changes of call volume. Call center management uses models to adjust agent staffing levels. Although specific methods for designing service systems vary from those used for designing products, there are similarities. This is an important concept to remember. The application of these methods helps prevent failures. Many times, when a catastrophic failure occurs, the issue has been that basic design and testing methods were not effectively used to design the product and service.

Operational experts such as industrial, manufacturing, and process engineers work concurrently with design teams to ensure new products and services can be economically produced with high quality. The advantage of using a concurrent engineering approach for design is that it enables process engineers to provide feedback to a design team regarding the best ways to produce new products and services. This communication is especially important if new production equipment must be designed or when modifying supporting production systems.

Important outputs from the fourth design step (process design) include creating preliminary process flow charts, product assurance plans, process failure modes and effects analyses (PFMEA), a preliminary quality control plan, requirements for new equipment, tooling and facilities requirements, gauges and testing equipment requirements, floor plan layouts, process instructions, measurement systems analyses, preliminary process capability studies, production part approvals, and packaging evaluations. If these activities are not properly executed, the result will be a higher likelihood of failure. The best product or service design cannot overcome poor production methods.

A pilot study is used to evaluate the manufacture of a product or a service process for a limited time and under very controlled conditions to verify it meets customer requirements. Pilot studies are used to evaluate the entire system including design attributes and production systems. The development team coordinates the pilot evaluation with production operations, quality assurance, customers, and key stakeholders. Pilot studies also expose remaining issues that require design or process modifications prior to commercialization. Specific activities include making a production trial run, evaluating measurement systems, conducting preliminary process capability studies, obtaining sample approvals from customers, conducting additional validation testing, evaluating packaging, creating a final production control plan, and obtaining quality planning sign-offs from customers. The result from successfully completing these activities will be a higher level of stakeholder support and customer satisfaction, and fewer failures.

A design process moves through these five steps (concept review and approval, product or service design, testing and validation, process design, and piloting and commercialization), using appropriate tools and methods for creating products and services. In parallel, a team must also manage several types of project risks. How well they identify and manage project risks also influences the likelihood of failure. Many of the catastrophic events to be discussed in upcoming chapters have a common theme in that basic design methods were not effectively used or project issues and risks were not effectively managed.

Project management activities, especially those related to the design of products and services, are subject to several types of risk. In fact, failures can often be traced back to specific project issues that were initially identified as potential risks, but not eliminated and managed prior to commercialization. Project risks include scheduling, cost, technology, performance, market demand and supply, legal issues, and regulatory concerns. Risks may also be interrelated. As an example, supply issues may adversely impact a project's schedule and cost. Legal and regulatory issues may adversely impact performance, schedules, and cost.

Project scheduling risk occurs if product or process requirements are not achieved by agreed-upon dates. There are different reasons why project schedules are at risk. Often schedule risk is caused by other types of risk. As an example, supply issues are caused by capacity limitations, production or distribution breakdowns, or shortages of skilled workers and professionals. These adversely impact project schedules. Supply issues also occur if materials increase in price, are no longer available, or were incorrectly selected and specified early in the design process. Market risks occur if original sales and marketing assumptions were inaccurate, customers go out of business or unexpectedly cancel orders, new competitors emerge, costs erode margins, or new technology renders obsolete the need for a product or service. Customers may also change requirements, causing specification changes and design modifications. There may also be technological and performance limitations related to new laws and regulations. There are many factors that may adversely impact a project's schedule or other important project goals.

A problem with not meeting schedules is that a design team and key internal stakeholders may be tempted to take shortcuts such as incorrectly reporting information or not completing important design activities. This behavior can result in design issues that eventually cause product or service failures. How well a design team handles scheduling and other types of risk depends on many factors. Using a professional project management and review methodology that periodically updates customers and key stakeholders is a basic requirement for properly identifying and managing these risks. Well-managed design projects also help improve the quality and reliability of new product and service designs.

Supply and capacity risks increase if prices for materials, labor, or project resources unexpectedly increase. Higher prices also reduce profit margins if selling prices cannot be increased. One tactic used by organizations to manage supply and capacity risks is to modify a design's components or production process to use new materials, methods, and technologies to maintain supply alternatives to control costs. But there are situations where projects may fail because critical resources are no longer available.

In situations in which products and services are designed to have very long life cycles, cost pressures may also become important. This is especially true from a total life cycle perspective. Costs are impacted by requirements for periodic maintenance and repair. Examples include commercial and military aircraft and infrastructure projects such as construction of roads, railways, bridges, and similar large-scale projects. If effective actions to maintain cost targets are not applied early when designing products and services, performance degradation may occur if changes need to be made to protect profit margins. This behavior contributes to failures. Technical risks occur if customer requirements are inaccurately translated into specifications, or new and unknown technologies must be used for products and services or their supporting processes. Technical risks are also incurred if a design only marginally meets specifications regarding functions, features, and other attributes. Development teams can easily get themselves into a no-win situation when a project relies on unproven technologies. Sometimes, there is no feasible technical solution for a problem. Technology risks can easily cause performance issues, but so can other factors. To the extent that technology risks can be recognized early, it may be possible to effectively manage them.

The design of new products and services requires a well-organized strategy for project management. This requires participation of almost every organizational function and the coordination of hundreds and sometimes thousands of people. Coordination of activities may also be required across several countries. However, despite due diligence and the best intent by design teams, failures sometimes occur. Often they can be attributed to poor communication, failed performance testing, or operational and distribution issues.[16] There may also be other reasons.

In my experience poor communication rather than technology is one of the most common reasons for product and service failures. Poor communication occurs if customer requirements are not correctly translated, project management protocols are not properly created, teams are not balanced or do not collaborate with each other, and few mechanisms exist for communicating project progress, risks, and issues to customers and key stakeholders. It inhibits a team's ability to accurately assess a project's schedule along with its cost and performance issues, and to identify technological and other risks. As an example, performance issues caused by poor communication occur when a new design's functions, features, or other attributes do not meet customer requirements and internal specifications, or these elements are contradictory or detrimental to other design attributes. ; They also occur if design modifications have not been reviewed or approved by customers and stakeholders; if there are defects in components and subsystems; or if these have not been properly integrated and tested. Poor communication causes testing issues to occur if internal defects are not properly identified, reported, and eliminated prior to commercialization. Poor communication causes support issues to occur if auxiliary supporting information such as customer and employee training documentation do not exist or are marginal, and field maintenance systems are not adequate to maintain products and services in the field. Poor communication contributes to distribution issues when packaging has not been properly specified and tested, when damage or deterioration occurs during transportation, or when products and services are not available at the time and place advertised. These are some of the many ways in which products and services fail from poor communication.

SUMMARY

Design teams across the world follow a structured and collaborative process for creating new products and services to ensure they meet and balance customer and stakeholder needs. There are thousands of new products and services commercialized every year. Most of them satisfy customers. Good designs, from a customer's perspective, are those that are easy to install, use, upgrade, maintain, and dispose or recycle at the end of their useful lives. Designs from a stakeholder perspective are those that achieve profitability targets because they can be efficiently produced, are easy to sell and install, have sufficient reliability (e.g., are available for use within their application environments), and are easy to service, upgrade, and dispose or recycle.

It is the interest of every organization, regardless if it is private, public, or nonprofit, to create designs that meet these criteria. Failures do occur. Whereas most are minor inconveniences, others cause catastrophic loss of life and property. Using best in class design methods is only the first step for ensuring that unexpected failures do not occur. However, even when using the most advanced technology, the best design practices and project management methods may not be able to prevent catastrophic failures. Nonetheless, they are our best chance for success. As an example, some recent catastrophic failures may have been foreseen and prevented, but others could not have been, even when using the most advanced project management methods and technologies. This is because there may be conditions that will cause unexpected and catastrophic failures for several reasons. Some may have been known in advance and only partial solutions implemented. Others may have been caused by negligent maintenance and repair. Still others may not have previously occurred and become a surprise for designers. These latter failures cannot be easily prevented.

In the next chapter, we will discuss cognition factors and group behaviors from a social psychological perspective. People make errors of perception, judgment, and understanding. Groups of people also make errors of various types. Errors cause failures both small and large in their effect. Most of the most catastrophic events discussed in upcoming chapters have as their root causes cognitive issues. We will integrate this chapter's information with that of the next chapter to show how new products and services can be modified to make them less prone to failure.

NOTES

1. History.com, *History of the RMS Titanic,* http://www.history.com/topics/titanic.

2. Kirk Johnson, "Denver Airport to Mangle Last Bag," *New York Times,* August 27, 2005.

3. Richard W. Stevenson et al., "Hurricane Katrina: Federal Response; Administration Steps Up Actions, Adding Troops and Dispatching Medical Supplies," *New York Times,* September 1, 2005; Centers for Disease Control, "H1N1 Vaccine Behind Schedule," *CBS News,* October 21, 2009.

4. Federal Drug Administration, "FDA Releases Results of Study on Defibrillator and Pacemaker Malfunctions—Part of Agency Drive," news release, September 16, 2005.

5. James W. Martin, *Operational Excellence: Using Lean Six Sigma to Translate Customer Value through Global Supply Chains* (New York: Auerbach, 2008), chapters 3 and 4.

6. The Microsoft *Encarta Dictionary,* http://encarta.msn.com/encnet/features/dictionary/DictionaryResults.aspx?lextype=3&search=complexity; Encarta World English Dictionary [North American Edition] 2009. Microsoft Corporation. All rights reserved. Developed for Microsoft by Bloomsbury Publishing Plc.

7. Merriam-Webster, "Design," *Merriam-Webster Dictionary,* http://www.merriam-webster.com/dictionary/design.

8. Tim Berry, "Product and Brand Failures: A Marketing Perspective," http://articles.mplans.com/product-and-brand-failures-a-marketing-perspective/.

9. C. Merle Crawford, "Marketing Research and the New Product Failure Rate," *Journal of Marketing* 41, no. 2 (1977): 51–61.

10. Jill Jusko, "Failure to Launch," *Industry Week,* September 1, 2007, http://www.industryweek.com/articles/failure_to_launch_14782.aspx.

11. "Dreamliner Costing Boeing $4B in Overruns," *United Press International,* October 15, 2009.

12. Douglas McIntyre, "The Dreamliner May Finally Get Off the Ground," *Daily Finance,* December 7, 2009, www.Weblogs.com.

13. "Audit Criticizes Caltrans Over Bay Bridge Costs," *Bay City News,* December 22, 2004.

14. Geoffrey Boothroyd, Winston Knight, and Peter Dewhurst, *Product Design for Manufacture & Assembly,* 2nd ed., rev. and expanded (New York: Marcel Dekker, 2002).

15. See ASTM International (www.astm.org), International Standards Organization (ISO) (www.iso.org), and similar organizations for numerous testing and qualifications standards for products and their components.

16. James William Martin, *Measuring and Improving Performance-Information Technology Applications in Lean Systems* (New York: CRC Press, 2009), 19–20.

Chapter 2

BEHAVIOR INFLUENCES
THE DESIGN PROCESS

Few people are capable of expressing with equanimity opinions
which differ from the prejudices of their social environment.
Most people are even incapable of forming such opinions.
—Albert Einstein

Several decades ago, people with communicable diseases were isolated to
protect their fellow citizens. The prevailing medical opinion, at that time,
was that quarantines would prevent widespread infection. Over the past
several decades, the manufacture and distribution of vaccines to immunize
people against diseases such as polio was orderly and efficient. However
most recently there have been problems. Although medical technology has
dramatically improved, its distribution and allocation has not always been
orderly or efficient. Examples include lack of health care for tens of millions
of Americans and others around the world and shortages of medical supplies including life-saving vaccines.

In 2003, the avian flu or SARS (severe acute respiratory syndrome) epidemic was moving through the Asian region. According to the Centers for
Disease Control (CDC), 8,098 people worldwide eventually became sick
with SARS during the 2003 outbreak and 774 died.[1] It was a very deadly
disease. When traveling to Hong Kong and Singapore, as I queued up in the
arrival line at immigration screening, infrared sensors measured my body
temperature. The temperature measurement was designed to detect the
presence of a fever within the temperature range a SARS virus was known
to create. In parallel, the Chinese and Singapore governments quarantined

citizens who contracted the SARS virus[2] to prevent its spread to the larger population. In contrast, when I returned to the United States, there was no inspection of people returning from Asia to see if they had body temperatures characteristic of being infected by SARS. The contrast in preventive strategies was striking to me. I thought to myself, what will happen if a more deadly virus is unleashed somewhere within the world? Will the opinions of a few people and self-serving politicians trump science?

I received an answer when the swine flu virus (H1N1) was unleashed in Mexico and migrated across the world. It caught the CDC and state and local health agencies by surprise.[3] Admittedly, the eventual creation of the vaccine was great science, but the manufacturing and distribution were poorly executed.[4] Estimates place the infection rate at 50 million United States citizens and estimates of resultant deaths range between 4,000 and 10,000 people in the United States who died within several months.[5] Most recently, the death toll increased over initial estimates. The opinion of several medical and scientific experts is that the United States is poorly prepared to protect its citizens against epidemics, or worse, future bioterrorism attacks.

The distribution of the H1N1 vaccine was spotty and there were shortages. Manufacturing capacity could not meet demand. The people who needed vaccination the most (the young, pregnant, and old) had to wait months. Complicating its distribution was that, in some situations, it was distributed to people who needed it less. In addition to manufacturing and distribution breakdowns, the communication of major activities associated with production and distribution of the vaccine were poor. Further complicating the distribution activities was that in contrast to management of previous epidemics, some medical workers refused to take the vaccine. The distribution of vaccine to prisoners living in cramped quarters was also disparaged, although it has been a commonly used strategy for containing epidemics.

What's happened to the ability of societies to protect citizens against epidemics? Although the ability to create new vaccines has never been greater, political responses to the more notorious epidemics have been confusing and disruptive. Also, manufacturing, distribution, and related activities have at time been inefficient. It is almost a certainty that a major viral outbreak will occur across the world and within the United States in the future. The current predictions are significant increases of illness and death for some of these outbreaks. The prevention and management of epidemics is one example where catastrophic failures are not caused by technology alone, but by individual behaviors and groups acting through political, religious, and cultural organizations. Many cognitive and group influences affect major failure events. This is why we need to understand some important topics of social psychology.

An interesting fact is that after the 2003 SARS epidemic had been successfully contained, several smaller outbreaks occurred. These were caused by accidents within viral research laboratories in Asia. Fortunately, the isolated outbreaks were successfully quarantined in China, Singapore, and Taiwan.[6] It is also interesting that viral and bacterial outbreaks from research laboratories have repeatedly occurred elsewhere. An example is the 1971 release of the smallpox virus in the Soviet Union. It was contained by quarantining and vaccinating thousands of people. But there were several deaths. There have also been other incidents and deaths caused by different bacterial and viral strains in the past several decades. Incidentally, some research laboratories, many of which are in densely populated urban areas, routinely store smallpox, the polio virus, the anthrax bacterial strain, and many other deadly bacteria and viruses. The problem is that if harmful viral or bacterial strains escape from these laboratories into highly populated areas, people are likely to become sick or die. Like the sword of Damocles, these laboratory storage facilities hang over our heads by a horse's hair. There will be laboratory accidents in the future; we just don't know where or when they will occur.

In parallel, viral and bacterial strains are continually mutating. This often occurs within the animals around us. Mutation rates accelerate within areas of high population density and where there is close proximity between people and certain animals such as birds and swine. These mutations continually test our ability to survive by probing our body's immune defenses. We win and lose these attacks over the years. It is the opinion of experts that pandemics will certainly occur because of viral and bacterial mutation in the future and with catastrophic consequences for human populations.

It is difficult enough to create the vaccines to protect us; we also need to create efficient manufacturing and distribution systems. These are easiest for us to control. But, unfortunately, these systems depend on people and organizations. People make errors of judgment and organizations are sometimes inefficient. There are also constraints of supply, people, and other resources. In other words, the problem is not always technical, but rather there are major contributing factors. Compounding the problem are breakdowns associated with manufacturing, distribution, logistics, and other systems.

Many years ago, people thought the causes for product failures were only errors of design, technology, manufacturing, or inaccurate supplier's customer requirements specification. The human contributions for error were often ignored. This situation has changed in recent years. Today people know product and service failures are caused, in part, by individuals, groups, and organizations in addition to technology. In fact, a careful study of the causal factors for many catastrophic events will show technology actually has small influence on causing failures. However, if technology is used correctly to design products and services, it can be a powerful enabler for safety by reducing risk. This is because cognitive and group influences can be neutralized to varying degrees by good design.

As an example, technology is often not efficiently utilized or it is misused. Examples include ineffective project management methods, poorly identifying customer and stakeholder requirements, not using good design and testing methods, overreaching past limitations of technology, and similar behaviors. Many of the underlying causes for failures are related to social psychological issues associated with individuals and groups. They were caused by ignorance, misinterpretations of important information, and patterns of dysfunctional and destructive behavior. Cognition research shows that ignoring or misinterpreting patterns and information is common. Unfortunately, cognition errors sometimes cause breakdowns within new product design processes as well as production, distribution, maintenance, and other supporting activities necessary to commercialize and use products and services.

Products and services are designed using currently available technology, tools, and methods. When they fail, blame is often placed on the design or application environments where unforeseen stresses act on a design in unexpected ways. The question is, "Why can't designers and design teams analyze, test, and modify new designs prior to unexpected failure?" There are some people who believe we expect too much from our technology and its supporting systems and there are others who think it falls short of its capability. The truth lies somewhere between these extremes. Although there are some failures that, in hindsight, no currently known technology, tools, or methods could have prevented, there are also many others that could have been prevented from occurring, but were are not.

This chapter has been written to explore the relationships between individuals and groups on the project management activities used to create new products and services. We will use a social psychological perspective to discuss perceptions, attitudes, and behaviors in formal and informal groups. The key topics are shown in the Figure 2.1 roadmap and defined in Table 2.1.

In *Star Trek, the Next Generation*, Councilor Deanna Troi is a key member of the Enterprise crew. Her responsibility is to provide counseling to crew members in a manner similar to today's psychologists. Her usefulness for helping prevent and solve complex interpersonal and behavioral problems becomes obvious if you watch episodes of this television and movie series. In contrast, I have never worked for an organization or participated with design teams where professionally trained people were responsible for helping manage the human aspects of a team's interpersonal relationships.

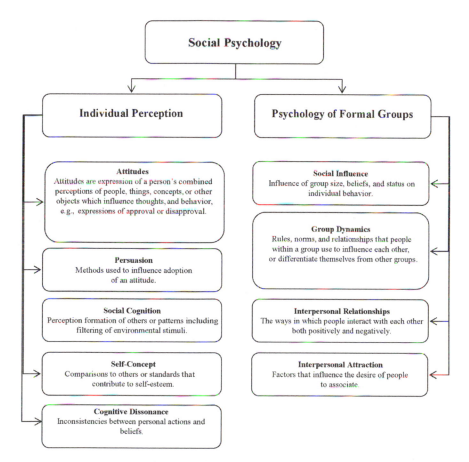

Figure 2.1   Key social psychological factors

In fact, few organizations employ social psychologists to help design products and services. Exceptions may be at the front end of a market research process or if behavioral issues occur and individual and group counseling becomes necessary.

Instead design teams frequently work in an ad hoc manner to facilitate their team behaviors. The facilitation is often learned haphazardly through seminars, on the job, or anecdotally. It is often thrown over the proverbial wall by human resources or training departments. Unfortunately, sometimes team facilitation must also be done within hostile or politically charged work environments characterized by dysfunctional behavior occurring in differing forms and degree.

Social psychology provides relevant concepts, tools, and methods that are proving to be increasingly useful to the design, production,

Table 2.1
Impact of social psychological factors on design teams

Psychological Factor	Definition	Common Example	Impact on Design Team
Attitudes	Expressions of approval or disapproval	Personal prejudices and biases that determine beliefs influencing the types of work activities, their priority, and how they should be performed.	In the absence of facilitation, incorrect work activities will be selected, prioritization will be ineffective, and required information may not be acquired or analyzed correctly.
Persuasion	Methods used to influence adoption of an attitude	Facilitative methods are used to obtain consensus for team behavior, members are removed or added to a team, members are counseled regarding their behavior.	Correct persuasive methods will move a team to a high performance stage; otherwise it becomes dysfunctional and fails to achieve its goals in a timely and efficient manner.
Social cognition	Perception formation of others or patterns including filtering of environmental stimuli	Teams that are not diverse, are not balanced with respect to required work activities, or do not use facilitative tools will filter out important information.	Incorrect goals will be selected and information will be incorrectly interpreted, resulting in wrong conclusions.
Self-concept	Comparisons to others or standards that contribute to self-esteem	Some team members have low self-esteem and others are egotistical. Failures to propose correct ideas, engage in group activities, and oppose incorrect ideas or behavior.	Incorrect goals will be selected or not prioritized and team issues will not be effectively facilitated.
Cognitive dissonance	Inconsistencies between personal actions and beliefs	Team members have not been persuaded to agree with group's goals and work activities. Cannot support the group.	Information is leaked. Work tasks not completed. Dysfunctional behavior occurs. People may leave the team.

Social influence	Influence of group size, beliefs, and status on individual behavior.	Team cohesiveness and its maturity stage depend on group cultural norms and values. Flexibility is required for multicultural teams. Group size must be managed to control dynamics.	People may engage in dysfunctional behavior if social norms and values cannot be effectively communicated to them.
Group dynamics	Rules, norms, and relationships that people within a group use to influence each other, and to differentiate themselves from other groups	The dynamics of a group change as its membership changes as a result group norms; values must be clearly communicated and facilitated.	If not properly facilitated, the group may break up into subgroups and engage in dysfunctional behavior.
Interpersonal relationships	The ways in which people interact with each other both positively and negatively	Related to group dynamics, interpersonal interactions must be facilitated to manage personal attitudes, social influence, and group dynamics.	If not properly facilitated, the group may break up into subgroups and engage in dysfunctional behavior.
Interpersonal attraction	Factors that influence the desire of people to associate	People have different reasons for wanting to join a development team based on perceived value of rewards and recognition.	People need to see an advantage of associating; otherwise, other priorities receive their attention.

distribution, and other activities of products and services. However, the methods have been used only sporadically to support team building, facilitation, and organizational change initiatives. As we analyze the causes for catastrophic failures we will show the lack of application of social psychological methods has been detrimental to the safe use of some new products and services.

Historically, social psychology's primary application in industry has been to investigate the emotional and subjective perspectives of how products and services contribute to consumer satisfaction.[7] Understanding consumer requirements, needs, perspectives, purchasing, and usage behaviors can help influence how products and services are eventually designed. Organizations also have different needs regarding how requirements are gathered from their customers and key stakeholders. As an example, gathering customer requirements for consumer products and services requires a consumer marketing approach regarding product and service functions, features, forms, aesthetics, and other attributes. In contrast, the requirements needed for building bridges and civil engineering structures are precisely defined by architects in consultation with only a few customers and stakeholders.

The impact of failures also differs. If a consumer product fails, it can usually be repaired or replaced with little cost impact, whereas a building or bridge failure may result in numerous fatalities and injuries, and a significant financial loss. But it is also true that some consumer products such as vehicles routinely cause injury and loss of life if they unexpectedly fail. Also, from an economic perspective, if thousands or millions of low cost consumer products fail, a significant financial loss may occur. Although social psychology methods are useful for ensuring customer requirements are accurate, they are also useful for managing the behaviors of design teams, and ensuring smooth interactions between customers, key stakeholders, and supporting functions within organizations. As we investigate the causes for catastrophic product and service failures, it will become obvious that many of them are classified as human error and group behavior. The concepts, tools, and methods of social psychology will also be shown useful for the management of the perceptions of the larger community as well as at design team, group, or organizational levels if major failure events occur.

People see the world differently. This affects their behavior as well as the formal and informal groups in which they participate. Facilitators know this fact and have designed tools and methods to help team members work together more effectively when designing products and services. As an example, group diversity is important when forming teams. It has been shown that diversity, if properly facilitated, increases a team's ability to see alternative perspectives to create more balanced design solutions.

The formal structure and methods of project management such as periodic design reviews, establishing goals and objectives, obtaining approvals, and creating and using similar methods also help facilitate and manage team interrelationships. Project management methods continue to evolve by creating formal and informal structures, enabling people to behave in ways that increase the reliability of design, production, and supporting processes. A group of people cannot be left to pursue an ad hoc approach for design. A structured project management methodology is a design team's best chance for ensuring it has an effective and efficient process for designing products and services.

However, even this strategy may not be enough to prevent failures when social psychological factors are ignored.

Social psychology shows us that even the best procedures, sophisticated tools, and control methods cannot prevent resourceful people from overriding a system's failsafe controls at some level. The Chernobyl disaster, which was briefly discussed in the Introduction, is a classic example where people purposely did not follow standard and agreed-upon procedures. Although it is also true the reactor could have been better designed (e.g., not had a large positive void coefficient based on other reactor models), human error and group behavior were the primary reasons for the Chernobyl disaster.[8] As an example, the plant personnel did not coordinate a critical test with the site's chief engineer, the workers purposely disabled the safety features of the reactor, false assumptions were made regarding the reactor status, and then as the situation quickly unfolded, the reactor's deteriorating conditions were misinterpreted or ignored by plant workers.

Complicating factors included disintegration of the reactor, the reactor's roof used a combustible material (bitumen) contrary to regulations, and the radiation detectors malfunctioned or their readings were ignored by plant personnel. These were all human errors at differing levels. The technical deficiencies of the reactor's design would not have caused an explosion if the safety systems were not disabled and proper procedures were followed. In retrospect, the Chernobyl event provides a strong lesson showing that a strictly technical approach may not always be sufficient to prevent future catastrophic failures. This is why it is important we understand individual attitudes and behaviors as well as group behaviors and their effects on design activities.

Attitudes, persuasion, social cognition, self-concept, and cognitive dissonance are major cognitive influences of teams that are designing products and services as well as the people using them. Individuals have perceptions. People comprising a design team, the many influential stakeholders who provide approval, resources, and information to a team, suppliers, and customers also have differing perceptions. The interplay between individual perceptions and varying degrees of influence and power within and between groups will often move a design team in predictable and stable directions. But they may also move a team in unpredictable directions and out of control. Sometimes, failure is immediately apparent, but at other times, it may not be seen for several decades. Technology is not often an issue. In fact, subsequent analysis after a catastrophic event often shows technology was misapplied or not properly used. The underlying reasons for failures are disproportionately human and organizational rather than technical.

Personal attitudes affect a person's behavior when reacting to the things in the environment, such as information, patterns, other people, and objects. Personal attitudes and behaviors are influenced by previous experiences, images, and beliefs associated with the things we have encountered in the past, those currently being encountered, as well as neurological limitations regarding how information is obtained and processed by the brain. In this context, a person's resultant behavior will be consistent with his or her attitudes. Attitudes evolve through personal experiences over many years. They are often seen as expressions of approval or disapproval if activated in response to stimuli within a person's immediate environment.

Design teams are vulnerable to personal attitudes such as prejudices and biases. These create beliefs influencing the types of work activities people are willing to do, their prioritization of activities, and decisions regarding how, when, and where the activities should be performed. Attitudes not aligned with the goals of an organization or a design team, in the absence of effective facilitation, are problematic. If left uncorrected, they will lead to people refusing to work with others, engaging in distracting behavior, doing the wrong work, or doing the right work but in the wrong ways. Agreeing on work activity prioritization will also become an issue. The effective result will be misinterpretation of information, errors of judgment, and mistakes. Interpersonal conflicts may also occur and cause various forms of dysfunctional team behaviors.

Attitudinal issues also exist with key stakeholders, customers, or suppliers. These issues may interfere with requirements translation and analyses. The inevitable result will be confusion, design rework, longer cycle times, and higher costs. If the design work is not done correctly, and poor work is not detected, errors and mistakes will also occur when customers use products or services. Although a project manager can do little to change the attitudes of team members, customers, or key stakeholders, tools and methods can be employed to ensure transparency of design activities. Project structure and information transparency are two important methods for managing design teams to control personal attitudes and behaviors. However, control may be ineffective if organizational policies and management controls are loose.

Attitudinal differences are productive for a team if diverse ideas help to broaden the types and quality of creative solutions. However, differences of opinion will also need to be discussed and eventually reconciled to ensure a team addresses relevant design issues. As an example, a team meeting for the first time will likely have differing opinions regarding the accuracy, relevance, or usefulness of available facts and information. There may also be differences of opinion regarding identification and prioritization of work activities or roles and responsibilities. One common facilitative aid to help a team communicate more effectively is to ensure information is factual and effectively organized and communicated to make it very easy to understand. There are several methods useful in this regard. Examples include organizing information into a hierarchal format and presenting it to a team visually to help everyone more easily understand its meaning. There are also several useful methods to help a team overcome cognitive influences.

Personal attitudes may have very positive or negative effects on the design of products and services as well as maintenance and usage. The recent failure of the I-35W Mississippi River Bridge in Minnesota provides one example. In this catastrophic failure, three people died, 176 were injured, and the bridge replacement costs and the local economic losses were estimated by Minnesota's Department of Transportation at $17 million in 2007 and $43 million in 2008 in economic loss, plus $234 million for bridge replacement costs.[9] After an exhaustive investigation, the bridge's failure was traced to several factors. These included the original design of the bridge, organizational issues, and personal attitudes of the various inspectors over many years. The report's summary was, "Probable Cause: The National Transportation Safety Board determines that the probable cause of the collapse of the I-35W bridge in Minneapolis, Minnesota, was the inadequate load capacity, due to a design error by Sverdrup & Parcel and Associates, Inc., of the gusset plates at the U10 nodes, which failed under a combination of (1) substantial increases in the weight of the bridge, which resulted from previous bridge modifications, and (2) the traffic and concentrated construction loads on the bridge on the day of the collapse. Contributing to the design error was the failure of Sverdrup & Parcel's quality control procedures to ensure that the appropriate main truss gusset plate calculations were performed for the I-35W Bridge and the inadequate design review by Federal and State transportation officials. Contributing to the accident was the generally accepted practice among Federal and State transportation officials of giving inadequate attention to gusset plates during inspections for conditions of distortion, such as bowing, and of excluding gusset plates in load rating analyses."[10]

From an attitudinal perspective, the bridge inspectors had preconceived opinions of the strength of the bridge components, as stated in a report to the Minnesota State legislature: "In an interview conducted as part of an independent investigation of the accident by the Minnesota State legislature, the MN/DOT Metro District bridge safety inspection engineer (a registered professional engineer and a specialist in performing fracture-critical bridge inspections) stated that he had observed the gusset plate bowing during inspections he participated in after joining MN/DOT in 1997. He said he consulted with another inspector about the bowing and concluded, 'That's fit-up, that's construction, that's original construction.' He said his first reason for reaching this conclusion was that in his undergraduate training he was taught 'gusset plates are overdesigned. The safety factors within those gusset plates are 2 to 3.'"[11] Technology, therefore, was not the cause of the collapse of the I-34 W Bridge. The cause was a series of human errors beginning with its design, the inadequacy of organizational policies governing its inspection, and the attitudes, biases, or preconceptions of its inspectors and engineers. This catastrophic event is an example in which personal attitudes were a contributing factor that resulted in a failure to raise the suspicions of the bridge's different inspectors over many years.

The attitudes of politicians and constituents often bend logic and facts to suit their own purposes. An example is the quasi-governmental entities Fannie May and Freddie Mac, which have conflicting responsibilities to shareholders because of a federal mandate to promote mortgage lending. In recent years the political pressure from the United States Congress encouraged these organizations to lend money to customers for mortgagees. It was obvious many of these customers should not have been extended credit. As a result of these poor lending policies reinforced by personal attitudes of politicians, executives within the organizations, and their customers, Fannie May and Freddie Mac lost $188 billion in nine quarters ($83.6 billion annualized) and required more than a trillion dollars of federal subsidies by the end of 2009.[12]

These policies contributed, in part, to the resultant speculative housing bubble. Exacerbating the situation was rampant unethical behavior by many individuals and organizations including some major banks, mortgage companies, and Wall Street firms. These conditions eventually contributed to the collapse of the United States housing industry in 2008 and 2009. In 2009, this practice was continued by the federal government in its $75 billion effort to extend credit to prop up near-delinquent mortgages to prevent foreclosures. The consensus among economists in early 2009 was that mortgage default was only a matter of time for many of these delinquent homeowners, who obtained mortgages through subsidized programs. As of 2010, these policies are thought by some people to be preventing a recovery for the housing industry.[13] Fannie Mae and Freddie Mac were once very successful programs, and most likely will be again in the future, but when

policies are politically based because they are clouded by personal prejudices and biases regarding the allocation of resources and risk estimation,
people lose money.

In summary, the attitudes of customers and stakeholders exert a high
level of influence on designers of products and services and their teams.
These attitudes can be positive or negative reinforcing. Negative attitudes
can be particularly disconcerting if they influence otherwise good design
practices in the wrong directions. Project risks and the likelihood of unexpected failure significantly increase in these situations.

People can usually be persuaded to modify personal attitudes or at least
behaviors to varying degrees. However, the effectiveness of persuasion depends on the person communicating information, as well as the information's format, accuracy, and relevancy to the person receiving the message.
Research has shown that the power position of the person communicating can also have a strong persuasive effect on a person's attitude and behavior. Power is a relative position gained through expertise, the ability
to control rewards and punishments, trustworthiness, and other relevant
factors. Power is gained through education, experience, relationships, usefulness, and assigned authority. It can also be increased through a series
of previously positive interactions that help establish perceptions of mutual trustworthiness between people. In other words, some team members,
stakeholders, suppliers, and customers will tend to have more power and
authority than others. This increases their ability to persuade others. As a
result a design team usually consists of members with differing power positions relative to each other, key stakeholders, and others.

A design team can be persuaded in the right ways based on the relevancy
and accuracy of information it receives. Information needs to be communicated simply and in a timely manner to a team because people are
persuaded differently by a message's content and delivery method. Effective communication is important to prevent disagreements between team
members, key stakeholders, and others. Communications should also be
consistent and reflect the intended message and audience. Some communications are directed at customers, suppliers, and key stakeholders, whereas
others go to team members. Messages can also be emotional or impersonal,
fact-based or propaganda, one-sided or interactive. The result is that design teams and individuals can be persuaded to varying degrees. Persuasion strategies are especially influential when new customer requirements
are being considered or design alternatives are being evaluated relative to
requirements.

There are several useful strategies for effectively persuading team members. One is to only rely on factual information presented in standardized
formats and frequently, a practice of complete transparency within an

organization. This approach helps reduce personal biases and reduces persuasive influence that may be negative. A second useful strategy is to communicate complicated information in person or in an interactive way such as video conferencing. In contrast, simple and routine information can be communicated using impersonal formats such as e-mail. If a team needs to periodically communicate information to customers, key stakeholders, and others outside their team, a good strategy is using standardized reporting formats that are distributed according to preestablished criteria. This makes it easier for people to understand the information and reduces unwanted persuasive influences. Effective communication helps gain support from people within and external to a team.

Persuasion also occurs in negative and detrimental ways. Examples include situations where customers, executives, key stakeholders, and team leaders influence design functions, features, and other attributes in ways not based on fact, but on personal opinions or prejudices. Powerful people may also abuse their relative power position to withhold or influence the distribution of resources, rewards, and recognition. They could also harass or punish team members. These types of dysfunctional behaviors increase the likelihood that new products and services will be improperly designed and fail. Design errors also occur if teams are not allowed to accurately capture customer requirements, are required to use marginal suppliers and materials, cannot fully integrate or test subsystems, are required to ignore unfavorable information or falsify testing results, and are not allowed to complete planned work activities, resulting in taking shortcuts or being forced to use unproven or risky technology. Persuasion is necessary to gain team consensus, but must be managed to ensure it has a positive rather than a negative effect.

Unfortunately, people are often easily and sometimes negatively persuaded by others. The recent 2009 financial crisis is a good example. People within several financial organizations were persuaded to engage in unethical behavior regarding allowable risk and investment strategies for their clients. Negative persuasive influences were prevalent across the industry and people were persuaded to take inordinate amounts of financial risk, such as taking advantage of easy credit when incomes could not match escalating mortgage rates. The result was that many people quickly became financially insolvent during the recent financial crisis. The financial crisis has temporarily altered the public's attitudes of necessary financial regulations and risk. As a result, people have become sensitized, for a while, to the dangers of not embracing personal fiscal responsibility. They will not be so easily persuaded to incur such risks in the immediate future. The slow pace of economic recovery in 2009 and 2010 is evidence of this fact.

Although there are differences of opinion regarding the specific improvements necessary to regulate the financial industry, few people would argue against the need for greater transparency and more effective regulatory actions to reduce the persuasive influence of powerful people and organizations. In the immediate future, fewer people will be so easily persuaded to engage in unethical conduct or take inordinate financial risk. Of course, over time the lessons will be forgotten and similar catastrophic financial events will reoccur. They always do.

It is an interesting fact that as financial transactions became highly overleveraged the situation was obvious to most people, although many people remained in a state of denial for several years prior to the eventual crisis. The regulatory systems designed to manage the many financial processes across the world also reflected a widespread pattern of denial that something could go very wrong. Today, some people blame the regulatory systems, while others blame the governments, the public and private institutions, and specific individuals who were associated with the crisis. Few individuals, groups, or organizations followed their own conscience when subjected to persuasive influences or personal attitudes and biases. In fact, they were easily persuaded to circumvent established organizational policies and procedures. In retrospect, additional financial controls needed to be created because the necessary checks and balances were clearly missing. But, then again they can be ignored in the future.

Although public attitudes regarding financial risks have changed because of the enormity of the failures, the reality is that people routinely offer little in the way of resistance when persuaded to do things. Research has shown that people selectively filter out information contradictory with their attitudes, but believe information, even if incorrect, if it is consistent with their attitudes. Although persuasion is more difficult in these situations, it can be successfully applied with good or bad intentions.

People will also behave contrary to what they believe to be right behaviors based on their personal attitudes. In other words, they can be made to behave inconsistently. Research shows attitudes are not always a good predictor of behavior if there are inconsistencies between a person's affective and cognitive components. The affective component reflects personal feelings. The cognitive component reflects logical thought. The affective and cognitive components must be in alignment for behavior to be consistent. According to cognitive research, the misalignment occurs because attitudes are a reflection of a general perception of a class of things whereas specific behaviors occur in response to a particular situation. The situation is a subset of the general class of things.

Returning to the recent financial crisis, people generally believe stealing is a bad thing. But there are different things that can be stolen and many ways to steal them. When faced with situational decisions regarding stealing another person's money, using a gun may appear wrong, but selling them highly leveraged financial assets may not. This in spite of the fact that only a few dollars may be stolen using a gun, but millions of dollars stolen through financial fraud. In fact, there are many types of financial fraud. Some include a financial advisor or similar person taking other people's money without disclosing all risks and fees (e.g., lying by omission), failing to understand the risk (incompetence), or purposely acting against a client's best interest in other ways (conflicts of interest). The result is that people are often defrauded by professional people who don't really see an ethical or legal issue. Note the distinction in these people's minds: criminals *rob or steal,* but bad professionals *defraud* people, which is the same as saying they indirectly steal people's money. "I am a good person because I don't directly steal client's money."

Persuasive influences are powerful if there is alignment for a behavior or misalignment regarding opposite behavior. As an example, the pyramid scheme used by Bernie Madoff over several decades is a notable example of attitude misalignment, persuasive influence, and a failure of the regulatory systems used by the Securities and Exchange Commission (SEC).[14] One estimate is that $65 billion was taken from investors. However, only a small amount of the money had been recovered by the government as of early 2010 after the discovery of the fraud. Madoff was found to be guilty of fraud, but it is also obvious there was a lack of regulatory agency oversight and very intelligent people were persuaded to act against their personal interest. The causal factors for inadequate regulation also should be identified and these regulatory systems need to be redesigned to help prevent future fraudulent activities. Persuading people improvements are necessary is not as difficult as it was prior to the financial crisis, given the extensive fraud and coincident SEC inaction. Prevailing public attitudes have significantly been changed by the crisis. But, political bickering remains a drag for financial reform. If the bickering continues, people will lose interest and nothing will be done to prevent similar fraud in the future.

Design teams are also subject to attitudinal and persuasive influences. Team members can be easily persuaded to accept certain facts even when false, but reject others, even if correct, by people having higher relative power. These types of influences derail a design process unless they are guarded against by transparency and structure. Facilitative methods are also useful for obtaining team consensus or managing difficult people. If necessary, disruptive or unethical team members can be removed from a team or counseled. These types of positively reinforcing persuasive methods will move a team in the right direction.

Social cognition helps us understand how people see, think about, and remember information within their environment. Information filtering is a key mechanism associated with social cognition. It is useful because it enables people to focus on more important (while ignoring less important) information. It evolved as an adaptive response animals use to focus attention on immediate survival threats. In humans, the filtering adaptation is partly responsible for creating a person's belief system because it influences the types of information that in part form a person's attitudes. Recall, attitudes influence behaviors and interpersonal interactions.

Because people are susceptible to filtering of information, design teams can also be impacted to a certain extent. The problem is exacerbated if a team is too homogenous. Group dynamics and persuasive influences act in concert with information filtering. This implies that if not facilitated by social psychological advisement, design teams will tend to believe some types of information but not others. Two immediate effects are that requirements are not accurately translated or test information may be incorrectly interpreted. Accurate requirement translation and test information are the basis for the effective design of products and services.

Design teams can use several strategies to help minimize the negative effects of information filtering. As an example, groupthink is a dysfunctional condition that occurs if team members reinforce each other's distorted views of reality. This occurs when there is little discussion of all issues and risks facing a project and when evaluating other types of information. The results will be overly optimistic or pessimistic team consensus rather than the truth. First, a diverse team having different perspectives and balanced skills should be created. Different people filter different types of information. A diverse team will tend to evaluate greater amounts and different types of information from its environment than homogeneous teams. However, a diverse team requires facilitative methods to ensure information is reviewed and analyzed in an unbiased manner. This ensures viewpoints of all team members will be heard and fairly considered by a team. The likely consequence is team members will tend to actively participate in group discussions and decisions.

The usefulness of a structured project management approach, that is, a set of activities organized into a schedule such as that displayed on a Gantt chart and reviewed at critical tollgates, has been explored in earlier discussions. Key stakeholders, suppliers, and customers should also be brought together to review the progress of a project to ensure nothing has been missed during requirements translation and subsequent design work. Finally, information should also be represented in easy-to-understand and standardized patterns to avoid filtering of important information. This is a useful method for helping a team and others quickly understand a project's technical content when working through its many design activities. If these types of facilitative methods are not used to design products and services, breakdowns occur. The result is that new products and services are not well designed.

In the past 30 years, I have been on many design teams. These teams were sometimes very successful and at other times failed. In retrospect, teams that failed had various issues. Sometimes, the voice of the customer (VOC) was ignored or selectively filtered. The result was that requirements translation was poorly done. These designs needed to be modified before being accepted by customers. Other times, we on the team were unable to create solutions because of personal, group, organizational, or technological challenges.

One interesting example is an electrostatic discharge issue encountered when a hydrocarbon fuel was filtered through a porous membrane. The team received several patents for solution to the problem. When a hydrocarbon such as gasoline moves through a porous medium such as a filtration element, electrons are stripped from the fuel and accumulate upstream of the filtration element. If the static electric charge is not continuously drained through a grounding connection then significant voltage can build up within the filter housing, potentially thousands of volts. Previous designs had been metallic, which prevented a voltage buildup. But the newer design was plastic. It could not provide a grounded pathway to dissipate the charge. This led to a catastrophic rupture of the plastic filter housing if the voltage sought a ground. A solution escaped us for several months. Eventually, it was found within a different industry: computer hardware. This industry had already solved the conductive plastic problem using a thin metallic fiber to prevent voltage buildup. We never would have found a solution if we continued to look within our team, organization, and industry.[15] This is an example that shows sometimes it is impossible to prevent failures if a team simply doesn't have prerequisite knowledge.

Several years prior to the electrostatic issue, I joined a different team in another organization manufacturing the first direct current (DC) motors for computer disc drives. At that time, there were three competitive motor designs. Each had differing unit costs and quality, but similar performance. They were used by the same customers and applications. One organization had a very simple design; it used a minimum number of functions and features, that is, only what the customer required. Not surprisingly, their motor was less costly and failed less frequently than competitors'. This was the best approach for designing. Unfortunately, design teams have a knack of convincing themselves that certain functions, features, and other attributes are necessary or needed by customers. They substitute their voice for that of their customers, which constitutes information filtering. Eventually, the organization with the simpler motor design dominated the industry. It was Japanese. This story has repeated itself in industry after industry over the past several decades.

How many times have you driven by a house or object, but only noticed it after many years? The same phenomenon is at work when people inaccurately interpret information from customers, stakeholders, other team members, test and evaluation reports, and other information sources. Everyone makes these types of mistakes. In fact, I have given people attending seminars a simple test to measure how well they read a paragraph of approximately 30–40 words. The exercise requires counting the number of times a letter of the English alphabet occurs within a paragraph. The letter appears as sentence or capitalized case. It is very common for more than 50 percent of a group to incorrectly count the actual occurrences of the letter. I have used this exercise with over 100 groups with similar results. It demonstrates human inspection is fundamentally flawed because of information filtering.

Sometimes information filtering causes a catastrophic failure. The I-35 W bridge failure occurred because of several factors. First, a design error was missed. Then routine inspections were conducted using false assumptions caused in part by information filtering. The Chernobyl disaster and many other such catastrophic events have also been partly caused by information filtering. It causes people to make incorrect decisions based on biased attitudes. It also suggests people need tools and other aids to enable them to overcome cognitive limitations.

In 2009 there was a catastrophic crash of Continental connection Flight 3407 near Buffalo, New York. Forty-nine people were killed by what in retrospect appears to be pilot error.[16] Winter conditions resulted in ice buildup on the aircraft's wings. The pilots were not able to compensate for the ice buildup by making equipment adjustments. Complicating the situation, the Bombardier aircraft was a new design requiring the nose of the aircraft should be pointed down rather than upwards if a stall condition occurred in flight. This recommendation was different than for older aircraft. When a stall occurred that evening, the pilots became confused. The standard operating policy of the airline also required manual rather than automatic pilot control in severe icing conditions. The pilots apparently ignored this recommendation. Complicating the situation, pilot training may have been marginal. The conclusion by the investigating board was the pilots were not situationally aware during the final moments of the crash. Fatigue may also have been an additional contributing causal factor for the accident. The pilots, for a variety of reasons, incorrectly processed information relevant for understanding their hazardous situation. The consequences were cata-strophic for their passengers and crew.

People create a personal image or self-concept by evaluating and com-paring their perceived versus expected personal status. Personal image or self-concept is formed by conditioning factors. These include cultural and group norms and values, as well as persuasion by others. A positive per-sonal image helps people satisfy their needs and wants in a constructive manner. A negative personal image distorts behavior. It can also be very self-destructive.

A personal image is influenced over time by comparing personal ex-pectations to the outside world. Comparisons are made through interper-sonal interactions, feedback from others, and self-examination relative to personal norms, values, and goals. These personal expectations represent a cognitive component called self-schema. The associated evaluative cog-nitive component is called self-esteem. As a result, people have a mental image of who and what they should be and their self-esteem is a reflec-tion of actual status versus an expected one. Positive gaps between expected versus actual condition result in high self-esteem and negative gaps in low self-esteem.

Self-esteem is relevant to how people interact within a design team. In fact, it is very likely that team members will have differing levels of self-esteem. Some will have high levels and others have low levels. Behavior is influenced by self-esteem. Ideally, every team member will have high self-esteem and be confident and mature. In combination with experience and education their ability to effectively contribute to their teams is enhanced. In contrast, people with low self-esteem tend to be overly agreeable or dis-agreeable with others or exhibit other behavioral problems. Overly agree-able team members will usually fail to actively debate important design issues. This behavior results in a loss of relevant team information because these team members do not provide important feedback or information to help their team.

This behavior also tends to provide a team with a false sense of security because important issues go unchallenged. Typical low self-esteem behav-ior includes self-deprecating humor, mistaking personal feelings of failure for reality, dwelling on negative aspects of any situation while ignoring positive conditions, and a lack of flexibility, that is, thinking in terms of all or nothing and no in-between. On the other hand, team members having an unreasonably high level of self-esteem (egotists) may tend to dominate team discussions or exhibit other forms of domineering behavior. Serious issues occur when egotists provide overly positive reports, even if contra-dicted by fact. The personal image of team members can greatly impact a team's effectiveness as well as the likelihood of a project's success or failure.

Facilitative methods such as transparency, project management structure, and team facilitation will help minimize the negative influences of these types of cognitive issues.

If situations occur that cause a person's cognitions to be in contradiction, then they will experience feelings of uneasiness or unpleasantness. These situations are explained by the theory of *cognitive dissonance* put forth by Leon Festinger.[17] The theory states people will either modify or attempt to rationalize their beliefs, attitudes, and behaviors to minimize or eliminate uneasiness or unpleasant feelings. An interesting fact of cognitive dissonance is that it may operate at a subconscious level. As an example, a person may not know they rejected important information because they cannot remember it. This makes it a very powerful influencer of personal behavior. If dissonance exists, people will create rationalizations for their thoughts and behaviors. As an example, a person who has been taught not to steal from others, but finds himself making omissions of fact by withholding relevant information or making false claims, may feel guilt. Guilt feelings make a person uncomfortable, producing dissonance, and in response create rationalizations for thoughts and behaviors. These rationalizations may appear as thoughts such as, "The other person was warned by fine print," "The information withheld was confidential," "The promotion of financial products is fair," and "Commissions are deserved." These statements are true only when there is full and complete disclosure of all information between people having equal power. Cognitive dissonance also occurs if people don't follow policies, then later feel guilty and begin to rationalize their behavior through thoughts such as, "Others do it," "The policy is silly," or "It does not apply to me." These behaviors have important consequences for why things fail.

People may also engage in constructive or destructive behaviors. Constructive behavior occurs if people modify their attitudes, beliefs, and behavior to the benefit of themselves and others. In other words, they are willing to engage in new behaviors. To the extent they believe new facts and change behaviors, dissonance will be minimized. But if they are forced to accept other's beliefs or behave in ways they have not really internalized, then dissonance will be operative. Eventually, they may change their behavior to reduce feelings of dissonance even if the new behavior is wrong. This occurs when teams influence individual behaviors that deviate from the team consensus. This influence could have either constructive or destructive consequences. Destructive consequences occur if others are harmed. Examples include knowingly falsifying facts, refusing to act on factual information that is in conflict with personal beliefs, or behaving in ways that inhibit team goals. In these situations, customer requirements, testing results, or other critical information in contradiction with personal beliefs may be ignored or rejected by some team members or an entire team.

A common expression associated with the influences of cognitive dissonance is seen by the phrase "not invented here." Many catastrophic failures
have occurred because people cannot accept that others have more knowledge or higher skills. If feelings of uneasiness are created, they will cause
people to reject new ideas and methods. Also, to the extent that products
and services rely on manual operations, dissonance becomes a powerful influencer for the likelihood of failure. However, there are ways to minimize
the influence of dissonance and its detrimental effects. These have been
previously discussed: information transparency, managing a team's attitudes and behaviors, not relying on only one person for work activities, and
implementing management controls that require minimal human interaction. Other useful strategies include creating diverse and balanced design
teams, using facilitative tools and methods to reconcile divergent opinions,
following a structured project management approach, and seeking periodic
feedback from people such as customers, key stakeholders, and others impacted by a team's work but who are external to the team.

Organizations and teams exert tremendous pressure on people regardless of their individual perceptions, attitudes, or personal goals. People who
will not conform to the norms and values of their organization or team will
likely be removed and replaced by others who are compliant. Control is
possible because organizations create policies and procedures and use reward and recognition systems to modify and control individual and group
behaviors. Organizations also create hierarchal power structures to ensure
opinions are not equally weighted. In an absence of mature cultures that
promote fair treatment, powerful stakeholders can manipulate goals, objectives, and the work activities of their employees. Unfortunately, key stakeholders are subject to the same cognitive issues as other employees. They
have attitudes and biases, filter information they have not been conditioned
to accept, and will take action to reduce feelings of dissonance. Unchecked,
the problems only become worse. As a result, design teams and supporting functions can be easily influenced by these influential people. Ensuring
employee behavior, at all levels of an organization, is consistent with an
organization's policies, procedures, and ethics is a constant challenge.

The phrase *design team* has been mentioned in several contexts. Let's
discuss it from a different perspective. Design teams are formal groups of
people brought together to create a product or service. A typical design
team consists of people having very different attitudes and perceptions of
the world around them. Their views of how work should be done, which
information is important, and other issues may become a source of conten-
tion. This is especially true if a team is diverse. As a result, to prevent errors
and failures, it is important to review important elements for creating these
teams and discuss potential issues. There is much to consider because the

interactions between members, key stakeholders, suppliers, and customers is complex. A review of some basic definitions will be useful prior to discussing the behavioral effects on a new product design teams.

First, design teams and key stakeholders should maintain integrity at all times. Integrity is based on a group's values, norms, and ethics. According to the Microsoft *Encarta Dictionary,* values are "the accepted principles or standards of a person or a group"; norms are "a standard pattern of behavior that is considered normal in a society"; ethics are "a system of moral standards or principles." In turn, a value system is "a set of principles and standards, which when applied, results in ethical behavior relative to accepted values and norms." Integrity is defined as "the quality of possessing and steadfastly adhering to high moral principles or professional standards as defined by a value system." So when we say a design team should have integrity, the implication is that it consistently adheres to the policies and procedures of its organization and its project management structure.

Integrity is especially important if project teams miss their schedules, costs exceed budgets, and product and service performance fails to meet customer and stakeholder requirements. Shortcuts are tempting under such conditions. An assumption is that an organization's work systems are ethical and reflect societal norms and values. This is the best that we can do here, since our assumption must be that societal norms and values are moral from a universal perspective. However, this assumption is not always accurate, as evidenced when new products or services are used for destructive purposes. History has many examples where resources were brought together do harm.

The discussion of several key topics in the previous section—attitudes, persuasion, social cognition, self-concept, and cognitive dissonance—provides a useful basis for discussing and explaining individual responsibilities and behaviors within the context of social influence. People can be embarrassed and persuaded into engaging in behavior they would not do if alone. There is much research supporting the theory of social influence, which attempts to explain how people exert influence on others. There are also different forms of social influence. First there is conformance of one's behavior in response to pressure from others. Usually conformance is implicit in that a person becomes attuned to expectations of others. When explicit, there are direct requests to conform one's behavior to rules or standards. Organizations routinely use explicit conformance to ensure personal compliance. A third form of social influence is obedience to rules or standards. Obedience occurs if there is an unequal power relationship between people so that one party can demand that others behave in certain ways. An interesting example of social conformance can be seen when coworkers begin to mimic each other's mannerisms, speech, and other behaviors. Social influence is situational and can also be positive or negative. Design teams need to be aware of its influence because it causes groupthink and suboptimal solutions because of group dysfunction.

Social conformance also shows interesting relationships between groups and individuals. First, culture is important. Some cultures are characterized as having a high degree of personal interdependencies whereas others are individualistic. Conformance has been shown to be higher in cultures having higher interdependencies. Second, group size impacts the likelihood of conformance. Individuals who are part of larger groups tend to conform to a higher degree than smaller groups. In this context, employees will tend to conform to a higher degree at an organizational level rather than at a team level because of group size. Relative expertise and power also influences social conformance. People defer to experts and people holding positions of power. Finally, group unanimity has a high influence on conformance. Research has shown that when all but one individual hold a common belief, there is pressure to conform. But a positive result is that other team members may feel free to disagree with group opinions if even one other person disagrees. This effect is more severe in groups consisting of less than six individuals and its effect levels off for larger groups. Design teams need one or more people having divergent views to prevent the team from developing groupthink. This is especially true when the pressure for conformance is high to accommodate project issues and risks. We will use these concepts of social influence to discuss how organizations, key stakeholders, and others influence design teams.

Groupthink occurs when consensus is very important to team members and the personal cost of a poor decision is low. There have been many examples where groupthink resulted in poor decisions and catastrophic events. These events are characterized as overt in that incorrect group decisions led to action or indirect in that a lack of action caused a poor response. Vietnam is an example where one poor decision after other resulted in a gradual buildup of the war with tragic consequences. Other examples include the invasion of Iraq to search for weapons of mass destruction. They were never found, but many people still insist they were there.

Examples where actions was not taken because of groupthink include Pearl Harbor and the 9/11 terrorist attacks. In both situations, the prevailing consensus was that such events would not occur. There are several characteristics of teams having groupthink. These include a cursory examination of information, rejection of disconfirming information that is at odds with a group's beliefs, insulation of the group from outside opinions, informal meeting structure, stress, a focus on limited solution alternatives, and a sense of not being wrong. There is also often a strong group leader who dismisses divergent opinions. The group may also have negative opinions of people outside the group. Solutions to combat the phenomenon are opposite the symptoms. Diversity, facilitation, and a structured project management strategy will help avoid many of the issues associated with groupthink.

Individuals make choices regarding personal behavior. They either conform or not to their groups' norms and values. In organizations, norms and values are represented, in part, by policies and procedures as well as individual, group, and organizational behaviors. People follow policies and procedures because of their desire for acceptance by others or an aversion to fear of social ostracism (including termination of employment). Acceptance by a group also has personal advantages such as personal influence, power, access to information, and other benefits. People may also have reasons not to conform to a group's demands. These include a conflict with personal values, norms, and ethics versus their group's required behaviors. In this context, a desire to avoid the feelings of cognitive dissonance exerts an influence on a person. Cognitive dissonance occurs if a person is compliant with a group's demands in contraction to personal attitudes and beliefs. Compliance can be obtained several ways including bribery, false promises, or coercion. However, enforcing behavioral conformance is not necessarily wrong, to the extent a team member's behavior would be dysfunctional and adversely impact a team or be in violation of organizational policies and procedures. Behavior must be ethical, based on correct information and aligned with organizational goals as well as society's expectations.

Several individuals in close proximity are not considered to be a formal social group in the classical sense. As an example, three people standing at a grocery counter are not a social group. Social groups share common values, norms, beliefs, and expected behaviors. They also interact in expected and predicted ways based on normative rules. In this sense and based on these criteria, a design team is a formal social group consisting of its leader and team members. An extended social group would consist of a team's customers, suppliers, key stakeholders, and supporting people. It should also be noted that in formal groups the roles, responsibilities, and interpersonal relationships within a team are often well defined. In design teams, structure is brought by project management tools and methods within the larger organization's culture and power structure. It should be noted that different social groups within the same organization will have adapted very specific group norms and values to help guide the behavior of their teams. These norms and values, while consistent with those of the larger organization, may differ from those of other groups within the same organization. As an example, accounting, purchasing, operations, and design teams can be expected to differ in the specifics regarding their behavior toward policies and procedures and internal group rules of conduct.

Design teams also mature as members interact with each other over time. This maturation process can proceed very quickly, move slowly, or cause a team to fall apart. One theory of team maturation is that teams undergo four maturation stages.[18] Figure 2.2 describes these stages as forming, storming, norming, and performing. The forming stage includes initial meetings and opinion sharing. After forming, a team enters a storming stage. This stage is characterized by conflicts between team members. Conflicts are caused by differences of opinion regarding information, team work activities, goals, and other topics. Differences of opinion may also result in disagreements and even arguments when facilitative methods are not effectively used by a group.

The norming stage follows the storming stage. It is characterized by a growing consensus between team members. Consensus is gained on work activities such as collecting and processing team information, roles and responsibilities, goals, and similar things. Performing is the last stage of a team maturation process. It occurs when team members understand and meet their roles and responsibilities. Although the time required to move through these team maturation stages varies, teams can quickly move

---

Performing Stage: Competent team members efficiently execute work tasks without conflict. Differences of opinion are successfully facilitated and resolved in the team's mutual interest.

Norming Stage: Interpersonal conflict is minimized using facilitative rules to control conduct. Mutual trust and cooperation between team members increases. Diversity of ideas must be reinforced to avoid groupthink.

Storming Stage: Competition between team members for power and influence. Interpersonal conflict may occur.

Forming Stage: Psychological motivation for acceptance based on attitudes and self-esteem. Avoidance of conflict with others.

Figure 2.2   Four stages of team maturation

through the four stages. Success is likely if team members worked together on other projects; they use a project management structure that clearly defines roles and responsibilities, and they utilize facilitative methods to reach agreement. However, it should be noted that not all design teams reach a performing stage. If they do not, there will be an increased risk that products and services are poorly designed and the likelihood of unexpected failures.

The dynamics of group interactions complicate interpersonal relationships and confuse roles and responsibilities. As an example, some team members may have formal power sanctioned by their organization whereas others have power that is situational or informal. Informal power refers to team members who receive greater power and influence than their titles, roles, or responsibilities may imply. Informal power relationships are usually created when team members begin interacting. Each team member brings attitudes, concepts of self, and personal experience. These personality attributes influence their behavior. As an example, some people may be passive, whereas others may be overly aggressive. Others are arrogant whereas others are insecure. A team leader must manage and facilitate these diverse personalities to ensure a team's success. Depending on the organization and team this task may be easy or very difficult. However, this is not as difficult as it may first appear because design teams usually operate within a well-defined organizational framework. Also, team leaders have at their disposal several means of positive or negative reinforcement that help influence cooperation between team members and others external to the team. However, failure to elicit cooperation increases the likelihood of miscommunication and human error. Eventually there will be design mistakes because of influences of dysfunctional behavior.

Dysfunctional behavior is seen if people arrive late or unprepared to meetings, do not participate in its discussions, behave aggressively by arguing or insulting other team members, or engage in rude behavior such as having off-line conversations. There are many other manifestations of such behavior. At the group level, dysfunctional behavior is seen if people are penalized for identifying legitimate issues, team members are not provided with necessary information, tools, time, or other resources needed to complete their work tasks, people are threatened, individual contributors are rewarded at the expense of others, and similar types of behavior exist.

Contributing factors that dramatically increase dysfunctions include not using an agenda or keeping meeting minutes, not establishing clear and realistic project goals and objectives, rewarding power based on who people know rather than their competence, not communicating effectively with customers, key stakeholders, and team members, and not providing team members with the necessary authority to complete work tasks. These types of issues will result in poor decisions.

Interpersonal attraction describes the desire of people to associate. It increases to the extent that team members share common values and a perceived fairness of personal rewards and recognition. People have different reasons for wanting to join a group. Interpersonal attraction also operates within a design team. People join these teams with an expectation that they will benefit as well as their organization. Because a design team shares common goals, the tendency will be for it to efficiently work together. But facilitative methods will always be necessary to ensure a team works through its maturation stages to ensure it accomplishes goals.

Whereas a design team is a formal group, informal groups also have an impact on how people positively and negatively interact. Positive interactions accelerate work activities. This is especially true if mutual trust exists between people. Trust is reinforced to the extent people share common norms and values. It is also increased if there has been a history of positive interpersonal interactions. Negative attributes of informal teams include the propagation of rumors, resistance to new ideas, enforced conformity to the group beliefs, and other dysfunctional behaviors. Although, informal groups often help design teams, they are no substituent for the rigorous project management structure necessary for creating new products and services.

Recall, a story was told of Kitty Genovese, who was murdered despite the fact there were bystanders present in nearby apartments. The reason no one called police was they each thought the other person was calling for help. This is a classic example of a group phenomenon called *diffusion of responsibility* (briefly discussed in the introduction to this book). It has been found to exist in situations where people are part of a large group, but without having clearly defined roles and responsibilities. The practical result is that if actions must be taken, each member of the group thinks others will become responsible for the actions. The result is that no action is taken by anyone. The Kitty Genovese story showed how a group of people did not provide necessary help to a young woman being viscously attacked one evening. Each of the bystanders, who were in their apartments and could not see each other, thought the other one was calling the police or providing assistance to the woman. There was a communication breakdown because this informal group lacked rules to guide interpersonal behavior: there were no clearly defined roles and responsibilities. In the intervening years since the tragic incident, sociologists have studied similar events showing the influence of diffusion of responsibility in other events.

However, a similar phenomenon should not occur within formal design teams having clearly defined roles and responsibilities. But the roles and responsibilities of people peripheral to a team such as customers, key stakeholders, and supporting personnel, if not clearly defined as part of a team's project management strategy, could result in similar issues. Diffusion of responsibility also becomes an issue when products and services are used by others.

SUMMARY

People within organizations have different attitudes and behaviors. These directly impact the design of products and services. Although organizational policies, procedures, and rewards and recognitions systems are designed to modify and control personal behavior, there are limitations. In fact, it's interesting to see the ways in which organizations attempt to ensure employees follow established policies and procedures. Even a cursory review of the many catastrophic events in the news shows that employees at all levels in an organization can easily ignore policies and procedures when they want to do so. Publishing a policy or procedure is very easy. Monitoring compliance is much more difficult for an organization. Ensuring that policies and procedures are followed all the time is almost impossible.

However, this is not always the situation. More than 30 years ago when I worked at United Parcel Service (UPS), the rules were very clear: perform work activities according to policy or be disciplined. Violate ethical guidelines and be terminated. Steal and be criminally prosecuted. The punishment was immediate and directly connected with UPS's policies and procedures. In contrast, over the past 30 years as I migrated from one organization to another, I have seen policies and rules routinely ignored and not enforced. Typically, they are applied to lower-level employees rather than higher-level executives. Organizations with a high level of process complexity are particularly susceptible to violations of policy and procedures. By design, UPS has very simple and standardized operations that enable it to quickly recognize abnormal behavior and take corrective action. Its policies and procedures are also simple and standardized as a result of their process design. This concept has important implications for preventing failures in complex systems.

People react differently to negative or poor working conditions. Various coping mechanisms are triggered in these situations. Examples include denial of the issues, making accusations against others, and engaging in rationalizing behavior (e.g., we will fix this later, it is not as bad as we think, they really don't have to know or they won't understand the complexity of the problem, etc.). The proven approach for keeping a team at a high performance level is to employ a well-structured project management methodology that requires frequent reviews by customers, key stakeholders, and others impacted by a team's work. In other words, transparency is important.

Although organizations want their work activities to be performed correctly and ethically, good results are not guaranteed. How many managers have you known who hide or distort information from subordinates, peers, and superiors to avoid embarrassment or to gain personal advantages by blaming others? This behavior hides design issues and risks. It may also inhibit the ability of a team to efficiently complete its work tasks. If managers or team members engage in these types of dysfunctional behavior, they negatively impact others. In some organizations, accusations and blame are sometimes assigned regardless of the cause for an issue. In these situations, there will be a tendency for people not to report issues and risks. Transparency and trust is particularly important for design teams because they should not become fearful of making their mistakes known, or reporting issues and risks to others.

NOTES

1. Department of Human Services, *SARS Factsheet: Basic Information about SARS* (Atlanta: Centers for Disease Control and Prevention), January 13, 2004.

2. Asia Society, *Close Calls: The Story of SARS,* August 26, 2008, www.asiasociety.org.

3. Rein Allday, "Distribution Plans Fall Short for H1N1 Vaccine," *San Francisco Chronicle,* December 14, 2009, www.sfgate.com.

4. Robert McCoppin, "Swine Flu's Lesson: We're Not Ready for Anything Virulent," *Daily Herald,* December 14, 2009, www.dailyherald.com.

5. "At Least 4,000 Swine Flu Deaths reported in the U.S.: CDC, 'Many millions' Have Been Sickened Since the Outbreak Began in April," Associated Press, November 12, 2009, www.msnbc.com; Arthur Caplan, "Opinion: Swine Flu Response Dismal at Best: Vaccine Delays, Priority Breakdowns Raise Fears about a Worse Crisis Ahead," November 9, 2009, www.msnbc.com.

6. David Brown, "SARS Cases in Asia Show Lab's Risks," *Washington Post,* May 29, 2004, www.washingtonpost.com.

7. David Windell, "Using Social Psychology in Product Design: How Can That Help?" November 22, 2004, posted by David Windell on Local Tech Wire, http://wraltechwire.com/business/tech_wire/opinion/story/1159985/.

8. International Atomic Energy Agency report, "Chernobyl's Legacy: Health, Environmental and Socio-Economic Impacts and Recommendations to the Governments of Belarus, the Russian Federation and Ukraine," in *The Chernobyl Forum: 2003–2005,* 2nd rev. (Vienna, Austria: International Atomic Energy Agency, 2006), http://www.iaea.org/Publications/Booklets/Chernobyl/chernobyl.pdf.

9. *Economic Impacts of the I-35W Bridge Collapse,* Minnesota Department of Employment and Economic Development, September 20, 2007, http://search.state.mn.us/dot/query.html?qp=url%3Adot.state.mn.us&qt=I-35W+Bridge+economic+impact&charset=iso-8859-1&col=state+portal+dvs.

10. Minnesota Department of Transportation, news release, "I-35W bridge Replacement Wins America's Transportation Awards' Grand Prize," October 30, 2009, http://www.dot.state.mn.us/newsrels/09/10/29-award.html.

11. "Collapse of I-35W Highway Bridge, Minneapolis, Minnesota, August 1, 2007," and "Highway Collapse of I-35W Highway Bridge Minneapolis, Minnesota, August 1, 2007," in *Accident Report NTSB/HAR-08/03 National PB2008-916203* (Minneapolis: Transportation Safety Board, Minnesota Department of Transportation, 2008), 63, 152.

12. "Fannie, Freddie Remain Problem Children for Feds," *Bloomberg News,* December 28, 2009, www.contracostatimes.com/business; Peter S. Goodman, "NYT: Loan Program May Have Made Things Worse," *New York Times,* January, 1, 2010.

13. Neil Irwin, "A Lost Decade for the U.S. Economy: Workers, Economists, Policymakers Will Be Chewing on the Lessons of the Aughts for Years," *Washington Post,* January 2, 2010, www.msnbc.com.

14. Peter Barnes and Adam Shapiro, "Report Criticizes SEC over Madoff Scheme," *Fox Business,* August 31, 2009, www.foxbusiness.com.

15. Patents 5,164,084, 5,164,879, and 5,076,920 covering electrostatic dissipative nylon 12/ stainless steel fiber filtration element and housing and 5,328,612 covering a thermoplastic filtration element. US Patent Publication (Source: USPTO) Publication No. US 5164879, November 17, 1992. Application No. US 7/724240 filed on July 1, 1991.

16. David Saltonstall and Richard Sisk, "Officials: Pilots in Buffalo crash of Continental Connection Flight 3407 May Have Been Distracted," *Daily News,* May 11, 2009.

17. Leon Festinger, *A Theory of Cognitive Dissonance* (Palo Alto: Stanford University Press, 1985). First published by Row Peterson, 1957.

18. Bruce Tuckman, "Development Sequence in Small Groups," *Psychological Bulletin* 63, no. 6, 1965: 384–99.

Chapter 3

UNIVERSAL PRINCIPLES FOR GOOD DESIGN

We build too many walls and not enough bridges.

—Isaac Newton

In the last chapter, we discussed important topics of social psychology. One topic was the interaction of individuals and groups within design teams. Another was informal and formal groups including customers and stakeholders. It was shown that even the most unique concept or creative design will fail if activities necessary to design it are mismanaged at a team, group, or organizational level. In this chapter we will discuss additional principles for good designs now from a social psychological perspective and cognition. The influence of cognitive factors on human perception and behavior is significant. In fact, the effects act equally on designers as well as the people using products and services. The effective application of social psychological principles helps ensure products and services have useful attributes but are also designed in ways that make it almost impossible to incorrectly use their functions and features. These principles will enable us to build a framework for explaining failures caused by errors of cognition and group behavior.

Failure prevention, from my perspective, depends principally on understanding and applying tools and methods from four areas. These are (1) correctly using technology, (2) successfully applying lessons learned from social psychological research including those of cognition and group behavior, (3) the application of organizational theory including organizational structure and culture, and (4) principles of effective training

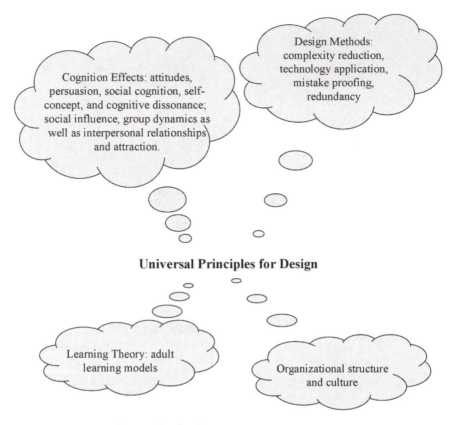

Figure 3.1   Universal principles for design

theory. Within these four areas, shown in Figure 3.1, are universal principles for good design. These are the principles we will discuss in this chapter.

Recall that chapter 1 discussed several important design methods including complexity reduction, technology applications, mistake proofing, and design redundancy as well as several other important concepts. Chapter 2 discussed cognition and group behaviors. Cognition included the effects of attitudes, persuasion, social cognition, self-concept, and cognitive dissonance as well as behaviors of informal and formal groups. Group behaviors included social influence and group dynamics as well as interpersonal relationships and personal attraction. Toward the end of this chapter, we will also discuss several related concepts associated with adult learning models. In combination, this information will be useful for understanding why things fail. Products and services should be designed in ways that teach their users how to properly use functions and features. Ideally, instruction should be intuitive.

Have you ever slept in a hotel room and tried to set its alarm clock? Over many years, I have encountered many different types of alarm clocks. They are overly complicated. Also, there are never instructions showing how to properly use them. Many nights I have had difficulty sleeping because I needed to rely on these devices and wakeup calls. This would not be a problem for most people. But, knowing people easily make errors of judgment and perception that cause mistakes, I like to have at least two sources of time. The alarm clock sitting in a hotel room is an integral part of my planning, but I can seldom use it because of the its many functions and features. It plays music, provides the time, and acts as an alarm. The world is full of similarly overly complicated products and services that confuse us. It is difficult to quickly learn how to use these products and services. Worst, in emergencies, when in stressful conditions such as poor lighting, loud noises, fires, vibration, and other adverse environmental conditions, people make errors. However, if best in class design principles were employed, people could use products and services in ways that help ensure they do not fail.

Recently, I visited the Zoo Atlanta with my daughter. The zoo has a fine primate exhibit with gorillas wandering within enclosures, separated from visitors by moats surrounded with concrete barriers. While touring the exhibit, a large silverback (mature male gorilla) sat across the moat looking at me from about 20 feet away. It probably weighed three to four hundred pounds. I wondered: how safe was this gorilla enclosure? In other words, what prevents this large gorilla from scaling the barrier and escaping? I did some research to answer this question.

I later found gorilla escapes are not uncommon. As an example, a CBS news report on May 19, 2004, from Dallas, Texas, described how a gorilla named Jabari escaped from his enclosure. According to the report, this enclosure "had been in the award-winning gorilla-conservation area, surrounded by a 16-foot concave wall, before the attack. . . . The animal injured four people, including a toddler, before being shot and killed by police. . . . 'He had to have scaled the wall,' said zoo director Rich Buickerood." But "this habitat is among the best in the country. This blows our minds."[1] It blows my mind too. Apparently, even some of the best-designed zoo enclosures may fail to keep animals inside them under certain conditions. In retrospect, I'm glad my daughter and I moved quickly past the gorilla exhibit.

People create mental models of the world around them. These help predict how events will unfold without spending a lot of time figuring out the situation. Mental models can be very useful, but also wrong when conditions change or are mistaken for different ones. Figure 3.2 shows that as a person faces a gorilla in a zoo, they make an assumption that the animal's enclosure cannot be climbed only because they have never heard of previous

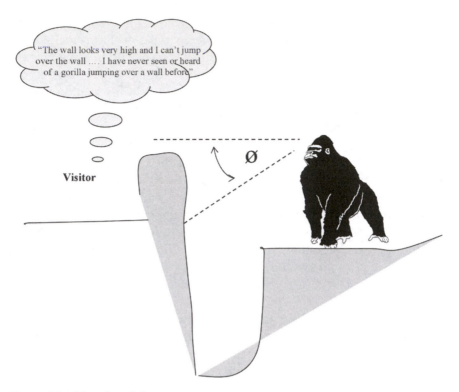

Figure 3.2   Mental models

escapes—a mental model has been formed. However, if the animal is able to climb its zoo enclosure because of a new condition such as aggressive behavior by visitors, there can be serious consequences. A mental model in this situation could be dangerous. Mental models control how decisions are made and work gets done every day all over the world. Things go well most of the time, but not always.

If you ever visited zoos you may have noticed how they are designed for your safety. Design intent can be seen in the many fences and physical barriers erected between people and captive animals. Each animal type has an enclosure that reflects its physical strength, agility, and likelihood of escape. However, despite these well-intentioned designs, different types of animals sometimes escape their enclosures. As an example, on December 25, 2007, Carlos Eduardo Sousa, Jr., a 17-year-old living in San Francisco, was leaving the San Francisco zoo with friends when a tiger named Tatiana escaped her enclosure. In the ensuing chaos and carnage, Carlos was mauled and killed. His two friends, brothers Amritpal and Kulbir Dhaliwal, were also clawed and bitten by the tiger. Police later found Carlos's body lying near the tiger's enclosure. After an investigation into the incident, police claimed the tiger was provoked by the young men. This may or may not be true. But an analysis of the tiger's enclosure showed the actual height of the moat wall was only 12.5 feet tall versus the Association of Zoos and Aquariums (AZA) recommended 16.5 feet.[2] But how did AZA calculate that the height standard should be 16.5 feet? Perhaps it should be higher. Regardless, the height of the original enclosure was an obvious design flaw because the tiger escaped its enclosure. Since the attack, the height of the wall surrounding the concrete moat has been increased to 16 feet and 4 inches. Also, three additional feet of glass fence with electrified hotwires have also been installed on top of the concrete wall.[3] To date, there have not been other tiger escapes.

According to the International Fund for Animal Welfare (IFAW), "There are an estimated 5,000–7,000 tigers living in captivity in the United States as well as another 10,000 or more lions, leopards, cheetahs, jaguars and cougars."[4] Only one half of these animals are kept in United States Department of Agriculture (USDA) approved enclosures. Many of these unapproved enclosures are in poor condition. According to IFAW, between 2003 and 2005, 56 big cats have escaped and 38 people have been mauled and bitten. Five additional people have been killed.[5] It should also be noted that these statistics are for the United States.

Although these serious incidents occurred, we should also put them into perspective. As an example, an Internet search for the most dangerous animals and specifically which animals are responsible for the most human deaths turned up some surprising statistics.[6] Worldwide, mosquitoes cause over 2 million deaths each year, snakes are responsible for more than one hundred thousand deaths and scorpions cause more than five thousand deaths. This article also lists statistics related to deaths caused by other animals. However, exposure to and risk from animals when in their natural habitats is one thing; but, when serious risks occur from visiting zoos it is unexpected. It should also be remembered that injuries and deaths at zoos occur for a variety of reasons. Poor enclosure design is one reason, but the processes associated with the day-to-day work activities such as feeding and transporting animals are also filled with numerous opportunities for failure. It should be noted that animal handlers and veterinarians are also injured and killed by zoo animals.

The proper design of products, services, and their supporting processes is important to satisfy customer needs and prevent or at least decrease the likelihood and effects of failures. In this context, in addition to causing personal or financial harm, failures also result in an inability to satisfy customer needs or value expectations. Recall that a customer's value expectations are broken down into several elements including those related to functions and features. Some failures have a minimum effect on customers, whereas others injure and kill them. Failures can also cause significant property and environmental damage. Because we want to understand the causes for product and service failures and create strategies for their prevention, it is important we understand some basic concepts related to errors and mistakes.

First, humans make errors when designing or using products and services. Second, it is important to understand why these occur so future errors can be prevented or better managed. Understanding implies an error or subsequent failure can be replicated and its causal factors or root causes are known. Third, we also need tools and methods to help people avoid creating or failing to recognize error conditions. These are the topics we will discuss. Another important matter is that people shouldn't be blamed for product or service failures unless the failures were intentional.

According to James Reason,[7] one leading expert, there is a psychological basis for human error, a concept called *error traps*. This concept implies that almost anyone performing a similar work activity within the same system would also tend to make similar errors. This is because error conditions exist in the system. Error conditions cannot be identified, prioritized, and eliminated if people do not come forward and report them. It has been found that many failures often occur after numerous near misses caused by existing error conditions. As an example, suppose there have been several recent incidents where people were almost hit by equipment in a warehouse. There could be many underlying reasons for the near misses. If the near misses are not reported, corrective actions cannot be taken to avoid an accident. In these situations, when an accident actually occurs, it may at first appear to be random, but an investigation would show it was not unexpected given several near misses. There are two important concepts to remember. Error traps need to be identified and eliminated. Near misses help identify them.

These concepts have important implications for the design of products and services. If one person makes errors when using a design's functions and features, then others are likely to have the same problem. As a result, it is always useful to identify potential improvements within a design relative to use, rather than focusing solely on improving the knowledge and skills of people. People make errors in large part because of inherently poor design functions and features, that is, design flaws, because designers do not always consider varying skills, education, and other human limitations. As an example, some people have poor eyesight, others are physically weak, while yet others are uneducated or unskilled. Physical and perceptual differences between people can also be significant. Good designers know these facts and design accessible products and services for their customers. Designers should also consider the interrelationships between technology, cognition, and learning behaviors. This is particularly important for preventing the misuse of products and services and subsequent failures. This approach to design is in contrast to a classical focus solely on technology.

Confounding the use of even well-designed products and services are the mental models of people using them. Mental models are formed, over many years, through life's experiences with similar situations. These models are useful because people are able to react quickly to new situations using information previously learned from similar situations in the past. This enables them to avoid stopping work or play to learn new information and behaviors. However, mental models are not useful if people are faced with a new situation that is mistaken for a former one, but is not in fact similar. These are errors of judgment or perception that cause mistakes or failures.

An example would be trying to open a door one way, pushing it open because of experience using similar doors, but having difficulty because the current door works differently in that it must be pulled to open it. Other examples include turning a screw clockwise (normal rotation for most uses) to tighten it rather than counter-clockwise for other applications, or misinterpreting new information patterns that had been interpreted differently in previous situations. Users of products and services have inherent expectations (mental models) regarding how products and services should be used in certain applications. It doesn't matter if user expectations are wrong. Designers must think ahead of how people will be interacting with functions and features to prevent failures. This requires they understand basic principles of cognition to predict likely user perceptions and behaviors. In other words, when people encounter a new product or service for the first time, its functions, features, and other attributes should be easy to understand.

A new product or service should be created from a perspective that if an error of judgment occurs in its use, the consequences will be negligible. In fact, there is a theory embodied in the field of mistake proofing that encourages a designer to work through a sequence of design activities to prevent errors or minimize their impact. Recall that we briefly discussed mistake proofing in the context of product and service designs. Now we want to discuss its principles in more detail as shown in Figure 3.3.

Mistake proofing is a formal set of concepts and methods used to prevent and detect errors. If errors occur, a supporting strategy is to prevent the occurrence of defects (mistakes or failures). An error is an unintended or undesirable result caused by overt action or a failure to take an action. A defect occurs when an error results in a failure to meet internal or external standards. Standards are represented as specifications in different forms such as written procedures. An important concept of mistake proofing is that certain conditions increase the likelihood for errors. Mistake proofing

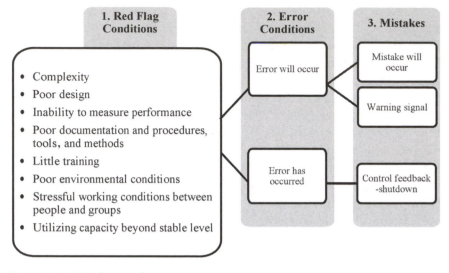

Figure 3.3 Mistake proofing

requires using a sequence of methods to prevent red flag and error conditions and the propagation of defects.

Red flag conditions contribute to the creation of error conditions and subsequent errors. Typical errors include processing omissions and additions, errors associated with setting up work, missing or extra components, use of incorrect components, working on the wrong work, and making measurement errors. Measurement errors are very common because people measure the wrong thing or the right thing the wrong way. This leads to false conclusions and increases the likelihood of defects. In fact, measurement systems exhibit varying degrees of bias, precision, stability, linearity, and other errors. People know much less than they should about the products and services they use because a measurement system usually consists of complicated combinations of equipment, standards, and people.

Errors may or may not lead to defects or failures from a customer perspective. As an example, if a component is left out of a shipping carton (processing omission error), but its absence is detected so it can be added to the carton prior to shipment, then from a customer perspective a defect has not occurred. How would such an error be detected? In some industries cartons are weighed to ensure they contain all needed components. In other industries checklists are used to audit orders prior to shipment.

In still other industries, predictive models may use information from sensors to detect an error condition and calculate the likelihood of a defect such as a burst pipeline. An error condition would exist if internal pressure approached the mechanical strength of the pipeline, but a pipeline rupture was prevented from occurring. In these situations, high pressures can be decreased to prevent a catastrophic failure of a pipeline. In a service process, error conditions include poor training, lack of procedures, and similar situations. A defect would be a failure to meet requirements of time, cost, or quality of service, which vary depending on the service system's design intent. Mistake proofing strategies help eliminate red flag and error conditions prior to defect creation or failures. They can be applied with good results to detecting error conditions within any system.

Additional red flag conditions include complexity, not using good design methods, an inability to measure performance of products or services, lack of product and process documentation and procedures, little use of best in class tools, poor training, deteriorating environmental conditions, and stressful working conditions such as those between people or pushing a system past its optimum capacity. Red flag conditions cannot cause error conditions if they are identified and eliminated from designs and processes.

If an error condition is detected, it may be possible to prevent a mistake. There are several common mistakes associated with designing products and services. Examples include incorrectly capturing customer requirements or translating requirements into specifications; these are set-up errors. Others include not using calibrated testing equipment (measurement errors), forgetting to include all information in a project folder (assembly errors), and providing information that leads to incorrect work procedures and procedures out of sequence (information errors). There are many ways in which products and services could fail.

Exacerbating problems are people's mental and physical limitations, which cause them to make errors of judgment leading to mistakes. Examples include misunderstanding information because of mental models and filtering, poor concentration and forgetfulness, distraction and fatigue, sensory errors leading to poor identification, delay of executing work tasks because of limitations of information processing, and making willful errors for various reasons. These are some of the reasons why some catastrophic events occur. There are many ways in which things can fail.

However, there are proven ways to implement mistake proofing methods to prevent failures. A useful approach is to describe a potential mistake or failure mode including where it occurs, why it occurs, its occurrence frequency, and its effect. This method is called a failure mode and effects analysis (FMEA). Recall it was described in chapter 1. When designing products and services, an FMEA analysis requires a review of its functions and features. These are analyzed relative to components and subsystems in products. In contrast, a process FMEA analyzes operations and work tasks. For both applications, the information is used to identify error conditions and their causal factors or root causes. Tools such as an FMEA and others can provide information that can be used to create effective mistake proofing strategies. They also help designers and their teams decrease the likelihood of failures. In summary, an important design goal is to prevent the occurrence of red flag and error conditions since they create conditions for errors or mistakes that cause failures.

There are also lower-level mistake proofing strategies. Depending on technology and design, processes create different types of defects. These defects also have varying occurrence frequencies. An important lower-level strategy, if a defect occurs, is to immediately recognize and eliminate the cause to prevent other defects from occurring. Some important second-level activities include establishing clear and easy-to-understand standards, establishing relevant operator training systems, and creating systems so people or machines can quickly detect and classify defects in ways that facilitate immediate corrective actions.

As an example, if error conditions occur, software verifies information is correctly entered into a computer by cross-validating zip codes to a specific city and state prior to accepting a credit card transaction. Even if an error condition occurs, a mistake or defect is not allowed to be created or affect a credit card transaction. The user is prompted to change information prior to a transaction being accepted. A third-level mistake proofing strategy is preventing defects from propagating to other operations. This is a containment strategy. At this level, compensating actions are taken to eliminate error conditions prior to creating a second defect.

In summary, mistake proofing is often applied at several levels, beginning with the design of a product or process, and is expanded throughout all associated production operations. The application of mistake proofing significantly decreases the likelihood of unexpected failures. At a higher level, mistake proofing integrates psychological, organizational, and technological factors to prevent systems from failing unexpectedly. Designers understand people have cognitive, perceptual, and perhaps even physical limitations. As a result, it is very likely they will make errors of judgment, causing defects. Mistake proofing is a useful tool for preventing failures. Best in class designs use this methodology to help people successfully use products and services.

If failures cannot be eliminated through effective design or applying classic mistake proofing strategies because of technological or operational limitations, then redundancy may be required to ensure backup systems engage if critical systems fail for any reason. Closely related to redundancy are safety factors or margins of error. These are used if the full effects of environmental factors are not known with certainty. In other words, safety factors compensate for variations of strength and applied stress within application environments. They decrease the likelihood of unexpected failures. Recall, typical stresses include mechanical, thermal, and similar types. Strength depends on a system's design attributes such as materials, geometry for mechanical systems, and other attributes.

Over the past 30 years, Toyota has been a major influencer of best practices for the design of products, services, and manufacturing processes. In fact, Toyota's engineering and production systems have been studied by operations and quality exerts around the world. They have also been adopted by many leading edge organizations, for good reasons. Toyota's methods reinforce important design and production concepts such as translating customer needs into highly differentiated, but also simply designed, products and services manufactured by very flexible, standardized, and stable production systems. But, risks can never be completely eliminated.

Although Toyota's philosophies, tools, and methods have proven to be highly effective, recently some Toyota vehicles experienced uncontrolled acceleration problems. Others, such as the Prius, experienced braking issues. These events posed a serious danger to Toyota's customers as well as its reputation and profits. As of February 2010, Toyota's vehicle recall costs for the acceleration problems were estimated at more than $2 billion, and 51 deaths had been linked to vehicle acceleration failures as of March 2010.[8] Recently, *BusinessWeek* published an article titled "The Humbling of Toyota." It discussed Toyota's legendary frugality and explored the possibility that extensive cost reductions, over several years, may have contributed to the recent vehicle problems. Incidentally, the cause of the acceleration problems was thought to be stuck accelerator pedals or floor mats and perhaps software.

According to Toyota, Prius brake problems were caused by a software issue. Software in these vehicles is important because, in addition to using the friction between brake pads and the rotor or drum to stop a vehicle, the electric engine is also used to slow the vehicle and generate electricity. Toyota has done many things right over the past several decades, but its recent vehicle failures have made people wonder if quality has slipped in recent years. Truly innovative designs intelligently reduce cost, but also increase quality and safety. Although Toyota's newest designs are partially to blame for its failures, its cost cutting over the past decade is thought to be another reason for the recent failures.

An important principle of good design is that customers should be able to easily use products and services. But this implies that designers know what customers need and how they will use a product or service's functions and features. It is important people have accessibility when using a product or service. As an example, one may notice that some websites seem to be better designed than others when navigating Web pages to find information. It's not easy to quickly find information when navigating poorly designed web-sites. Unfortunately, some people have more difficulty than others because of physical limitations. Imagine you are nearly blind and can't easily see a computer screen or words appear blurred and fuzzy. Unfortunately, this is reality for some people. In fact, font sizes on some websites make them nearly unreadable even for people with good eyesight. Or perhaps a person is color blind and cannot differentiate red from green icons? Other website issues may be the use of overly complicated phrases containing words that are difficult to understand, or slow Internet service speeds. In these website applications, good designers will research and know the needs of all poten-tial users to design websites to ensure people can use them without making errors.

There are similar examples where accessibility is a problem. They include handicapped people attempting, with difficulty, to reach light switches or elevator control buttons, people being automatically locked out of their au-tomobiles, or automated teller machines that fail to complete transactions. Language may also be an issue if people must read complicated instructions not in their native tongue before using a product or service. Poor accessibil-ity increases the likelihood people will make errors. Unfortunately, people often blame themselves when they have a difficult time using products and services. But the fault usually lies with the design of the products and ser-vices they use. In contrast, accessible designs enable people to use func-tions and features without error. Also, people should not need to spend inordinate amounts of time trying to understand how to use products and services.

Designs should lend themselves to easy interpretation and use. As an example, a sharp pointed object is intuitively useful for making holes. In-tuitively, a round object can be rolled across a surface. Also, a flat object can intuitively be used for pressing, grinding, and compression. To the extent physical appearance matches functions and features they will be easier to use in practice. This attribute is called an affordance. Affordance reduces the likelihood of human error because people are less likely to misinterpret a design's function.

A product or service's form and geometry should provide easy-to-under-stand clues regarding its functions and features so users require little or no training. If you examine a computer mouse, you will find it is designed so people can place their fingers across its left and right control buttons. The cursor on the computer screen responds naturally to movement of a mouse across a flat surface. Also, the roller track located between the left and right control buttons enables a user to intuitively scroll through a computer's screen. Unfortunately, designers do not always effectively use affordance. Common examples are using several similar buttons for different functions and features or an inconsistent use of geometrical shapes or colors causing confusion.

Accessibility and affordance are the first two design principles we need to remember. But they are not enough. Designers also need to apply other important principles. Many of these require an understanding of cognition. Unfortunately, designers, and especially technically focused engineers, are not usually taught the relevance of social psychology to design. The practical result is that minor or serious errors and mistakes are inevitable if people misinterpret how to use products or services. A major reason why the things we trust fail is that they are designed without regard for the people who use them.

In this section we will discuss several principles of technical design. The underlying theme is that functions and features should work regardless of who uses them. The discussion is broadly divided into methods and principles related to reducing complexity and ensuring a high quality of information transfer. As an example, the ability of people to easily understand and use functions and features depends on their quantity, that is, the device's complexity, and how the functions and features are technically designed, that is, the quality of information provided by designers regarding usage. There is also synergy between these concepts. Fewer functions and features (simplification) will make information transfer easier. In other words, people more easily understand how to use products and services. However, simplicity doesn't imply a product or service should be stripped of useful functions and features to the point of having less overall utility. In fact, there are several design methods that provide a full range of functions and features, but in an organized way to reduce complexity. Information quality and ease of transfer also depend on the content and the physical representation of information. In this context, technology, cognition, and organizational factors as well as basic learning principles are especially important for creating and maintaining safe designs under all application conditions.

According to Hick's Law, an increased number of alternatives will lengthen the time a person requires to make a decision. This has important implications for the ways people use products and services. It also is a consideration if people need to process information and especially in crises. High information complexity, in a crisis, often leads to information overloading when there is a need to make decisions under stressful conditions. High complexity results in numerous decision alternatives that must be simultaneously considered for successful execution. Humans have limitations.

Complexity reduction is a useful principle for good design. In addition to facilitating decision making, reducing complexity directly lowers design and product usage costs. It also decreases the likelihood of errors because there are fewer components. As an example, the likelihood of misassembled components will be higher when assembling a hundred rather than two components. Also, mental effort is reduced when not using products and services within confusing environments characterized by distracting sounds, light, and other external stimuli. Simplification of product and service designs should always be the desired goal since benefits are immediate and sustainable over time.

A methodology for simplifying the design of products (design for manufacturing, or DFM) was popularized by former University of Massachusetts professors Boothroyd and Dewhurst in the mid-1980s.[9] The methods also have direct analogies to service systems. Up until mid-1980, screws, adhesives, and other fastening systems were widely used for product design and assembly. Although still used, their use is limited. Product designers had seldom used DFM principles on a widespread basis before mid-1980. The DFM methodology was immediately popular because of its usefulness for reducing product complexity.

A DFM seminar begins with a presentation and an exercise. The exercise requires creating a baseline analysis of the number and types of components and assembly operations required by a current product design. The information is entered into a simple Excel model. The design team is then taught the basic principles of DFM. The exercise is repeated, but an analysis is done to identify the best ways to combine functions and features. Strategies include creating fewer components to replace several others and using simple and mistake-proof assembly methods such as snap fits rather than adhesives or screws. DFM offers other innovative methods that help simplify and standardize assembly operations. When a product, redesigned using DFM, is compared to the current design, the results are often surprising. As an example, in mid-1980, Ford Motor Company claimed more than $1 billion in savings using DFM methods. Other organizations have also reported achieving significant financial as well as operational benefits.

The IBM Pro Printer, designed and manufactured in the 1980s, is a classic example where several DFM methods were successfully used.[10] The redesigned printer had 79 percent fewer components than the previous version. The number of components was reduced by combining several functions into one, reducing the number of materials, and eliminating screws and other difficult-to-handle components. The final printer design was integrally molded plastic made up of components that could be easily snapped together rather than bolted, screwed, or otherwise fastened. The result was a reduction of the amount of time and cost required to assemble the printer using automated assembly methods. The new printer could be automatically assembled in less than three minutes.

The DFM concept enabled IBM's manufacturing operations to remain within the United States rather than be outsourced to countries having lower labor rates. The DFM concept is an important methodology for designing, producing, using, and maintaining systems safely. It has 10 key principles.[11] Several of these are incorporated into Table 1.3. These include (1) eliminating unnecessary components, (2) using standardized materials, components, and procedures, (3) combining several functions into one, (4) eliminating different materials, (5) eliminating screws, fasteners, adhesives, and secondary operations, (6) ensuring easy visual and vertical alignment of components for assembly, (7) mistake proofing operations to prevent errors, (8) ensuring testing is accurate and easy, and (9) ensuring ease of service, maintenance, and disposal of products or services. The overall approach of DFM is to simplify, standardize, and mistake proof the design, production, and use of new products. The extrapolation to service applications is also straightforward.

There are other simplifications useful for analyzing processes to identify ways to decrease cost and cycle time, and eliminate operations that contain work activities causing problems. One common method is creating a process value flow map (VFM). The exercise requires a cross-functional team that is knowledgeable with the work activities being analyzed to build a process map. The team consists of people who do the actual work activities, facilitators, and subject matter experts (SMEs). An evaluation is made to determine if every work activity adds value. Those that do not (called non-value-adding) are removed from the process to simplify it. A work activity is valuable if required by a customer, if it has three characteristics. These are it physically changes the work moving through it, and if it is done right the first time. Value-adding operations are needed by customers and should not be eliminated from a process. This is in contrast to a second category of operations that do not have value. There is also a third category that is useful for process analysis. It is called business value adding. It includes operations that do not meet one or more of the three value criteria, but must be done because of regulation, law, or technical constraints.

Once a value flow map is created, process measurements are taken at every operation. Examples include the duration of each operation's cycle time, its quality measured by yield percentages, operational availability, or machine uptime, and similar information. Because people routinely interact with processes, simplification is important for helping reduce the likelihood of errors and mistakes.

Simplification is achieved by using fewer components, eliminating secondary operations such as adhesives and fastening systems, and presenting functions and features to users in easy-to-understand ways. Simplification also depends on standardization of materials, components, and procedures. Standardization implies there is always one best material, component, or procedure that should be used every time within the framework of a current design. This reduces variation. Simplification can also be achieved combining several design functions and features into fewer components (modularization). Modularization implies functions and features are integrated into one unit, which increases system reliability. These are the goals of DFM methods.

Several other principles are also helpful for simplifying designs. The first is the use of connected objects by linking them. If objects are connected, when one moves, the objects linked to it also move. Connecting objects is useful in complicated visual systems that require people to monitor several interacting objects. An example is an air traffic control display where planes are displayed with their routings. A second principle is a consistent use of objects in ways that reinforce familiar usage patterns. Both design strategies help people simplify decision making within complex environments by making changes easier to identify and understand. This reduces the need to continually analyze interacting objects within a system. Both strategies take advantage of the ways people process information to simplify decision making. Fewer errors and mistakes will be made as a result of using these principles.

Constraining movement of action by limiting the range of functions and features to a few choices or levels is another useful simplification principle. Limiting the range of variation is also a useful principle. Examples of its uses are widespread. As an example, consumer electronic devices constrain movement of power, volume, channel selection, and similar controls. A digital control on televisions and radios that only allows discrete levels is one version of the concept. Constraining the movements of controls, valves, levelers, and similar components to certain ranges will reduce the likelihood that incorrect settings will be selected. The principle is used in many other applications. As an example, valves controlling liquid and gas flows within nuclear facilities may require some valves to be manually turned by people using a wheel and screw. Sometimes their range of movement must be constrained to ensure flow rates are kept within predetermined ranges to prevent catastrophic failure.

However, a balance should be reached relative to design flexibility and usability. Designs that present a large number of functions and features to users are more difficult to use without making errors of judgment and mistakes. However, reducing complexity below a level for optimum utility cannot be done. This is called a trade-off decision. There are two design principles that can help in these situations. First, functional mapping can be used to create a one-to-one correlation between functions and features needed by users. The mapping should be intuitive and not require relearning. An example is the iPod designed and manufactured by Apple. Its design incurs little need to read directions. A single button is pressed and scrolled to select different functions and features to play music and access other functions. Updating is also easy because the iPod is periodically synchronized with a computer's ever-changing song list. That is all a person has to do to keep their song list up to date. Functional mapping helps reduce errors.

Another useful design strategy is to match functions and features to a user's current knowledge. In other words, users are presented with basic information, functions, and features with an option to proceed to more advanced levels. The relationships are hierarchal and easy to understand. This enables people to quickly begin using a product or service with minimal training because they are familiar with its higher-level basic functions and features. In time, once they learn and become familiar with these basic functions and features, they can learn to use the more advanced ones. This strategy reduces informational overloading. There is less stress and the likelihood of errors is reduced. An example of this design strategy is commonly seen in software. Software has numerous functions and features that can quickly become overwhelming. However, users can begin using basic features such as opening and closing files or simple formatting prior to using more advanced features. In fact, many of the features and functions of a software product may never be used by most people.

Standardization was briefly discussed as useful for reducing complexity, because it helps reduce the variability of product and service performance in design, production, and usage. It is easier to produce and use products when components, materials, and work procedures are the same every day. This is in contrast to situations wherein every component is unique and requires specialized handling and processing.

A lack of standardization creates situations where mistakes are easily made and the likelihood of subsequent failures increases. But it is not an excuse to deprive customers of functions and features they need and want, otherwise they will not purchase products and services. It is always important to capture customer needs and translate these into the features and functions they need. However, providing these in the simplest ways should always be the goal of good design.

Let's examine a well-known example showing how standardization can be correctly applied in practice. Southwest Airlines has grown its business by delighting customers in a very competitive industry. It provides the basic service of transporting people to their destinations safely, inexpensively, and comfortably. It also provides other value-adding services at additional cost. As an example, people can purchase priority boarding for a nominal charge. Southwest is also profitable. If you take a cursory view of their operational strategy you will notice a high degree of standardization. They use common aircraft throughout their system.

This reduces pilot and maintenance training as well as repair and maintenance costs. They also fly to fewer cities where demand is stable and costs are lower than larger airports. Their frequent flyer program is also very simple: one free flight for every 10 purchased flights. In contrast, their competitors use much more complicated service systems. These are characterized by using several different types of airplanes that require different process workflows designed around more complicated training and maintenance.

Which organizations have the correct operational designs? The answer depends on their marketing strategies, the customer promises they make, and the types of customers they want to attract. Since Southwest Airline's systems are simpler, they will be less costly to maintain and their likelihood of failing will be lower than the more complicated service and operational systems of its competitors. As a result, customers will see fewer failures, excluding weather and airport issues, which airlines cannot control. However, not all customers want to fly with Southwest airlines.

An effective and efficient strategy for process design is to design operations at the customer facing portion of a process to meet marketing promises. But the back end of a process should be simplified, standardized, and mistake proofed to provide consistent operational performance at lower cost. The front end should be designed so customers receive functions and features they need and want, but in ways that make their user experience stress-free and easy. However, even in these systems service systems should be designed for high value and consistency.

Modularity was briefly discussed in an earlier section. Its importance for simplification requires more discussion. If two subcomponents can be combined into only one, there will be less complexity from a user perspective. Fewer components within a product or fewer handoffs within a service system increase a system's reliability by reducing the number of required components. How is modularity achieved in practice? Prior to the widespread application of DFM methods, designers routinely used components that required complicated assembly operations. The materials were also costly, as was assembly labor. Over the past several decades, in parallel with many technological breakthroughs there was also a growing popularity of plastic and other materials because their physical and chemical properties continued to evolve. Practitioners of DFM were able to take advantage of these technology improvements. This enabled manufacturers to integrally mold several single subcomponents into one. Design modifications also enabled a consolidation of the number of materials used to manufacture a product. In addition, fastening systems such as screws, nails, clamps, and adhesives were no longer required for assembly when modularization was applied. Modularity provides significant advantages for both manufacturers and users since there is less complexity to understand and manage. Process designs can also be modularized by reducing and combining operations to reduce overall complexity.

The ability to see work, including materials and tooling, also helps reduce errors. Think how important visualization is when repairing a leak under a kitchen sink. There are two options: work on one's back facing upwards and see the bottom of the sink to repair connections, or remove the sink from the counter, repair the connections, and then place it back into the counter top. From experience, the latter approach is sometimes less tiring and can be more efficient than the former because the work is easy to see. But this depends on the required repair. As another example, people use light, magnifying glasses, and similar tools to help them more easily see objects. The ability to visualize conditions dramatically reduces the likelihood of errors or mistakes being made by people doing work because they can more easily see how to do the work or the cause of a problem.

Prior to widespread use of DFM, products were assembled in very complicated ways. Screws and bolts were inserted in places that were difficult to access and inspect. Assembly mistakes were routinely made by line workers. A lack of visual access also became a significant issue when organizations began to employ robotic assembly machines. The movements of robots were relatively inflexible when compared with those of humans. As a result, designers were forced to find ways in which robotic machines had direct access to components to complete assembly operations. The result was the DFM concept of vertical assembly and alignment to correspond with the up-and-down motions of robotic machines. Once design modifications were made to ensure access and vertical alignment, the robotic and automated assembly machines performed work more consistently than humans. This decreased the likelihood of error conditions and defects. The concepts of visual access to work tasks and vertical alignment of components and tools have been popularized across many different industries with great success over the past several decades.

Designers of mechanical or structural components also use the alignment principle when designing products to ensure mating components fit together along a common line or plane. One useful strategy is to design mating components asymmetrically so they fit together only one way. Alignment is an effective mistake proofing strategy because little skill is required for assembling components. It is particularly useful in a crisis situation where people must react quickly by assembling or disassembling such things as hoses when there is a fire, pneumatic lines, and similar equipment. It should also be noted that once aligned, mating components may then be joined using methods such as a quick connect, snap fits, or other fastening strategies.

The principle of component alignment also has applicability in services. As an example, there should be no possibility of misinterpreting instructions or how to enter information into manual or electronic forms. A common way this mistake proofing is done in practice is to match information fields along a common line to prevent transcription errors. Another practical application is ensuring people can move only one way to continue through a process unless alternate pathways are created to manage capacity.

Products and services fail because designs may be marginal or incapable of performing within their application environments. They may also be misused, not properly maintained and serviced, or improperly disposed and recycled. The best-designed products and services will fail if they are not properly maintained and serviced. The proper disposal after their useful life is also important. This is because some products contain dangerous substances and pose significant environmental risks. In fact, some catastrophic events have occurred because of improper disposal of hazardous materials. As an example, on December 6, 1983, a resident of Ciudad Juárez, a city in the Mexican state of Chihuahua, took materials from a radiation therapy machine containing several thousand Cobalt-60 pellets. The truck used to transport the radioactive material became contaminated as well as the 5,000 metric tons of salvaged steel it was transporting.[12] The radioactive steel was eventually used to manufacture furniture that was later sold in Mexico and in the United States. These types of incidents, where environmental damage occurred, have been quite common.

There are also design principles to ensure effective maintenance, serviceability, and disposability of products and services. These are usually integrated into a strategy called total life-cycle design. Total life-cycle design attempts to ensure products or services are well designed, easy to maintain and service, and if they are not needed can be easily disposed of by users, or if necessary by professionals. Maintenance systems ensure products or services are available for use with a predefined probability. In this context, availability depends on a system's reliability. In critical systems, the probability systems will be available, that is, their reliability should be very high. Maintainability consists of combinations of preventive and corrective activities. Preventive activities are designed to provide service at specific hours of use based on a system's design. Corrective maintenance is done after a failure occurs. Different systems have different types and frequencies of required preventive and corrective maintenance.

A common example of preventive maintenance is changing an engine's oil and conducting diagnostic checks after a certain number of usage hours. A common example of corrective maintenance is changing light bulbs in a commercial facility. Using a minimum cost model, replacement bulbs are inserted only after a predetermined number have failed. But it should be noted that there are enough functioning bulbs to meet all regulatory and safety requirements. Some systems require combinations of both approaches, whereas other types of systems rely exclusively on preventive maintenance strategies. Aircraft, nuclear power plants, and similar critical systems cannot be allowed to unexpectedly fail.

If corrective maintenance is used either by design or default, there are important work activities that must be done. These include diagnosing the problem, removing failed components, repairing the system, and verifying the repairs are correct. In complicated systems, maintenance activities are usually also very complex, which increases the likelihood of error conditions and subsequent mistakes. Having poor or no maintenance systems are a red flag that systems will likely unexpectedly fail in the future.

Periodic maintenance is also required for software products and their services. Actually, software is a good example of how maintenance can be automatically and cost effectively performed. A well-known example would be the periodic updates Microsoft downloads to computers. They are automatic and easy. In contrast, other software and information technology systems usually require more extensive maintenance by professionals and the hardware must be physically maintained by people.

Service systems that are combinations of physical objects, people, and information systems must also be maintained. Let's examine a restaurant as an example. A restaurant is designed to provide food and services to customers. There are also different types of restaurants ranging between fast food and fine dining. They contain several processes or workflows. Examples include cooking, serving food and drinks, billing, and providing utensils. People working in a restaurant also have differing roles and responsibilities and use different information systems. Examples include placing orders to the kitchen, serving food, cleaning up, invoicing customers, and collecting feedback. These systems rely heavily on manual work tasks. As a result, they can quickly deteriorate if standards are not created, and audited on a frequent basis. In fact, failures are often associated with service and supporting systems rather than a technical failure.

In summary, the more complex a system, the higher the likelihood it will fail. As a result, the best design strategy should be to create simple, standardized, and modularly designed products and services that require simple and standardized maintenance. This is the best designers can do to prevent failures from a technical perspective. Cognitive influences must also be considered.

In the previous section we discussed design principles from a technical perspective. In this section we discuss them from a cognitive perspective. Although the application of best-in-class technical design principles helps create simple and standardized designs, more is needed to increase the likelihood of correct usage to avoid failures. Social psychology shows us the human brain reacts to information in predicable ways. Sometimes these reactions are very good, but, at other times the consequences from failure can be serious.

It is known that psychological patterns caused by conditioning can also be used to communicate a design's function. This design principle is called archetype representation. These are usually culturally dependent patterns. Many types of products and services are designed using archetypal patterns. As an example, marketing research is done to identify feelings of satisfaction, power, influence, sex, hunger, thirst, and similar feelings invoked by images and sounds. The marketing goal is to influence purchasing intent and behavior. Common examples include using well-dressed people to convey feelings of wealth or large men to convey feelings of power, using skull and crossbones on a label to warn of a poisonous substance, or using dark images to evoke feelings of caution or danger. Archetypes can be used to influence behavior to either avoid or interact with functions and features of products and services.

Designers also should consider biases consumers often have developed from using similar products or services. As an example, people become used to turning screws clockwise to tighten and counterclockwise to loosen them. But some products use a counterclockwise motion to tighten and clockwise motions to loosen screws. The existence of biases requires designers to inform users if work activities that run contrary to the norm are required to use a product or service. Perhaps a warning label should be used in situation where screws must be turned counterclockwise? A second example would be to contrarily use the colors green, yellow, and red within the United States. People within the United Sates have been conditioned to interpret these colors as green to go, yellow to slow, and red to stop. If designers should revise the use of these colors in a contrary manner, then people may misinterpret a system's status. This would create an error condition and increase the likelihood of user mistakes. Designers should understand the ways personal biases influence behavior relative to intended use of products and services because errors occur if people misinterpret the correct meaning and usage of features and functions.

The law of *prägnanz* recognizes the fact that people interpret ambiguous information as complete; that is, people create and see patterns where there are none. The effect occurs when a person mentally fills in blanks between visual elements arranged as a shape or pattern, although the pattern is incomplete. One example would be to see a pattern formed by a series of lines containing intermittent blank spaces. People tend to mentally fill in the blanks between the lines and perceive the actual and imagined lines jointly forming a shape or pattern that does not exist. This perceptual effect can be either useful or dangerous depending on the application. It is useful if the design intent is to convey information in this manner, but dangerous if people misinterpret the intended pattern. It's usually best to not leave anything to chance in these circumstances; designers should not create partially completed patterns and then leave interpretation to users.

This phenomenon is also called closure because people mentally close a shape's outline. Associated with closure is a design principle called continuation. People tend to more easily understand how to use a design's functions and features when these are arranged in straight lines so as to be perceived as being more connected or related. This implies designers should consider arranging functions and features in this way to show related functions and features unless there are good reasons for not doing so.

Recall, we discussed several social psychological topics including cognitive dissonance in earlier chapters. Advertising professionals use cognitive dissonance to create feelings of discomfort. These feelings are caused by perceived differences between what a person thinks or does versus what, in their mind, they should be thinking or doing. Examples include showing pictures of well-dressed people, or people who purchased new automobiles, electronics, and houses, to induce buyers to purchase these same products. In these applications, the images are designed to create feelings of inadequacy. Purchasing the product or service will decrease the level of dissonance and the person will feel better.

A contrasting application is showing images of people in desperate circumstances needing help. The goal of these messages is to manipulate people into taking actions to reduce dissonance feelings. Many organizations asking for donations use this strategy. Designers can also use cognitive dissonance to create positive and negative feelings regarding product or service usage. Positive feelings make people feel good when they complete intended actions and engage in useful or safe behavior. Negative feelings make people feel uncomfortable if they behave in ways not intended, useful, or safe from a designer's perspective.

People often misinterpret visual information. A physiological example is caused by visual cortex adjustments of brightness and color variation when viewing an object. These are called correction errors and a primary example is constancy (shown in Figure 3.4). Constancy occurs if the visual cortex attempts to maintain a constant image as the size and color of objects change relative to their background or environment. Correction errors also occur when the brain minimizes variations of light or sound. Correction errors increase the likelihood of failures when alarms and controls are not highly differentiated from normal or safe conditions. A common design principle is to use color to compensate for the effects of constancy. Examples include using red colors to convey danger and green colors to convey calmness and

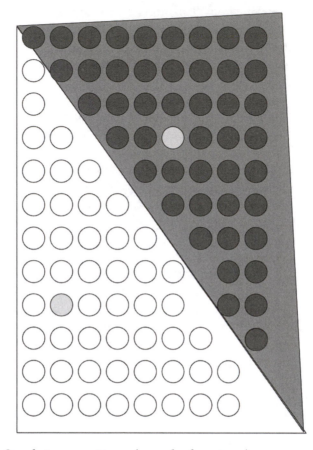

Figure 3.4　See what we expect to see (example of constancy)

normality. But the use of color is culturally dependent. This implies that designers, to the extent color is used for making decisions, should understand how users perceive and interpret colors. This is also true for service systems to the extent physically colored objects are used for making decisions or they are made based on variations of light and sound.

If you have gazed at a picture that produces two different distinct objects depending how it is viewed, you experienced a phenomenon called a figure-ground relationship. It is also called the Gestalt perception principle. Other previously discussed Gestalt principles of perception included closure, continuation, and the law of *prägnanz*. Gestalt principles imply designers should be careful when designing products, services, instructions, and similar objects that must be visually interpreted to ensure evaluation is unambiguous. These concepts are important for failure prevention. In other words, important information should stand out from its background to prevent perceptional failures and reduce the likelihood of errors because people perceive patterns differently.

Fitt's law states a person's ability to visually recognize a target or to physically move to it depends on its distance. This implies smaller objects further away will take longer to move than closer and larger ones. Graphic icons located on a computer screen are examples of the effect of Fitt's law. If an icon is very small and a display screen's resolution is high users, will require more time to interact with the icon. Designers should understand that Fitt's law has important implications for the design of controls and similar decision support systems. The effects of Fitt's law are especially important when people are in emergency situations and must quickly interact with physical or virtual objects. It is also an important consideration when designing interactive computer display screens because people must point and click on objects to execute commands.

Graphical attenuation is another useful design principle. It is used to quickly focus a person's attention. Designers use graphical accentuation to highlight important words, symbols, and numbers to alert users to important information and increase the likelihood they are recognized. Everyday examples include changing the color, size, and type of font when writing text. Bolding and underlining text are other examples. This methodology is also important when designing safety features or providing instructions to users in emergency situations.

The Guttenberg layout comprises design principles based on the fact that people in different cultures develop different reading preferences. As an example, people in Western countries visually scan an object from the left, top down, and diagonally to the lower right quadrant. People will tend to ignore homogenous information not arranged in this manner, increasing the likelihood of reading errors. The implication of that important information (including safety instructions) should be organized in this manner in Western countries and perhaps differently in other cultures to increase readability.

Designers can also use framing of positive and negative images to reinforce ways in which people interpret information. Positive images are used to influence people to take an action and negative images are used to influence them not to. As an example, showing the negative results from not following procedures such as showing images of burn victims or accidents would be an application of negative framing. Recently, there have been suggestions that packaging of tobacco products should show images of people dying or the effects of disease from heavy usage. In contrast, showing images of green plants or water would, in most applications, convey positive imaging. Additional examples of framing are images of a fire to convey the thought that an object can burn, using an image of a flower to convey the thought that an object is healthy, and using images of radioactivity to alert people to dangers of opening sealed containers holding such materials. Alternatively, images could be used to show the location and proper use of safety equipment. But images are also culturally unique. This implies they are interpreted differently by people of different cultural backgrounds. As a result, caution should be exercised when using these methods because the likelihood of failures will be increased if improperly used.

Iconic accentuation uses symbols having universal meanings to convey important information. It is effective because symbols are easier to interpret by people than words. But icons should be culturally neutral. Common examples include highway signs showing turns, inclines, and slippery road conditions, or pictures of fragile objects, such as a glass, to show breakable objects. If designers effectively use iconic accentuation, people will be less overloaded with extraneous information. They will also be less likely to make errors or mistakes. As an example, people will make decisions faster when in complex operating environments or emergency conditions. But the meaning of an icon must be unambiguous to users of a product or service.

Informational overload, especially in a crisis, can be dangerous. When it occurs, more effort is necessary to perform a work activity and it is less likely to be completed successfully, if at all. Effort includes mental processing, physical action, or a combination of both. Iconic attenuation reduces mental effort to help minimize mental fatigue. There are many applications. If you look overhead from an airplane seat, you see several icons such as the one for lights, the one on the call button for the flight attendant, the icon for wearing seat belts, and the icon that means no smoking. These are well-known icons. In summary, icons are useful for conveying complex information, but a limitation is that they may be culturally dependent. This implies they should be supported with additional communication aids if the consequences of failure are expected to be severe and catastrophic.

Designers can also accentuate similarities or differences between objects. These differences can be either qualitative or quantitative. This design principle is called object comparison. It also helps decrease mental loading by increasing the ability of people to discriminate between objects. Typically, one of the objects is a standard or benchmark compared to one or more objects. Examples include comparing weight, size, and volume against a standard, or placing information on the same graph for easy comparison. Comparisons can be made under controlled conditions—apples to apples, so to speak.

Designers also use object orientation to convey information in complicated, visually dominated systems for easier interpretation of meaning. Imagine looking at many similar lines on a computer display screen. The most important line should be oriented at a different angle than the others for easy identification. The principle is also true when locating features on products and services or conveying information about how to use them. If people do not have sufficient orientation information, they will make errors of judgment. The likelihood of failures increases because people perceive similarly appearing objects as also having similar functions and features. However, if objects are similar, that is, used in the same way, making them resemble each other is a good strategy. Otherwise, they should be dissimilar in form and appearance.

A design principle related to object orientation is proximity. Proximate objects are also perceived as having similar functions and features. This principle suggests placing objects having dissimilar functions and features separate from each other to decrease the likelihood of error. As an example, an alarm clock radio should have an alarm's functions and features organized in one place and the radio's functions and features organized in a different location.

People have cognitive and physical constraints that affect their ability to take in and process information within complex working environments. Several cognitive limitations were discussed in the previous chapter. Some of them included information filtering, attitudes and bias, and cognitive dissonance. In this section, we will show how several design principles can be used, in part, to help mitigate the negative effects of cognition. Designers need to understand these principles so they can design functions and features to compensate for cognitive limitations. Unfortunately, products and services are not always designed to account for cognitive factors. As a result, ineffective designs are prone to error; mistakes occur, often at the worst of times, when people are overwhelmed by circumstance. It is important to simplify, standardize, and use well-established cognitive principles to ensure efficient utilization of products and services as well as their safe operation. The design principles discussed in this section are useful for preventing failures if manual operations are required or if there are human and machine interfaces including the use of products and services.

In the previous two sections of this chapter we discussed design principles from technical and cognitive perspectives. If these design principles are effectively incorporated within products and services, people will be advantaged because they will not need to exert effort to understand their operation when they are used. The most effective designs do not rely on human interpretation or learning for effectiveness. In fact, people should immediately be able to intuitively use basic functions and features. They can use more advanced features if needed over time (an application of the principle of hierarchal design). The application of these key design principles is focused on overcoming limitations of cognition as well as innate human behavioral responses. Recall these are caused by how people perceive and react to objects, information, and conditions within their environment. People do not always perceive these objects, information, and conditions the same way, so it is not surprising they will not always behave similarly. As a result, behaviors cannot be predicted with certainty in complicated and stressful situations. This is why the application of good design principles is important as a first step for preventing catastrophic failures.

The ability of people to quickly learn to use a design's functions and features is a third important design principle. Recall, we mentioned that when people first encounter a new product or service, it is especially important they have the ability to quickly grasp its intended functions and features and how to use them to prevent errors and mistakes. In this context, there are different strategies for training people to quickly use a product or service. First there could be formal training showing people the best way to use a product or service. Second, there are ways in which people can be taught to immediately use a product or service when first encountered. The latter approach is always a good strategy because people often forget what they have been taught. This is because, although up-front training is usually both useful and necessary, it must be continuously repeated and will never be completely reliable. Of course an assumption is that people are taught correctly. This is not always the situation.

Extensive research exists describing how people learn. There are several theories. One theory is Fleming's VARK model. The acronym VARK represents visual, auditory, reading/ writing, and kinesthetic preferences. Adult learning theory is based in part on the VARK model. Visual learners prefer pictures, slides, and similar methods for transmitting information. Auditory preferences include listening to discussions and lectures. These people are stimulated with sound. Some people easily understand written and abstract information and so have a preference for reading books, using printed materials, and conducting online information searches. Kinesthetic learning preferences are evident if people need to touch and handle objects to see interrelationships or interact with objects and other people within their environment. Effective training will present information in several forms that encompass each of these learning preferences. The correct use of adult learning theory is important when designing training materials to show people how to do safe work. Unfortunately, learning experts are seldom consulted and training is often haphazardly done.

Have you ever heard the phrase *information overload*? It is a fact; most people remember only small amounts of information if briefly exposed to it. Research has shown that approximately 7 ± 2 bits of information is optimum.[13] This is important for designers to remember when creating operating instructions. In situations where people are under stress, the likelihood of errors and mistakes increases if safety information and instructions are not brief and simple.

This concept leads to an important design principle called chunking. Chunking is a process for breaking down a long list of information (symbols) into smaller sequences that are easier to remember on a short-term basis. The usefulness of chunking, when designing products and services, is that users are not required to remember long sequences of symbols such as letters and numbers. This reduces the likelihood of errors and mistakes.

Password creation is a common example where a balance must be maintained between simplicity and security. In this application secure passwords require nonrepeating combinations of numbers, letters, and symbols that are difficult to remember. To balance a need for secure versus easy-to-remember passwords, supporting systems are often created to send users forgotten passwords via e-mail. Alternatively, users may be prompted to provide information only they would know, such as a pet dog's name, a parent's name, and similar information to obtain their lost password.

In addition to chunking, mnemonics is a useful design principle that makes use of jingles or familiar information in ways that help organize otherwise difficult-to-remember sequences of symbols so they can be easily remembered. Familiar patterns take advantage of longer-term memory to help people compensate for the limitations of shorter-term memory. This is a common strategy for remembering long passwords: create them using easy-to-remember information only known by users. We use mnemonics to help remember information that cannot be otherwise broken into smaller sequences.

Because people have a difficult time learning complicated sequences of symbols or other information, it makes sense to use the simplest written words and sentences. A well-known principle for publishing newspapers in the United States is to set the average reading level to an equivalent sixth-grade level for United States students. Technical designers seldom remember most people have limited educational levels and even if their educational levels are advanced, technical jargon is not something people can easily understand because they have different areas of expertise. In some organizations, lengthy procedure manuals filled with complicated terms and acronyms are common. There is a relationship between informational complexity and failures. This is especially true for new employees.

People also more easily remember information at the beginning or end of a message than in the middle. This is called the principle of relative position. There are several useful design principles for compensating in situations that require users to be provided with complicated information. In these situations, information can be presented in hierarchal patterns using figures, diagrams, or pictures. As an example, complex behavior can be shaped using a visualization approach that uses a sequence of graphical representation of discreet activities. These activities as a whole visually show how to complete an activity. Visual assembly instructions can also be used to shape the correct process sequence to show how to perform a complicated activity. An example is airline safety instructions, which show step-by-step operations for removing and inflating a life vest to survive a water landing. The instructions are highly visual and do not depend on a traveler's spoken language or complicated written instructions. In these applications, shaping complex behavior is more useful than relying on complicated verbal or written instructions.

The principle of information hierarchy is also useful for communicating complex information to help people learn faster because people more easily understand information if they see its interrelationships (hierarchy). A common example of the principle to help people use complicated products and services presents information to users at basic, intermediate, and advanced levels by matching a user's education, experience, and skills levels to functions and features. This design strategy makes it easier for people to access and quickly understand the most important information when using products and services. Over time they access more complicated information as needed. Recall, electronic and software products have functions and features that are accessed using a hierarchal design strategy. As an example, in software design, drop-down menus offer users additional options as they are needed. This design strategy helps reduce errors and mistakes. Unfortunately not all product and service designs present functions and features to users in this manner.

The principle of informational redundancy is closely related to information hierarchy. Redundancy requires information be presented in different forms to reinforce understanding of message content. Adult learning theory is based, in part, on this principle. People learn and retain information when they see it in several different forms rather than one. As an example, in a training workshop, people retain information to a greater degree using a combination of lectures, familiar examples, team breakout sessions, and testing and applying learning over time.

The likelihood of error is also reduced if people are periodically exposed to information, using a combination of reinforcing methods. Repetition of action is a useful learning strategy because it requires people to repeat an activity several times to increase information retention. However, a problem with the reinforcement of a set of actions is that a reflex response is created within people. This may inhibit their correctly interpreting and responding to new situations and information in the future. An example is the crash of Continental Connection flight 3407 near Buffalo, New York. Recall, the pilots turned the nose of the aircraft upwards rather than down as the new aircraft design required because they were trained to use older aircraft.

Dynamic feedback and verification of actions is another useful strategy for reinforcing learning because it immediately shows users the effects of their actions. This enables them to adjust subsequent actions until the feedback corresponds to the expected result. It is useful when a change of one object's status is used to modify one or more other objects.

In complicated systems, feedback in the correct form is very important. However, the feedback systems must be carefully designed because the underlying relationships (models) may be complicated (e.g., nonlinear) as well as positively or negatively reinforcing.

These situations make it difficult for people to correctly understand the phenomena taking place within a system. Sometimes counterintuitive results are obtained when users change the status of a system's objects. As a result, both a correct model and training are necessary to provide information to help people understand a system's design and its current status, and to enable them to control its dynamic performance.

A similar design principle called verification of action also provides feedback relative to a system's status to a user. However, an important difference between dynamic feedback and verification is that, for verification, one or more confirmatory actions are required prior to initiating or executing a prior command or instruction. Also, dynamic feedback must be modeled and users presented with correct system status. These design principles increase user learning, help reduce the likelihood of errors, mistakes, and unexpected failures, and in the case of verification of action help to directly mistake proof use of a product or service.

Training theory recognizes the fact that internalized information will be more easily recalled in the future. This suggests people should be trained over an extended period of time and training should be periodically repeated to ensure information can be recalled when needed. Finally, use of operant conditioning is useful to increase learning retention. Operant conditioning recognizes the fact that positive reinforcement increases the likelihood a behavior will be practiced in the future and negative reinforcement decreases its likelihood. This principle becomes important when trying to reinforce the safe use of products and services. Integrating these design principles into training activities helps improve the skills necessary to safely use products and services. Best-in-class instructional design uses the methods discussed in this section (chunking, mnemonics, repetition, redundancy) to present information in ways that enable people to learn more efficiently and retain the information when needed. This will create better-trained people as well as safer and more efficient operations.

SUMMARY

This chapter discussed the application of several important design principles from the perspectives of technology, cognition, and learning. These are important topics when attempting to understand why products and services fail. Designers should use best-in-class design methods to reduce the complexity of products and services. In this context, standardization and mistake proofing are very important. There are other technical tools, methods, and concepts that need to be carefully considered and applied. Cognition is also very important. It is an often-neglected part of designing because many designers are oblivious to the subject. They simply have not studied social psychological topics relevant for designing products and services people use. Closely associated with technical design and cognition, learning theory teaches there are good and bad ways to instruct people to use products and services. People have difficulty learning new things. It is important that correct methods be used to reduce the likelihood of failure. In the next chapter we will discuss organizational culture, which also has an enormous impact on product and services failures, either through direct intervention or by inaction.

NOTES

1. Tatiana Morales, "Gorilla Escapes, 4 Injured, 2 Women and 2 Children Hurt In Zoo Escape," CBS News, Dallas, Texas, March 19, 2004, www.cbsnews.com.

2. Kevin Fagan, Cecilia M. Vega, John Coté, and Marisa Lagos, "Tiger Grotto Wall Shorter than Thought, May Have Contributed to Escape and Fatal Attack," *San Francisco Chronicle,* December 28, 2007.

3. Patricia Yollin, "S.F. Zoo's Big Cats Meet People Again," *San Francisco Chronicle,* February 22, 2008.

4. International Fund for Animal Welfare, *Fatal Attractions: Big Cats in the USA,* http://www.ifaw.org/Publications/Program_Publications/Regional_National_Efforts/Big_Cats_in_the_USA/asset_upload_file827_14706.pdf.

5. Bob Smithe, "Most Dangerous Animals: Which Animal Is Responsible for the Most Human Deaths?" www.AssociatedContent.com, September 19, 2008. http://www.associatedcontent.com/article/1019088/most_dangerous_animals_which_animal.html.

6. James Reason, *The Human Contribution: Unsafe Acts, Accidents and Heroic Recoveries* (Burlington, VT: Ashgate, 2008), 111–13.

7. Chris Isidore, "Toyota Recall Costs: $2 billion," www.money.cnn.com, February 4, 2010, http://money.cnn.com/2010/02/04/news/companies/toyota_earnings.cnnw/.

8. Alan Ohnsman, Jeff Green, and Kae Inoue, "The Humbling of Toyota: A Combination of High-Speed Growth and Ambitious Cost Cuts Led to the Quality Lapses that Have Tarnished the Once-Mighty Brand. How It All Went Wrong,"

BusinessWeek, March 9, 2010; "Toyota: Software to Blame for Prius Brake Problems," www.cnn.com, February 4, 010, http://articles.cnn.com/2010-02-04/world/japan.prius.complaints_1_brake-system-anti-lock-prius-hybrid?_s=PM:WORLD.

9. Geoffrey Boothroyd, Winston Knight, and Peter Dewhurst, *Product Design for Manufacture & Assembly,* 2nd ed., rev. and expanded (New York: Marcel Dekker, 2002).

10. Geoffrey Boothroyd, *Assembly Automation and Product Design,* 2nd ed. (New York: Marcel Dekker, 2002), 15.

11. James William Martin, *Operational Excellence—Translating Customer Value through Global Supply Chains* (Boca Raton, FL: Auerbach, 2008) 95–97.

12. Susan Combs, Texas Comptroller of Public Accounts, "El Cobalto," *Bordering the Future,* July 1998, http://www.window.state.tx.us/border/ch09/cobalto.html.

13. George A. Miller, "The Magical Number Seven, Plus or Minus Two: Some Limits on Our Capacity for Processing Information," *Psychological Review* 63 (1956): 81–97.

Chapter 4

SUCCESSFUL DESIGNS DEPEND ON ORGANIZATIONAL CULTURE

Of all human inventions the organization, a machine constructed of people performing interdependent functions, is the most powerful.

—Robert Shea

On the evening of May 31 to June 1, 2009, over the Atlantic Ocean northeast of the Brazilian coast, Air France A430-300 (F-GLZKL) was torn apart in a violent storm with a loss of 228 people.[1] The actual causes of the catastrophic failure have not been officially determined, but the fault warnings analyzed after the accident showed several technical problems had occurred during the final moments of the ill-fated flight. These problems included an inability to accurately calculate airspeed as well as a sudden loss of cabin pressure.

It was also known that prior to this accident there had been problems with the pitot tube sensors manufactured by Thales; but not those of Goodrich, its competitor. These problems were associated with Air France's A430-300 (F-GLZL), Air France's A340-300 (F-GLZN), and possibly Air France's Flight 447 as well as planes flown by other airline carriers. Investigations of the Thales design indicated the pitot sensor drainage holes may have become clogged when exposed to icing conditions, which rendered the sensors unreliable for calculating a planes' airspeed. In fact, prior to the accident, Air France and other airline carriers had already begun retrofitting Airbus A330's with Goodrich pitot tubes as a precaution. These retrofit activities were being done at the time of the catastrophic accident.

Air France had begun retrofitting its pitot sensors, but it should be noted that these sensors had not been implicated with certainty as the cause of any accident. However, the pitot tubes continue to be replaced across the world by major airlines. Will this prevent another accident such as Air France's flight A430-300 (F-GLZKL)? No one knows for sure. In parallel, the European Aviation Safety Board recommends that air crews should always expect situations that cause inaccurate estimates of a plane's airspeed. But, it also noted that the consensus of leading experts is that although an airplane may still be operational in such situations, it would only be in a limited manner, if airspeed sensors fail.

How an organization responds to these tragic events reveals a great deal about how well they are organized, their culture, policies, and procedures, as well as the ethics of their employees. Air France, its competitors, and suppliers such as Thales and Goodrich as well as industry and governmental agencies all acted professionally both prior and after the horrific event. How far should an organization go to prevent unexpected failures? The answer depends, in part, on the specific situation or application. Some failures cause a loss of life, injuries, and extensive property and environmental damage, but others do not. One thing is certain: the vast majority of organizations can and should go much further in their efforts to prevent unexpected failures. The many events discussed in this book substantiate this opinion.

The aviation industry is an example of how well organizations can perform if they are proactive when analyzing and preventing failures. Most organizations within this industry provide good examples of ethical behavior regarding product and service design, production, and maintenance. But not all do. As an example, Southwest Airlines flew planes having fatigue cracks and despite this fact, the Federal Aviation Administration (FAA) relaxed Southwest Airline's maintenance schedules.[2] This situation was very disappointing because many of us fly with this airline.

Recall that earlier, we discussed the tragic accident that occurred on February 12, 2009, near Buffalo, New York, under winter conditions late at night when Colgan Air's flight Continental Connection 3407 crashed. The National Transportation Safety Board (NSTB) concluded in its final report that "the pilots were not adequately trained to handle a warning that the plane was going too slow or to recover after they lost control. The investigation identified unprofessional actions by the pilots, a system that allowed pilots with questionable qualifications to fly passengers, and regulators who failed to act on years of safety recommendations."[3] Unexpected and catastrophic events occur when public, nonprofit, or private organizations tolerate or encourage shortcutting and unethical behavior. In this chapter we will discuss some of the ways in which organizations and their employees cause failures.

In the design of an aircraft, systems must have a large margin for safety because of the severe consequences of failure. There are several ways safety margins can be practically achieved. Systems, subsystems, and components can be designed in ways to ensure high reliability. Reliability requirements are calculated through testing and applying advanced statistical models. Design redundancy is also used to increase the reliability of systems. Redundancy uses two or more parallel systems to ensure the functioning of an aircraft when one subsystem fails. Examples include having more than one communication system or the ability to manually lower landing gear if electronic and hydraulic systems fail. The result of these and other design strategies is that aircraft reliability is very high and few accidents are the result of technical failure. In fact, some airplanes are still flying more than 50 years after their manufacture. When there are accidents, the root causes are usually human errors or the application of environmental stresses beyond anything expected by designers. Air France flight A430-300 (F-GLZKL) may have fallen in this latter category under conditions of severe weather, which may have caused mechanical stresses on the aircraft's structure that exceeded its structural strength or pilot error.

Organizational structure and culture directly impact the design of products and services through a variety of ways. The effect can be positive or negative. The effect also depends on the many situations in which employees and stakeholders, with influential roles and responsibilities, make decisions regarding design, production, and supporting activities by providing resources and approvals. These types of influences vary over time and by organization. In smaller organizations the design process is highly dependent on people including their education, experience, skills, and ethics. In larger organizations, there are formal design review systems controlling and managing the design of products and services. But formal systems can also be circumvented and ignored, or erroneous conclusions can be drawn by people for many reasons.

An organization's structure and culture influence project management, procedures, and policies as well as the roles and responsibilities of design teams and supporting functions. Organizations control resources such as the materials, information, and employees supporting a design project. This implies that design activities should be aligned with an organization's strategic goals and integrated into process workflows. Integration of design activities should result in higher organizational productivity by increasing the effectiveness and efficiency of the many interrelated activities necessary for designing products and services. In this context, effectiveness is defined as doing the right things, that is, the alignment of design activities with an organization's strategic goals and objectives. Efficiency is doing the right things well (e.g., good management of the design teams).

The likelihood of failure will be lower to the extent organizations do the right things well.

Organizations are created for a variety of reasons. The Microsoft *Encarta Dictionary* defines the term *organization* from several perspectives, including: "a group of people identified by a shared interest or purpose, e.g. a business"; "the coordinating of separate components into a unit or structure"; "the relationships that exist between separate components in a coherent whole"; and "the effectiveness of the arrangement of separate components in a coherent whole." There is no restriction concerning the structure or purpose of an organization. In other words, commercial businesses, nonprofit organizations, and public institutions are all organizations containing process workflows that transform inputs such as materials, labor, information, energy, and similar resources into outputs such as information, services, and products. The degree of control, how various functions and operations are organized relative to each other, the types of intergroup cooperation, culture, and many other factors determine the usefulness of one type of organizational structure versus another for achieving goals. This chapter will discuss how different organizational structures and cultures strengthen or weaken the ability of design teams to manage design activities with consequential impact for failures of products and services.

F. E. Fiedler's contingency theory states there are different ways in which organizations make decisions and organize their work tasks in response to internal and external environments.[4] The Hersey and Blanchard situational leadership model is also useful for analyzing the impact of organizational structure and leadership styles on personal relationships within organizations.[5] These theories show how an organization's structure and its preferred leadership styles are relevant to internal decision making. One type of organizational structure will often be more appropriate than others relative to the types of work that need to be performed as well as external competitive and regulatory environments. Organizations can deploy different structures to maintain their competitiveness.

Figure 4.1 shows task and relational components of the contingency model. These create four leadership styles that differentially influence a design process. The styles include decisions made solely by a leader, decisions made using information from others, combinations of decisions made by a leader and followers, and decisions made by followers in an empowered manner. The four leadership styles are matched to the inclination of followers to be directed by a leader. Followers are classified into four groups that are combinations of competence and a willingness to complete assigned tasks. The goal is to match a leader's style with the situational awareness and goals of followers. As an example, if followers or employees are not competent (don't have the required knowledge or training) and do not

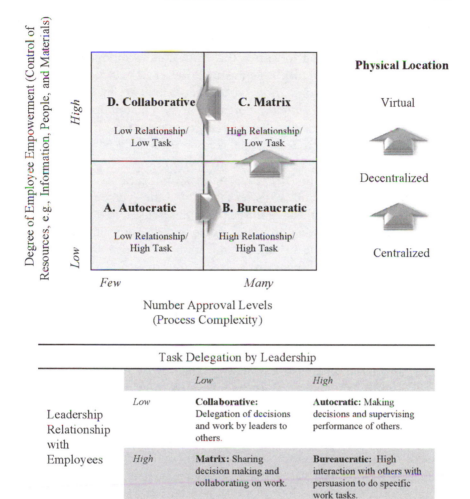

Figure 4.1   Organizational structures

want to assume responsibility for their decisions, then a leader must make decisions. In contrast, when people are very competent and want to make decisions, then a preferred leadership style will be collaborative or follower-made decision making. It is important to understand that in regard to organizational influences on design teams, the correct leader-follower relationships are necessary for the effective and efficient design of products and services. Missteps will cause unexpected failures.

A few years ago, I received a call asking if I would help a small manufacturer of an electromechanical device that had a very high failure rate. After discussing the situation with the manufacturer's design engineers I found a critical subcomponent had been internationally resourced to a new supplier for half the standard cost of the previous subcomponent. There was no analysis completed to determine the reliability of the sourced subcomponent. The decision to source this critical subcomponent to a new supplier, without any factual basis except lower cost, was made solely by the owner of the company. These types of decisions are made by leaders and key stakeholders in autocratic organizations. The opinions of professional employees can be easily overridden for convenience. In the absence of strict and formal controls, people make poor design decisions if the personal consequences for poor decisions are minor.

The Microsoft *Encarta Dictionary* defines *autocratic* as "a ruler who holds unlimited power and is answerable to no other person" and "somebody who dominates others." *Autocratic* in this sense implies an organization is dominated by one or a few people and decisions are made with little consensus with others in the organization. *Bureaucratic* is defined as "relating to the way administrative systems are organized" and "applying rules rigidly within an administrative system or government." Pockets of autocracy may also exist within larger organizations having bureaucratic or other organizational structures. In these latter situations executives make their own rules, ignoring organizational polices or recommendations from subordinates.

In organizations where work is highly standardized and requires a great deal of control, autocratic or bureaucratic structures are preferred when applied at organizational levels closest to the work tasks. An assumption is that work tasks have been proven to be the best or optimum. However, this doesn't imply localized work teams should not be creative within proper limits. There are examples where, although organizations are controlled by a few people, they are not micromanaged at lower levels of the organization. Wal-Mart, Motorola, Disney, Hewlett-Packard, and similar family-controlled organizations are examples. Although autocratic and bureaucratic structures may be useful in limited competitive environments, if only a few people make design decisions, things will be missed.

Not all functional groups within organizations are always aligned with respect to their goals and objectives and similar measures of success; one example is the organizational silo. Organizational silos have differing measures of performance, goals, and objectives. There are also many handoffs that increase system complexity and the likelihood for errors. As an example, in organizations functionally organized as silos, sales and marketing may be tasked with increasing revenues. In parallel, operational groups may be required to reduce costs and capacity. If these groups fail to communicate with each other, there may not be sufficient capacity to satisfy customer demand to increase revenue. The result will be lost revenues and customer dissatisfaction. Sales may also not sell products and services that are easy to schedule and manufacture, resulting in higher cost.

Without proper organizational policies, procedures, and controls, cooperation between different organizational functions may be difficult or impossible. The result will be lower performance. Performance issues may become exacerbated if one functional group, to the detriment of the larger organization, is able to force other groups to accede to unreasonable demands by resorting to political maneuvering. Cooperation between organizational functions can be improved by aligning goals and objectives and holding frequent meetings of key stakeholders and work teams and engaging in similar useful behaviors.

Organizations can also deploy matrix structures to help manage projects. Using a matrix management approach, people from different organizational groups or functions are formed into work teams focused on projects. These teams have modified reporting requirements to both functional and project managers. An advantage of using matrix management is it encourages sharing decision making and collaborating, across functions, on project work activities. However, there are some unique issues associated with this management approach. First, team members often have other roles and responsibilities that compete for their time. As an example, an engineer may contribute to several different project teams, each requesting work, or the engineer's functional manager may also not allow full participation with the teams. Overworked and stressed designers may do shoddy design work. If errors and mistakes are made, then the likelihood a new product or service unexpectedly fails will be higher.

Whereas teams managed using a matrix approach will collaborate at a project level, organizations using a collaborative management structure will encourage project teams to self-organize. Individuals are also encouraged to share knowledge with others, but also respect work task prioritization and goal alignment. Collaboration structures are becoming more popular because products and services have much shorter life cycles than even a few decades ago. People must quickly form into high-performance work teams across the world. They often do so without meeting each other. Also, design teams increasingly consist of people from different countries and cultures. A major characteristic of collaborative structures is that there is an alignment of resources to local work activities where employees determine the best way to do their work. However, to successfully implement a collaborative structure, employees must have the necessary knowledge and skills and a desire to self-manage. Leaders must also be willing to delegate decisions to lower organizational levels.

Several decades ago, design teams worked within a single country and traveled between facilities to create and maintain business and personal relationships. I recall that international travel in the 1980s was relatively rare and required special permissions because of cost and liability. This situation has changed since the 1980s. It's rare that design work does not require international travel and especially to locations such as Asia.

Organizational structures continue to evolve, in part because of technology enhancements, but also because of international trading policies. This evolution has changed the ways in which people are physically and virtually located, and the location of facilities and other assets. As an example, design teams are centralized, decentralized, exhibit combinations of centralization and decentralization (hybrid), or are virtually located. Their interactions also vary from face-to-face interactions to using e-mails, webcasts, and teleconferencing. Strategies for designing and producing products and services have also evolved from highly standardized, mass-produced products and services targeted to a few cultures to mass customization where practical for many cultures and consumer preferences. Mass customization creates a higher variety of products and service without significantly increasing cost. Localized consumer preferences and short product life cycles are the driving forces for many of the organizational changes we see. These concepts are captured in Figure 4.2.

Organizational culture overlays managerial and employee behavior through polices and procedures that capture formal and informal knowledge regarding the "ways to do things here." In addition to organizational structures, culture influences behaviors at individual, group, and organizational levels. This makes it relevant when trying to understand why products and services fail. Integral to an organization's culture and specific to roles and responsibilities are the ways in which an organization organizes its people, machines, materials, and other objects for planning and controlling the day-to-day activities associated with work. Organizational behavior consists, in part, of interacting activities performed by employees and coordinated by managers.

Managers create value by coordinating the activities and work of others. Integral to this work are several roles. These include organizing people, machines, materials, and other objects to do work, planning work activities, and controlling the day-to-day activities associated with work. Managerial roles and responsibilities require coordinating and influencing skills as well as gaining a basic knowledge of how work is done and the interrelationships of work processes.

The combined effect of people, their roles and responsibilities, and the ways in which they influence each other, including power relationships, determine organizational behavior for good or bad. Organizations do wonderful things. The products and services we use every day are designed, produced, and distributed by them. But they will sometimes, if unchecked, do bad things. Many of the catastrophic events discussed in this book are the result of organizations failing at many levels. The failures are often caused by not following policies, ignorance, excessive risk-taking, fraud, and other criminal acts. Organizational behavior is situational in that under certain conditions it may change to match perceived threats or opportunities. In this regard, it is similar to the behavior of individuals and small groups seeking survival.

Earlier, we discussed social psychology's relationships to individual and group behavior. This discussion must now be expanded to include several topics of general sociology. These include the effects of formal and informal groups relative to organizational culture, the relative power and

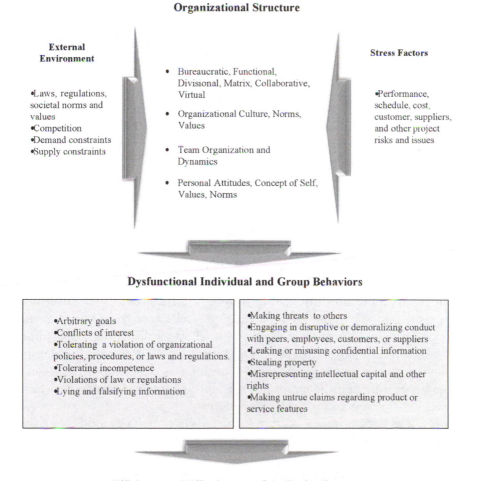

Figure 4.2   Organizational influences on the design process

influence of stakeholders, communications between people, personal and group conflicts, and intergroup behavior. Anthropological research is also important to these discussions because it shows how people develop comparative values and attitudes, and how organizational cultures behave and evolve over time.

In recent years there has been a growing globalization and diversification of organizations. This has complicated interpersonal and group relationships, especially of global organizations. It has also affected how people work together. First, relative power relationships between corporate offices and local country organizations evolved in the past several decades. It used to be that local country organizations were managed completely by expatriates. Sometimes these expatriates were culture deaf. They misunderstood local traditions and cultures or had a low level of trust for their culturally diverse employees. Much of this has changed, so now management roles and responsibilities have moved across the world more from a decentralized or virtual context. As an example, it is common for a virtual work group anywhere in the world to consist of people with different religious and political beliefs as well as diverse cultural perspectives.

Relative to catastrophic failures, globalization can be good or bad depending on circumstances and resultant individual and group behaviors. As an example, most organizational cultures are dominated by a single leader who is usually male. There is little consensus building within these organizations. Since people everywhere, regardless of their culture, are affected by similar cognitive factors, reliance on the judgment of a few individuals can be risky. At another extreme, some organizations are highly diverse. This may force them to embrace beliefs or pursue activities that are not optimal, but that satisfy all members of the group. Sometimes the best technical solution is not chosen because of competing interests.

At an individual level, the capacity to perform work is summarized by ability. Ability to do work, that is, to meet the requirements of a role and its associated responsibilities, depends on intellect, physical strength, and flexibility. There are different types of intellectual dimensions that influence how well a person will do certain types of work. However, this doesn't imply that anyone cannot be trained to do certain work, only that some people are inherently better for doing some types of work, unless they have tools to help them or the work is redesigned.

As an example, I might want to be an airline or fighter jet pilot or compete in the World Series. Unfortunately, my motor skills and ability to think quickly are poor. I could be trained for a long time, but would always fight inherent limitations. Some types of work require strength. Although I can use machinery to move heavy objects, I may not be able to perform the required work, even with machines, at a normal pace. Other types of work require flexibility when assembling objects. I am not very agile when performing these types of tasks and become easily distracted with routine work, so I also wouldn't be very reliable staring at a control panel in a nuclear facility hour after hour. These facts have important implications for preventing catastrophic failures because people may need training, tools, and equipment to enable them to perform work for which they otherwise are not naturally suited. The likelihood of failure will be lower if inherent physical limitations of people are considered when designing work roles and responsibilities. This is an organizational and individual responsibility.

Some systems depend on color perception to make decisions. One example is the common traffic light in the United Sates. If its light is green, this signals motorists to move forward; a yellow light is a signal to slow down, and a red light signals to stop. Approximately 2 to 6 percent of males cannot distinguish between green and red colors. These percentages reflect an underlying genetic condition caused by an X-linked recessive gene. However, many people don't know that color blindness can also be caused by several diseases. Some of them are degenerative and gradually develop without a person becoming aware of the condition. They include Parkinson's disease (which affects the light-sensitive nerve cells in a retina), Kallman's disease (which affects the pituitary gland and hormones that enable some genetically linked diseases), Leber's hereditary optic neuropathy (LHON), and cataracts.

There are some work activities that could be adversely impacted by color blindness and lead to failures. These include situations in which color-blind electricians make mistakes when working with different colored wires; people making mistakes when relying on bi- and tri-color LEDs (light-emitting diodes) to make decisions; workers evaluating chemical tests requiring color changes (e.g., test strips and maps); and computer displays where information is presented using red and green colors. If color-blind people are expected to be working within systems requiring color evaluation, then features need to be redesigned to help prevent mistakes or they shouldn't be performing the work tasks.

There are several dimensions of intellect. Some people have a natural ability for very fast and accurate calculations. My wife, an accountant, is intuitively very good with financial calculations. She can quickly add numbers and do arithmetic without using a calculator. I also recall meeting several groups of people over the years having similar abilities. One group consisted of finance managers and directors at Ford Motor Company, where I was training them in a Six Sigma quality improvement seminar. In the class exercises in which they were required to count, they achieved perfect scores. Engineers engaging in the same exercises typically achieved only 50 percent correct responses. In a different context, other people can more easily understand verbal and written communications. Lawyers, auditors, and engineers are typically these types of people. There are also dimensions related to memory, spatial visualization, and abstract reasoning. Organizations have many different types of roles and people naturally gravitate to some roles versus others for many reasons including ability. However, the implication is not that people cannot be trained for different roles. They can, but some people are better at some roles than others.

In addition to intellectual abilities there are also relevant physical abilities that influence how well people perform work in certain roles. First there is relative strength. Some types of work require exerting force to turn values, pick up objects, and take other types of physical action. Examples are police and fire roles, which require strength to arrest people or rescue people from burning buildings. Some people will have greater strength than others. Lower strength can to a certain extent be compensated for, but not always. There are also different attributes regarding strength. Sometimes people need to maintain their strength over extended periods of time. Other times physical force must be quickly expended and at a maximum level.

In addition to various forms of strength, work may require flexibility. Flexibility requires moving body parts to extreme positions or repeating flexing motions. There are several other relevant physical attributes influencing how well people perform work tasks. These include an ability to maintain balance or equilibrium, maintaining stamina to perform work for extend periods of time, and simultaneous coordination of several different physical actions. Some people are better at certain physical activities than others. Training and tools may mitigate physical influences, but not always. Also, physical ability is not necessarily dependent on gender. Many women are stronger than men and have greater stamina.

To the extent a role and its responsibilities require certain intellectual and physical abilities, the prerequisites must be met, but without discrimination. Unfortunately, intellectual and physical requirements, unrelated to work requirements, have often been used to unfairly discriminate against people in the past. As a result, a role's correct intellectual and physical requirements must be carefully determined. Nonetheless, ignoring the fact that some roles do have minimum requirements can lead to errors, mistakes, and serious consequences.

People have expectations regarding roles and responsibilities and how others treat them. These expectations influence individual and organizational relationships. Examples include work satisfaction, employee involvement, empowerment, and commitment. Research has shown that employees who are satisfied with their work, are involved, have the necessary authority to correctly perform work, and are committed to an organization's success will tend to perform at higher levels than employees not having these personal attributes. Attitudes and work satisfaction are very relevant to creating and maintaining safe work environments.

Employees with low work satisfaction will usually not remain with an organization or will move to different roles within an organization. However, if they do remain in their current role, they may engage in various behaviors. They could be vocal employees who voice dissatisfaction to improve working conditions, which could be constructive behavior, or actively sabotage their work areas and fail to correctly perform work, or ignore deteriorating conditions (e.g., destructive behavior). Low job satisfaction has important implications for safety. Destructive behaviors may lead to catastrophic failures.

Unfortunately, many employee satisfaction surveys show low satisfaction levels. Typically, levels are less than 50 percent. One reason often sited is that employees do not feel safe in their workplace. There may be several other problems that are organizationally dependent. However, managers often shrug off employee satisfaction survey findings. Employees usually get things right. Unfortunately, organizations often refuse to listen and instead create excuses for inaction. Organizational research has consistently shown organizations having higher employee satisfaction are more productive and safer.

Many years ago, I attended a seminar on leadership. Prior to attending the training we completed self-assessments. Our managers and peers also completed assessments of our attitudes and behaviors. Once we were immersed in the week-long seminar, we were formed into teams to engage in group activities. In the first team activity, people having a similar personality classification were grouped together using a Myers-Briggs Type Indicator (MBTI) classification. The practical result of the team activity was none of the teams, all containing people of a similar personality type, successfully completed project assignments. In the next activity, teams consisted of diverse personalities were formed to complete group exercises. The practical result was a breakdown of communication between team members because of personality differences.

Project assignments were not successfully completed by diverse teams. In the third and final team activity, the diverse teams were facilitated to ensure people communicated and respected each other. These projects were finally successfully completed by each group. These lessons have remained with me for many years. High-performance work teams need to be diverse and be properly facilitated to be successful. Groupthink is dangerous when trying to prevent or solve problems requiring innovation.

How organizations treat people influences the ways employees perform roles and responsibilities within a workplace. People have differing expectations of their required work activities. The differences between their expectations and how they are actually treated influences their perceived stress, work satisfaction, ability to lead and follow others, interpersonal behaviors, creativity, flexibility, and ability to manage others, as well as plan and comply with organizational policies and procedures. There needs to be a balance between personal and organizational needs to ensure employees perform well. Unfortunately, organizations are sometimes dominated, to their detriment, by dysfunctional personalities such as egotists, sociopaths, dominating or weak personalities, and others. The workplace is very complicate in this respect.

The ability to motivate employees to do work and follow policies and procedures is divided into personal needs and hygiene factors. Motivation refers to the tendency of a person to move toward a goal with persistence and intensity. Some people are more motivated than others when pursuing certain goals. A. H. Maslow, in his book titled *Motivation and Personality* (third edition), discussed motivation as a hierarchy of needs. This hierarchy evolves from a subsistence level (needs such as food, shelter, and clothing) to safety, social, esteem, and finally self-actualization needs. After the first few levels of the hierarchy, people begin to differ regarding their personal needs. Motivating them requires understanding their needs. Hygiene factors are influenced by organizational polices and how employees are actually managed.

There is another theory describing employee motivation. Theory X assumes people dislike work and must be coerced into performing it whereas Theory Y assumes people are self-motivated to perform work and need little coercion to do so. Organizations embracing either of these theories will tend to treat employees in contrasting ways. Employees within Theory X organizations will be tightly controlled and punitive measures will be routinely applied to influence behaviors. Employees in Theory Y organizations will be less controlled and encouraged using positive reinforcements to perform work. There are also other theories describing how organizations influence and motivate employees.

According to David A. McClelland in his book titled *The Achieving Society,* there are three individual needs. These are achievement, power, and affiliation. People have different affinities for these needs. How organizational polices and behaviors enable employees to fulfill needs creates satisfaction or dissatisfaction as well as constructive or destructive behaviors. Also, when organizational policies and behaviors affect employees, a dynamic occurs. Employees compare their treatment, status, and need fulfillment to expectations created by internal and external organizational factors. This dynamic is described using equity theory. When people make comparisons between their conditions of employment relative to that of others employed in similar conditions, they try to minimize perceived discrepancies.

Discrepancies cause them to evaluate how fairly they have been treated by their organization as far as salary, benefits, and working conditions relative to others in similar circumstances.

Motivation theory teaches us that roles and responsibilities must be carefully designed based on required skills, the scope of the work, and its importance. In addition to these attributes, the degree of autonomy and feedback are important motivating factors. Research has shown that the attributes of a working role have an effect on behavioral outcomes. This implies different people are motivated in different ways and some roles will meet their needs to a higher degree than others. To increase employee motivation and satisfaction, organizations can at times redesign work, rotate people between different roles, or allow them to move to other organizational roles. Role and work redesign enlarges the scope of an individual's role to include more work tasks, which encourages seeing the larger picture, increasing the control of current work (enrichment), or changing a work environment (enabling flexible time, telecommuting), and making similar changes.

Changes to roles and responsibilities can also be augmented through employee empowerment. Empowerment enables employees to make a greater number of decisions regarding how they work. Employee motivation greatly impacts individual and group behaviors and has an important influence on safety. Unfortunately, many employees continue to remain disengaged from their organizations. There are many reasons including the fact their management does little to modify roles and responsibilities based on research. As an example, employee surveys have shown that between 10 and 20 percent of employees are actively disengaged from their organizations. This group of employees is unhappy at work and will often exhibit dysfunctional work behaviors. This fact has important implications for workplace safety.

There are different roles and responsibilities within work groups that define expected behaviors of their members. The expectation of a group is that each of its members behaves in a consistent manner as defined by their roles. Individuals assigned to roles also have personal attitudes and perspectives regarding required group behaviors. There will be conflict if team members are perceived as failing to meet responsibilities in ways expected by one or more members of their group. This behavior is considered a violation of a team's norms or accepted standards that are used to control personal behavior. In this context, groups exert tremendous influences on individuals. This can be good or bad. To the extent an individual attempts to deviate from proven standards that ensure safe and efficient operations, group influence is positive. However, if individuals are bullied or coerced into taking shortcuts, cheating, or otherwise not following correct work methods, then the outcomes will be negative. It should be noted that some of the catastrophic events discussed in this book were caused by negative group behaviors.

Groups have several characteristics that influence safe work practices. They have advantages when solving complicated problems that no single individual would succeed in solving. But there are also pressures to conform to a group's norms and expectation for individual behavior. Research has also shown that individuals working in groups exert less effort than when working alone. The size of a group also influences completion of its work tasks. As an example, small groups tend to be more efficient than larger ones except when brainstorming causes of problems or if solutions need to be identified.

A work group is not always a work team. Examples of work groups include accounting, sales, or production. The work leaving a work group is additive, that is, the sum of its parts. In contrast, a work team collaborates and interacts in ways that usually increase its creativity and productivity. In high-performance work teams, the whole is more than the sum of its parts. Teams can also be organized in different forms. As an example, there are cross-functional, self-managed, virtual, and focused problem-solving teams, to name a few. Cross-functional teams are formed through association of people from different parts of an organization (e.g., work groups) to work on a specific problem and goal. Self-managed teams coordinate work activities without a direct supervisor. Virtual teams are cross-functional teams who conference and collaborate with each other from different locations.

Research has also shown that there are also several attributes that determine the effectiveness of teams. First, a team's composition is important. Composition is determined by factors such as the skills and knowledge of team members, the assignment of roles and responsibilities, the diversity of its members, and personal attitudes and behaviors. Second, a team's effectiveness depends on the tools, methods, and technologies available and applied to do work. How work is designed also impacts a team's effectiveness. Third, the organizational reporting structure in which a team works influences its effectiveness. As an example, the best team using the most advanced methods may not be able to overcome interference by key stakeholders. Organizations should create an atmosphere of mutual trust to increase the effectiveness of work teams. Finally, a team must be facilitated to ensure everyone is working on common goals and objectives. Facilitation is also important to ensure conflicts are quickly and effectively resolved. Team effectiveness should not be left to chance. Effective work teams help organizations identify and prevent errors and mistakes.

Sending the right messages at the right times can be difficult. Several catastrophic events discussed in this book occurred because communications failed. People were provided with inaccurate information, or they misinterpreted information, or information was provided too late to prevent catastrophic failure. Effective management requires people to create verbal, written, and visual information through appropriate channels. It should also be consistent with other messages over time. Verbal communications can be transmitted face to face, or through conferencing, speeches, and similar channels. Written communications can be transmitted via e-mails, through letters, and visually in graphical forms such as posters and advertising.

Communications can be made using formal and informal channels. Formal communications are planned and coordinated by professionals to send clear and consistent messages regarding polices, goals, and objectives. Informal communications also occur between groups and individuals. They can be top down from senior to less senior people, upwards, or lateral. They can also be jointly shared amongst several groups and individuals, shared using a hierarchy in which information is passed from one organizational level to another, or they may be channeled through a single group or individual. The right types of transmittal patterns depend on a communication's content and intended audience. Sometimes information needs to be tightly controlled to ensure its accuracy whereas at other times it needs to be freely shared so people can make comments or quickly be informed. The transmittal patterns and actual form of communications depend on the type of information. Less information is transmitted using e-mails, memos, and reports, than via conferencing and interactive blogs. Face-to-face meetings including videoconferencing provide the greatest amount of informational content. However, the correct communication vehicle depends on the specific message, audience, and intent of the message. Effective communication helps reduce the likelihood of error. If properly coordinated, it will also help manage catastrophic events.

Some elements of leadership have been discussed; but there are several relevant theories of organizational leadership, such as which attributes make good leaders, that are useful for understanding why things fail. Leadership is complicated because different styles naturally fit certain organizational cultures better than others. External and internal environments also influence needed leadership styles. As an example, some leadership styles encourage creativity. But if costs are increasing in a highly competitive environment, perhaps a different leadership style is needed (for example, one that exerts more control). In different situations, where internal and external factors are rapidly changing, we often see leaders joining and leaving organizations. Whereas a particular leadership style may have failed in one organization it may be just what is needed in another. Leaders are subject to the same cognitive issues as other employees. This implies errors will be made.

In the Fiedler Contingency model, discussed in F. E. Fiedler's book titled *A Theory of Leadership Effectiveness,* organizational performance is influenced by leadership style and the ability of a leader to control an organization. The degree of leadership effectiveness is controlled by three situational factors. These are leader-member relations, task structure, and position power. Relationships between leaders and employees depend on the levels of mutual trust and respect. Work task structure depends on the level of formality. Structured work tasks are designed using written and formal procedures. Unstructured work tasks can be done in differing ways. Position power describes the degree of control a leader exerts on employees or followers. Control is exercised using incentives such as salary and promotion or disincentives such as termination, demotion, and salary reduction. This theory implies task-oriented leaders require either a low or high degree of control whereas leaders strong in relationship building are more effective in situations where there is an average level of control, not too much or little. Although a leadership style may work in one situation it may fail if circumstances change.

There are also several other leadership theories. As an example, the path-goal theory, created by Robert House, stands in contrast to the Fiedler theory in that leadership styles are thought more flexible. In this theory, leaders direct work, provide support for followers (e.g., through empathy), accept information to make improvements (resulting in participative and better decisions), and set standards (achievement oriented). Some leaders differ in maturity. Immature leaders may stick to preferred styles regardless of the circumstances or needs of their followers. More mature leaders exhibit a broader range of behaviors, which are matched to circumstances based on experience. Most recently, Dr. House has extended his theories to describe leadership from global and cultural perspectives. This information is discussed in his coauthored book titled *Culture, Leadership, and Organizations: The GLOBE Study of 62 Societies.*[6] Leadership styles and behaviors directly influence an organization's behavior regarding the risk it takes and how safe it is to work in.

Power relationships are created when people join informal and formal groups. Power is the ability of people to control the behavior of others. Informal and formal power relationships are created if people are dependent on others. There are also different forms of power. First, there is legitimate power. It is created when people, such as employees, join an organization having a hierarchy of roles and responsibilities. This is explicit power. It can be used by people with authority to reward or punish people for certain behaviors. Sometimes power may be used to influence people fairly or unfairly, that is, coercively. People also gain power, relative to peers, if they have specialized skills, expertise, or access to needed resources. This type of power occurs anywhere within an organization. Power is also at times situational in that it is conferred on people by circumstance. Emergency situations sometimes create situational power. Power within and between groups can also be conferred, exchanged, or withheld using various tactics and behaviors. As an example, it could be conferred or withheld legitimately through policy and expertise; it could be exchanged by people who are dependent on each other.

Politics within an organization influence power relationships relative to defined roles and responsibilities. Power relationships are not always obvious. They also cause constructive and destructive behaviors. Politicking to create personal networks, in a constructive manner, helps speed the flow of information within an organization and creates mutual trust. But it also confers on certain individuals and groups power that can be used destructively or to thwart established rules of conduct such as following effective policies and procedures necessary for safe operations. Destructive behaviors result from ethical lapses, ignorance, or dysfunctional group dynamics including groupthink. Politics often leads to interpersonal and group conflict.

Minor conflicts are seen as petty gossip in which behaviors of others are criticized (not being a team player), disagreement regarding how work is done, and similar types of complaints. The level of conflict is increased when individuals perceive higher rewards and successful outcomes result from a behavior even if it is destructive. It also flourishes in situations that have ambiguous definitions for roles and responsibilities, unfair reward and recognition systems, or in which people have alternatives to work, have scarce skills and expertise, or are prone to be politically motivated. Conflict, when constructive, enables people to see different perspectives. However, research has also shown that conflict can have detrimental effects on work performance. These include stress, miscommunication, fatigue, work dissatisfaction, and lower performance. Higher turnover also occurs if there are alternative sources for work. Safety is often compromised in these situations.

Several types of conflict can occur between individuals working in teams, groups, and organizations. Examples include groups working toward different or competing goals, work task conflicts within or between groups regarding which work should be performed, interpersonal conflicts based on attitudes and behaviors, or disagreements as to how work should be performed (process conflict). Conflicts occur according to known patterns. Recall the discussion of red flag conditions in the context of mistake proofing? These conditions must exist for an error condition to exist. In turn, error conditions must exist for errors and mistakes to occur. Similarly, the process of conflict moves through several stages. These include the creation of a conflict condition, personalization of the condition, creating adaptive behaviors to mitigate the condition, interpersonal behaviors associated with the conflict condition, and lower or higher group performance depending on successful resolution of the conflict.

In the first stage, conflict conditions are created because of poor communication, opposing roles and responsibilities (structural conditions), as well as personal attitudes and behaviors regarding how roles and responsibilities should be performed. Poor communication causes confusion and differing expectations. Structural conditions also become an issue if one role impacts another. An example would be a quality inspector arbitrarily rejecting work of a production person. In the absence of policies and procedures or properly communicating the reasons for rejection of work, a conflict condition will be created that may or may not lead to an overt confrontation. People also have biases from previous experience or preferred ways of behaving. Interpersonal conflicts occur if people have differing attitudes and behaviors, unless they are properly facilitated.

In the second stage, conflicts occur if one or both people personalize their differences. The more emotional the attachment to an opinion or position, the greater the perceived stress, anxiety, and frustration levels associated with having to change it. Difference may cause hostility between individuals. Facilitation can reduce personalization of a conflict. Differing opinions are not a bad thing if everyone is respectful and listens to each other. Internalization of a conflict may also lead to disruptive behaviors.

In the third stage, people can avoid a conflict, make accommodation for it, collaborate with each other, compromise, or decide to simply compete to win their position. Avoiding may be a useful strategy if there is no reason to take other action. But if it delays or prevents a needed resolution, it is destructive. Accommodations can also be made. An example would be not interfering with another's opinion or behavior although you don't agree. Sometimes there are no alternatives, especially when people are equal in their relative power and influence. Collaboration is a very useful strategy because the perspectives of others are incorporated into a mutually agreeable solution. This solution may be superior to original positions. People can also compromise by giving up their original demands. This may or may not be useful. It becomes destructive if needed work activities are not performed. Finally, people can decide to compete with one winning and the other losing.

In the fourth stage, overt actions are made by the people in conflict. These reflect the outcomes of the third stage such as avoiding, making accommodations, collaborating, compromising, or competing. Depending on the decision from the third stage, the resultant behaviors may be no further conflict, minor disagreements, verbal attacks, or physical violence.

In many situations conflicts become apparent only when they have reached the fourth stage. Several methods have been developed to work through fourth-stage conflict. These include face-to-face meetings (e.g., problem-solving sessions), arbitration from third parties, by order, eliminating the cause for the conflict adding resources, eliminating work, restructuring roles and responsibilities, and issuing policies and procedures.

In the fifth stage, the final outcomes are achieved for good or bad. The conflict may remain unresolved and slowly destroy a group or organization, or it may be successfully reconciled, resulting in a more mature and cohesive group or organization. The outcomes from conflicts have direct effects on how people work with each other and on organizational safety.

Organizations have cultures that embody the shared values of their individuals. These cultures influence the ways in which people interact with each other or with outsiders, and how work is performed day to day. Culture is also a strong influencer of an organization's design, production, and safety processes. As a result, it affects how organizations prevent and respond to catastrophic failures. Organizations have cultures that promote core values shared by most of its members. There are also subcultures within organizations. Examples include separate businesses, business units within a business, and work groups or functions and informal groups. Teams are influenced by an organization's cultures and its subcultures. These entities often have differing measures of performance, goals, and objectives. Sometimes, when an outside business has been acquired, unique subcultures may exist that are different from an organization's dominant culture or its subcultures. This may or may not be a problem. If the newly acquired organization can be easily integrated into the larger business, assimilation will occur over time. However, if the new business is not smoothly integrated, the complexity of the combined organization increases. Error conditions also increase. In this context, some cultures are stronger than others and do a better job of this than others because their core values are widely practiced by their members. Strong cultures evolve by practicing behavioral patterns that increase organizational success as shown by longevity, profits, market share, growth, and similar measures of success. Organizational culture has importance relative to actions taken to prevent failures as well as manage them.

Employees move through a socialization process consistent with an organization's culture after they begin an association with a team as well as informal and formal groups. Through this process, they are exposed to attitudes and behaviors of coworkers that shape perspectives of how work should be performed and the interpersonal behaviors necessary for success. These learned behaviors are reinforced in several ways. New employees can be assigned a mentor, or left to fend for themselves, receive formal or informal training, or be provided with specialized tools, methods, and instructions to accelerate their socialization process. Over time, the socialization process continues as employees hear stories, do their work, interact with other members of the organization, and take part in rituals such as parties, reward and recognition ceremonies, and similar group activities.

In successful organizations, cultures become accustomed to success and take it for granted. However, issues will arise if an external competitive environment changes and historical assumptions are challenged. In other words, an organization may be successful today, but not tomorrow. This implies that strong and successful organizational cultures, if not adaptable, will tend to deny and avoid making necessary changes. These tendencies can be reduced if organizations, especially those that are globally dispersed, accelerate deployment of policies and systems that promote global and local adaptation. Examples include promoting diversity of many types, leveraging and sharing information, and ensuring active participation of all employees.

In their book titled *Managing the Unexpected*, Karl E. Weick and Kathleen M. Sutcliffe discuss several characteristics of high-reliability organizations (HROs).[7] These types of organizations include aircraft carrier operations, emergency medical treatment, the nuclear industry, and similar critical and high risk industries. The authors benchmarked these industries as well as others and the organizations within them to create several audit lists of shared cultural characteristics that these high-reliability organizations share. The common theme that emerges is that culture greatly matters when considering ways to prevent catastrophic failures. Several HRO characteristics include actively seeking near-miss and failure information, an assumption that a system is unsafe until proven otherwise, creating systems to quickly see near-miss and failure patterns (connect the dots or see the big picture, create shared beliefs that influence safety, communicate and support all aspects of ethical behavior). Culture dwarfs individual behavior in regard to safety. Organization cultures and the systems they create directly influence the likelihood of catastrophic failures.

From a different perspective, Yossi Sheffi in his book titled *The Resilient Enterprise* discusses the extensive planning for failure that resilient enterprises engage.[8] He discusses situations where small things such as loss of a supplier can affect competitors differently based on organizational culture. In one story, two competitors within the consumer electronics industry lost their supply of a key component because their mutual supplier's manufacturing plant had a fire. One competitor had planned for this worst-case scenario and quickly dominated the source of supply. The eventual result was a significant increase in market share for the more aggressive and well-organized supplier relative to its competitor. The author presents many examples where supply chains and their organizations successfully survive catastrophic events via better planning and the design of logistical systems. In this context, organizational culture played a major role for enabling resilience. The implication was that some organizations anticipate unexpected events to a higher degree than others and they react more successfully. These organizations exhibit high degrees of reliability and resilience.

Organizations have been forced to change their policies in the past several decades. There are many reasons. Their workforces have become more diverse with respect to differences in national origin, culture, race, ethnicity, age, and gender. In parallel, technology has expanded. In fact, it's difficult to believe that in only 15 years the Internet has become popularized and many people use personal computers. Technology has enabled remote and mobile working and collaborative relationships through virtual teams. There have also been macroeconomic and political forces shaping the structure of organizations. International competition has dramatically increased and there have been major disruptions of socialization patterns as reflected in blogs, chat rooms, and online social networking.

However, despite the increasingly competitive world around them, some organizations and their employees are reluctant to change learned behaviors. Resistance to change has several causes. One is that learned behaviors have proven successful over many years. Another is employees tend to be insulated from competitive environments. As an example, only a few people are concerned with this month's sales or the risks associated with design, production, and distribution of products and services. Overlaying the resistance to change are fears of the unknown, selfishness, and information filtering. At an organizational level, resistance to change is reinforced if there are several hierarchal levels, if roles and responsibilities are overly formalized, if people remain in positions for very long periods of time, if there is too much security and complacency, if there are very complex processes, or if procedures, controls, and policies allow work to be done only in certain ways, regardless of whether they are efficient.

Change is very difficult even under the best circumstances. It can become very difficult for individuals or small groups to navigate through a complex organization or gain the support and resources necessary to implement changes. Proposed changes may also threaten existing power relationships because newer power relationships are created. But, despite the obstacles for change, there are proven methods to implement it. John Kotter in his book titled *Leading Change* presented eight steps to implement successful organizational change.[9] As a summary of the eight steps, change is promoted when there is a reason for it (e.g., burning platform, a vision is created and communicated showing the way forward, people are empowered to pursue the changes, short-term wins are generated, and continual improvements are made to accelerate the change initiative). Over time the goal is to convince people that new behaviors will be rewarded by success in the new environment just as older behaviors were rewarded by success in previous environments.

Organizations also control reward and recognition systems and use this power to directly or indirectly influence the behavior of design teams, employees and stakeholders. Typical demonstrations of power include threats of demotion, withholding of resources and information, dismissal, lawsuits, and similar actions for unsanctioned behavior by employees. Organizations using power in destructive ways blur team roles and responsibilities. This causes a deterioration of team cohesiveness and effectiveness. Interference usually begins with influencing a project leader or a few key stakeholders. These people then manipulate or coerce team members to engage in various forms of detrimental behavior (e.g., usurp a team's agenda, become surrogates for customers and stakeholder requirements, modify a team's project goals, or manipulate information used for reporting project status and team performance). Sometimes a team's leader and members may not become fully aware of being influenced by others. Also, a team may engage in unethical behavior without their organization's knowledge. These are issues of personal ethics.

Ethical issues also appear in several forms. There could be a failure to report important information, such as testing and validation results, to stakeholders and customers. This behavior is more likely to occur if teams are not cross-functional or are heavily influenced by one or a few individuals. Usually these people have personal interests in withholding or distorting information in light of a bonus, increased sales, or fear of discipline. An example would be several engineers who collectively control testing and validation systems, and who work for a vice president of engineering. The information released by this team may be reviewed, questioned, and modified by this vice president prior to its dissemination. Information could be withheld or falsified with only a few people knowing.

Another example would be a production manager overruling a quality assurance decision to hold back product that does not meet testing requirements. These types of situations are not uncommon (high-ranking individuals overruling and substituting their judgment for that of lower-ranking technical experts). This behavior is unethical if engaged in for personal benefit, but it may also reflect ignorance or incompetence. Table 4.1 describes several of the most common ethical issues faced by design teams.

In contrast, high-performance organizations engage in different behaviors. According to Karl E. Weick and Kathleen M. Sutcliffe,[10] the process for recovery of airplanes aboard an aircraft carrier is characterized by the routine transfer of authority to lower-ranking ranking individuals having

Table 4.1
Impact of ethical issues

Ethical Issue	Examples
Conflicts of interest	Favoring suppliers, customers, or stakeholders to the detriment of the team and organization by means such as receiving money or other benefits to influence attitudes or behavior.
Tolerating violation of organizational policies, procedures, or laws and regulations	Allowing others to make statements, provide information, or behave in ways that subvert team or organizational strategic and tactical goals.
Tolerating incompetence	Allowing other team members to make repeated mistakes of judgment or action because of a lack of experience, education, or interest (e.g., ineffective team leaders, inexperienced designers, poor sourcing strategies).
Violations of law or regulations	To make statements, provide information, or engage in behavior that endangers people and property or is illegal (e.g., to avoid meeting requirements, reduce development cycle time, or avoid redesign to evade performance and cost issues).
Lying and falsifying information	Knowingly presenting information that does not accurately reflect the truth regarding requirements, project status, testing results, and similar information.
Making threats toward others	Engaging in abusive verbal or physical behavior to control another person's statements or behavior (e.g., threatening loss of employment, group status, or physical and emotional safety).
Engaging in disruptive or demoralizing conduct with peers, employees, customers, or suppliers	Verbal statements or behavior that cause deterioration in goodwill between customers and key stakeholders, and that reduce team cohesiveness (e.g., increased communications required to facilitate team member interactions or explain misinformation to those outside a team).
Leaking or misusing confidential information	Knowingly making available confidential information to third parties not authorized to possess the information (e.g., causing confusion by telling customers or key stakeholders of team issues yet to be resolved and prior to scheduled briefings, or telling suppliers sourcing information).
Stealing property	Taking intellectual or other property that belongs to a third party, illegally or without the owner's permission (e.g., taking trade secrets or other proprietary and confidential information from customers or suppliers).

(*continued*)

Table 4.1   *(continued)*

Ethical Issue	Examples
Misrepresenting intellectual capital and other rights	Claiming ownership or special rights to trademarks, patents, or proprietary information that knowingly or unknowingly belongs to third parties.
Making untrue claims regarding product or service features	Claiming levels of performance, cost, availability, or other product and service attributes to third parties that are not true (e.g., incorrect testing results to customers, key stakeholders, or governmental regulatory agencies; or making false statements of any kind reading price, promotion, production, distribution, quality, performance, and other capabilities).

immediate situational knowledge and expertise rather than to higher-ranking officers not having up-to-date situational information. Deferring to experts who are situationally aware decreases the likelihood of human error, mistakes, and failures. It's also ethically motivated behavior.

There have been several studies of organizational ethics in different situations. A general conclusion is that many organizations have ethical issues. It was found that these unethical practices result in lower productivity and decreased revenues as well as higher operational costs.[11] As an example, an article by Ronald W. Clement titled, "Just How Unethical is American Business?" found that 40 corporations in the Fortune 100 listing have been guilty of significant unethical conduct.[12] What is interesting is that despite ethical guidelines, some organizations show a bias for influencing behaviors of lower-level employees, but not management.

Ethical issues are also created if design or other types of teams are forced to meet arbitrary or unrealistic goals. Goals should be set in a balanced way to ensure a team resolves all issues in a professional manner.[13] Conflicts of interest present real problems for teams because people are unreasonable. Typical behaviors are seen as not agreeing to specific team goals, not agreeing with a group consensus regarding the best way to achieve goals, and refusing generally to believe testing data, information, or other analyses that are accepted by a group as accurate. This behavior is in contrast to employees who, for the right reasons, challenge a group's consensus. In other words, a group may be behaving unethically or simply be wrong, but one or more of its members may not.

Conflicts of interest become especially problematic if executives or team leaders engage in this behavior because of their influence over others. Autocratic and bureaucratic organizations are especially prone to conflicts of interest. Another example of a conflict of interest would be favoring certain suppliers, customers, or stakeholders to the detriment of an organization (e.g., receiving money or other benefits to influence attitudes or behavior). There may also be situations in which team members or internal stakeholders have conflicting goals and objectives. Although it is difficult to identify these situations, their impact can be significant.

Overlooking violations of organizational policies and procedures is another type of ethical issue. It is also difficult to read a newspaper without seeing some incidents of violations of regulations and law. These types of ethical violations can be insidious in nature. Violations of law or regulations occur if team members or others make statements, provide information, or engage in behavior that endangers people or property, or is illegal. Examples include people making false statements, providing confidential information to others who should not have it, or behaving in ways that subvert team or organizational goals.

Lying and falsifying information occurs if people knowingly present information that does not accurately reflect the truth (e.g., customer requirements, a project's status, testing results, and similar information). It also occurs if people withhold information (an omission). These types of violations are illegal and catastrophic failures have occurred because of these behaviors. Falsifying testing, quality assurance, technical, financial, and similar information may cause teams and organizations to draw incorrect conclusions or not take actions necessary to prevent injury, death, or property loss.

The behavior of team members, employees, suppliers, customers, or key stakeholder could also become abusive, threatening, and even dangerous. Examples include engaging in verbal or physical acts to control another person's statements or behavior (e.g. threatening loss of employment, group status, or physical and emotional safety). Other forms of abusive behavior include disruptive or demoralizing conduct causing a deterioration of goodwill between team members, customers, or key stakeholders. This has the effect of reducing a team's cohesiveness and causes extra work for everyone (e.g., using increased time to facilitate team interactions or to explain misinformation to those outside the team).

Unethical behaviors also occur when people misuse confidential information or provide it to third parties not authorized to possess it. Examples include telling customers, suppliers or key stakeholders of team issues yet to be resolved or telling them cost or competitive performance information. Organizations need to guard against this behavior, even if it is inadvertent.

Stealing property occurs if people obtain or use intellectual or other property that belongs to others without the owner's permission (e.g., taking trade secrets or other proprietary and confidential information from an organization or its customers and suppliers). Misrepresenting intellectual capital and other rights is a form of theft in which people claim

ownership or special rights to trademarks, patents, or proprietary information that knowingly or unknowingly belongs to others. This is also a
form of lying. Closely related to misrepresentation is making untrue claims
regarding product or service features. These acts occur by claiming levels
of performance, cost, availability, or other product and service attributes
that are not true. Examples include publishing inaccurate testing results
to customers, suppliers, employees, key stakeholders, or regulatory agencies, or making false statements of any kind regarding price, promotion,
production, distribution, quality, performance, and other capabilities. Ethical behaviors depend on creating transparent organizational cultures that
promote these behaviors. Unfortunately, it only takes one or two unethical
executives, team leaders, or team members to derail a team and even their
organizations.

Organizational cultures occur in different forms. Even organizations
within the same industry and region can be very different, but still successful from a competitive perspective. So how do we begin to sort how an
organization's culture and behavior influences the ways it designs products
and services to create safe products, services, and systems? It's one thing
for an organization to purposely not heed effective and established industry practices and to eventually get itself into trouble, or to flout laws and
regulations with serious consequences including catastrophic failures. But,
apart from the obvious ethical violations, how does organizational culture
influence product and service failures when there are no outward signs of
impending trouble?

Organizations have many ethical employees who work hard to do the
right things. But things do not always go right for a variety of reasons. As
an example, let's review recent catastrophic events involving BP. which was
formally known as British Petroleum, and its partners. BP is an energy company that was pieced together through the acquisitions of companies such
as Amoco and Arco in the United States and others across the world.[14] It is
difficult for an organization to properly integrate other organizations into
its parent organization. Integration in this context refers to information
technology, engineering, and other management systems as well as culture.
To complicate the situation, BP and its partners, like many other large organizations, rely heavily on contractors and consultants to do work. These
factors increase the complexity of their systems and its ability to manage,
control, and deploy its procedures and policies. Also, they must also operate within extreme and hostile environments where oil and gas are located
and produced.

Considering these facts, it should not be unexpected that BP and its competitors occasionally experience catastrophic failures.[15] In fact, as I wrote
this book, BP and its partners were in deep trouble regarding the 2010 Gulf

of Mexico oil spill caused by the Deepwater Horizon oil rig explosion. Lisa Myers and Rich Gardella in their article titled, "Deepwater Horizon Rig: What Went Wrong?" discussed preliminary findings of independent investigator Dr. Robert Bea.[16] According to Dr. Bea, an industry expert, several factors contributed either independently or in combination to cause the catastrophic explosion. These were improper well design, improper cement design, early warning signs that were not properly analyzed and resolved, removal of a pressure barrier, and design flaws and maintenance issues with the blowout preventer. Other news sources have provided similar information. It should be noted that these were only preliminary findings at the time this book was being written, which must be proven.

Exacerbating the situation was a lack of federal oversight of the drilling permits and related activities. Further complicating the situation is that three organizations were involved in the incident. These were BP, Transocean, Ltd., and Halliburton. BP leased the Deepwater Horizon rig from Transocean, Ltd., and Halliburton provided drilling services. In a *Wall Street Journal* article titled "BP Tries to Shift Blame to Transocean," two BP executives claimed that Transocean's employees were in charge of operations and monitoring the well at the time of the explosion.[17] Halliburton was in charge of pouring the cement slurry that prevents oil or gas from leaking from a well. Adding to the confusion was the blame shifting by all parties and poor communication of the recovery efforts to the public.

In his book titled *A Failure to Learn,* Andrew Hopkins discussed the reasons for BP's Texas City explosion, which occurred on March 23, 2005, killing 15 workers and injuring more than a hundred others.[18] Recently, he reiterated his original conclusions, with respect to the 2010 Deepwater Horizon explosion and oil spill, that BP may have marginalized its safety efforts. In a different article, John McQuaid argued that another potential reason for the explosion and resultant difficulties controlling the leaking oil was that the organizations had not properly put the project risks into perspective.[19] Another article written by Juliet Eilperin for the *Washington Post* discussed the fact that the United States Interior Department exempted BP from a requirement to file a detailed environmental impact study to begin the Deepwater Horizon drilling operation.[20] However, it should also be noted that the U.S. Department of the Interior routinely grants several hundred waivers each year to BP's competitors for Gulf of Mexico oil production operations. After the catastrophic event, it's now obvious the assumptions regarding risk were underestimated by everyone. However, it is difficult to understand why BP and its partners had no contingency plans, other than to actuate a blowout protector, if something went wrong. Perhaps this is an industry practice that needs to be changed?

As we look to cultural factors to explain why this event occurred, we must remember that the magnitude and catastrophic nature of the explosion is not atypical of the oil and gas exploration industry. BP has not been alone in underestimating the environmental impact arising from a major accident such as occurred in the 2010 Deepwater Horizon event. In fact, this book discusses other catastrophic events associated with the oil and gas industry as well as others. Many of the events superficially appear to be difficult to predict. We will show in the next few chapters that many of these events should not have been unexpected.

The environmental disaster that occurred in the eastern Gulf of Mexico this year used well-known technology, but errors and mistakes were still made by the organizations and people involved. A long list of contributing factors has been pieced together. Technology was misused. Risk analysis and contingency planning were poor. The response plan and control technologies either failed or were not up to par for such dangerous operations deep under the ocean. The information is troublesome and frustrating. In the aftermath of the event, investigations of the 2010 Gulf of Mexico oil spill and behaviors of the U.S. Department of the Interior, BP, Transocean, and Halliburton have shown a truly ugly side of these high-risk operations. Blame shifting is also not helpful for resolving these situations, but unfortunately an analysis of catastrophic events shows it is a common behavior. An organization's culture becomes more transparent when catastrophic events occur. As an example, a British Broadcasting Corporation article titled "BP Accused of Buying Academic Silence" stated that BP attempted to retain environmental scientists and restrict the information they could disseminate. The information would be controlled by BP's lawyers.[21] We each of us can judge for ourselves the causes of this event as well as the behaviors of the organizations involved. But organizational culture dominated the behaviors that increased risk and influenced the management of containment and cleanup activities.

SUMMARY

Collapsing bridges and buildings quickly come to mind when people think of unexpected catastrophic failures. Or they may think of accidents involving aircraft or trains. The causes are usually blamed on technology or simple human errors and mistakes. However, in this chapter we have shown that organizational structure, culture, and ethics are major factors that determine how people work together to design products and services. In many ways organizational culture is the most important determinant of why things fail. This is because organizations determine how products and services are designed and used. They also determine who is employed, how resources are allocated, policies and procedures, and enforcement of ethical guidelines.

Organizations use different methods for organizing and managing design teams. They are typically industry-specific with minor variations between organizations in a given industry. This does not imply that organizations alone can prevent unexpected failures, but only that within a given technological environment they have the largest impact on the likelihood and responses to failures.

In this chapter our focus has been on the effects of organizational culture on group and individual behaviors including team diversity, ethical conduct, and resolution of conflict. People will be less likely to engage in unacceptable behavior if organizations correctly define and manage the roles and responsibilities of individuals and teams. In this context, an organization needs the right project management structure, policies and procedures, and enforcement of ethical standards of behavior at all levels. Although a design team will usually be able to manage dysfunctional behavior amongst its members, it will have difficulty overcoming interference from its senior management and key stakeholders.

In addition to formal policies and procedures and ethical standards, organizations should also strive for workforce diversity and transparency. Diverse teams tend to create a larger number of solutions to resolve design challenges. They are also required if designing products and services to satisfy local customer needs around the world. But they need to be facilitated to prevent dysfunctional behaviors and conflicts. Poorly facilitated conflict causes increased levels of stress, fewer solution alternatives, poor team and stakeholder communication, lower team morale, and slower decision making. In turn, these conditions increase the likelihood that errors and mistakes will occur and cause catastrophic failure.

NOTES

1. Robert Wall and Jens Flottau, "Despite No Firm Link, Pitot Tubes Spotlighted in Flight 447 Investigation," *Aviation Week and Space Technologies,* June 14, 2009; Mark Sappenfield, "Air France Crash: What Is Known So Far," *Christian Science Monitor,* June 14, 2009.

2. Drew Griffin and Scott Bronstein, "Southwest Airlines Flew 'Unsafe' Planes," CNN Special Investigations Unit Records, March 7, 2008.

3. Alan Levin, "NTSB Blames Pilots in Buffalo Crash," *USA Today,* February 3, 2010; Jerry Zremski, "Colgan Pilots Fault Airline's Stall Training, February 22, 2010," *Buffalo News,* May 9, 2010.

4. F. E. Fiedler, *A Theory of Leadership Effectiveness* (New York: McGraw-Hill, 1967).

5. P. Hersey and K. H. Blanchard, *Management of Organizational Behavior: Utilizing Human Resources,* 2nd ed. (Upper Saddle River, NJ: Prentice Hall, 1972).

6. Robert J. House, Paul J. Hanges, Mansour Javidan, Peter W. Dorfman, and Vipin Gupta, eds., *Culture, Leadership, and Organizations: The GLOBE Study of 62 Societies* (Thousand Oaks, CA: Sage, 2004).

7. Karl E. Weick and Kathleen M. Sutcliffe, *Managing the Unexpected: Assuring High Performance in an Age of Complexity,* University of Michigan Business School Management Series (San Francisco: Jossey-Bass, 2001).

8. Yossi Sheffi, *The Resilient Enterprise: Overcoming Vulnerability for Competitive Advantage* (Cambridge, MA: MIT Press, 2005).

9. John P. Kotter, *Leading Change* (Boston: Harvard Business School Press, 1996).

10. Phillip E. Varca and Masha James-Valutis, "The Relationship of Ability and Satisfaction to Job Performance," *Applied Psychology: An International Review* 42, no. 3 (1993):265–75.

11. Simon Webley and Elise More, *Does Ethics Pay?* (London: Institute of Business Ethics, [1993]; Ronald W. Clement, *Just How Unethical is American Business?* (Bloomington: Kelley School of Business, Indiana University, 2005).

12. M. E. Schweitzer, L. Ordonez, and B. Douma, "Goal Setting as a Motivator of Unethical Behavior," *Academy of Management Journal* 47, no. 3 (2004): 422–32.

13. BP Business Summary, Yahoo Finance, http://uk.finance.yahoo.com/q/pr?s=bp.l.

14. Richard Mauer, "BP Has a History of Safety Failures: Profit, Corporate Culture Called Putting Earnings over Maintenance, Environment," *Anchorage Daily News,* May 8, 2010.

15. Lisa Myers and Rich Gardella, "Deepwater Horizon Rig: What Went Wrong?" MSNBC, May 21, 2010.

16. Russell Gold and Guy Chazan, "BP Tries to Shift Blame to Transocean," *Wall Street Journal,* May 21, 2010.

17. Andrew Hopkins, *Failure to Learn: The BP Texas City Refinery Disaster* (NSW: Australia: CCH Australia Limited, McPherson's, 2009).

18. John McQuaid, "The Gulf of Mexico Oil Spill: An Accident Waiting to Happen," *Yale Environment,* May 10, 2010, 360.

19. Juliet Eilperin, "U.S. Exempted BP's Gulf of Mexico Drilling from Environmental Impact Study," *The Washington Post,* May 5, 2010.

20. Robyn Bresnahan, "BP Accused of 'Buying Academic Silence,'" BBC News, July 22, 2010, http://www.bbc.co.uk/news/world-us-canada-10731408.

21. Jason Linkins, "Oil Spill Lawsuits: BP Spending Big to Acquire an Army Of Expert Witnesses," *Huffington Post,* July 16, 2010, http://www.huffingtonpost.com/2010/07/16/oil-spill-lawsuits-bp-spe_n_649335.html.

Chapter 5

THE REASONS WHY
THE THINGS WE TRUST FAIL

A problem well defined is a problem half-solved.
—Charles Kettering

Failure investigations take different forms depending on their type and severity. As an example, an investigation of the causes for an automobile accident involves few people and is primarily focused on technical details. In contrast, large-scale disasters, while following a similar investigatory strategy such as the one shown in Table 5.1, usually involve a much larger number of people, each having different perspectives of cause and solution. These situations create subjective, emotional, and political elements that complicate investigations.

The 2005 Hurricane Katrina disaster is an example showing the discrepancy between failure analyses that differ from a purely technical focus to those having a larger social, economic, and political impact and focus. The hurricane impacted, over a large area, the Gulf of Mexico including the city of New Orleans. The bipartisan congressional committee that investigated the Katrina disaster summarized their investigation in a report titled, "A Failure of Initiative: Final Report of the Select Bipartisan Committee to Investigate the Preparation for and Response to Hurricane Katrina."[1] The Select Committee conducted extensive interviews of key witnesses and organizations in an attempt to understand the activities leading up to the event as well as the subsequent relief efforts. In addition to interviewing, diverse sources of information were also used to reconstruct the event. The contributing issues included a failure to maintain the protective barriers

Table 5.1
Generic failure analysis—services and products

Step	Key Goals	Key Deliverables
1. Plan for failure	Stakeholders, roles and responsibilities	• Who should be notified? • Who is authorized to notify outside people? • Who conducts investigations? • Who receives investigation reports? • Who is responsible for follow-up? • What is the procedure for conducting the failure analysis?
2. Secure the failure site	Physical evidence and witnesses	• Protect material evidence so it is not damaged or lost. • Obtain timely information from witnesses.
3. Gather information		• Personal observation • Witness statements • Conditions at time of incident • Location of actors, equipment, and materials.
4. Interviews with key actors		• Determine cause of failure to prevent future occurrences • Identify and interview key actors at scene • Open-ended and relevant questions
5. Re-create event sequence		• Conditions that were hazardous • Behavior resulting in unsafe activities • System breakdowns

6. Root cause analysis	Identify contributions of key actors including people, systems, design, and others	• Level 1: Actual damage or injury
		• Level 2: Direct causes of level 1
		  • Stress factors
		  • Design factors
		• Level 3: Indirect causes of level 2
		• Individual, group psychological, and organizational factors
		• Customer and stakeholder requirements
		• Prototyping and design
		• Production factors

7. Recommendations	Summarize all learnings	• Introduction (using information from steps 1-4)
		• Recreation of event sequence
		• Findings (root cause analysis)
		• Recommendations
		  • Effective control strategies
		  • System improvements
		• Summary

(levees), and failure to effectively communicate information, in a timely manner, to the people needing it, as well as the poor management of the evacuation and relief efforts. Several types of failures (communications, evacuations, relief efforts) worked synergistically to help create the disaster that took the lives of more than 1,800 people and caused more than $90 billion in property damage.[2]

The hurricane began as Tropical Depression 12 over the Bahamas on Tuesday, August 23, 2005. It quickly increased in strength over the next several days, becoming a Category 1 hurricane on Thursday, August 25, with winds of 80 miles per hour. Eventually it made landfall as a Category 3 hurricane on Monday, August 29, in Louisiana near the city of New Orleans. The resulting storm surge, caused by its winds, inundated the city and surrounding areas. More than 50 levees failed, causing widespread flooding of New Orleans.

In the failure analysis of the event, the major reason the levees failed was because of design flaws. They had been constructed using an "I" rather than a "T" wall design. The "T" wall design has a horizontal base of concrete that helps prevent soil erosion. The levees could have been redesigned or strengthened years in advance of Hurricane Katrina since the "I" wall design had been identified as a potential issue in the mid-1980s, but they were not. In fact, several years after the Katrina disaster, there is still much work to be done to reinforce them and complete other important recommended actions to prevent or mitigate future hurricane damage. New Orleans is still vulnerable to powerful storms, although there are currently fewer people living in the city and surrounding areas that would be impacted.

The Select Committee in its preface stated the purpose of the investigation was to understand the following: "Why situational awareness was so foggy, for so long; why all residents, especially the most helpless, were not evacuated more quickly; why supplies and equipment and support were so slow in arriving; why so much taxpayer money aimed at better preparing and protecting the Gulf coast was left on the table, unspent or, in some cases, misspent; why the adequacy of preparation and response seemed to vary significantly from state to state, county to county, town to town; why unsubstantiated rumors and uncritically repeated press reports—at times fueled by top officials—were able to delay, disrupt, and diminish the response and why government at all levels failed to react more effectively to a storm that was predicted with unprecedented timeliness and accuracy."[3]

The losses associated with this catastrophic failure event can be understood by analyzing several factors: technical (design of the levees), behavioral (politicians disagreeing on how best to manage the relief efforts and people refusing to leave the devastated area), and failure to take mitigating actions (organizational disaster planning or communicating in a timely manner to reduce loss of life in the impacted areas). The technical causal factors of these events are usually easier to identify. It is also easier to make technical recommendations for prevention. Behavioral and organizational causal factors are more difficult to identify and analyze. As an example, the Army Corps of Engineers fully analyzed the events and contributing factors surrounding the Hurricane Katrina disaster and issued a summary report in mid-2009. The report discussed the required design changes necessary to prevent future structural failures and thus to prevent future loss of life, injuries, and significant property damage. Specific recommendations were design changes of current levees, building additional levees, recommendations for where to build future housing, and modifications to the design of buildings.

This type of failure analysis report is usually well researched because it has a technical basis. The root cause analysis and identification of solutions is easier as a result. In contrast, analyzing and reporting factors influenced by behavioral and organizational factors are usually incomplete or subjective. As an example, the Select Committee did not identify the lower-level causal factors for the Hurricane Katrina disaster or create actionable solutions. In fact, in its conclusions, the Select Committee identified only the most obvious higher-level causes. These were, "Tardy and ineffective execution of the National Response Plan; an under-trained and under-staffed Federal Emergency Management Agency; a Catastrophic Event Annex that was never invoked, and doubt that it would have done the job anyway; a perplexing inability to learn from Hurricane Pam and other exercises; levees not built to withstand the most severe hurricanes; an incomplete evacuation that led to deaths and tremendous suffering; a complete breakdown in communications that paralyzed command and control and made situational awareness murky at best; the failure of state and local officials to maintain law and order; haphazard and incomplete emergency shelter and housing plans and an overwhelmed FEMA logistics and contracting system that could not support the effective provision of urgently needed supplies."[4]

The final report should have provided a detailed list of lower-level causes and actionable solutions to be useful for preventing future catastrophic events. The fact that root causes and solutions were not identified by the report implies a similar future event may occur in the region. Most likely there will be additional loss of life, injuries, and property damage. Given that many of the root causes for the catastrophic event were behavioral (ineffective political leaders) and organizational (poorly functioning governmental agencies), we need to analyze these factors in more detail for effective solutions. Technical solutions alone cannot prevent future catastrophic events.

Social psychological and organizational influences should be investigated to determine how individual, group, and organizational behaviors, and also roles and responsibilities, should be changed. It should be noted that because the same organizations are responsible for predicting and managing catastrophic events across the United States, similar mismanagement should not be unexpected in the future.

In this chapter we will discuss why the things we trust fail. Perhaps the best way to begin such a discussion is to review how products and services fail using commonly accepted principles of failure analysis, well-known examples, and concepts discussed in earlier chapters. The goal is to integrate these principles to create a failure analysis framework to discuss failures of products, services, and logistical systems to prevent failures or mitigate their damage. The discussion will include diverse events, across different industries and applications, rather than only those having strictly technical causes. The influence of organizational cultures and safety subcultures as well as ethics will also be integrated into this framework.

The recent April 20, 2010, Deepwater Horizon explosion and oil spill in the eastern Gulf of Mexico has been an ecological disaster for several of the states bordering the gulf. Costs were already more than $650 million as of May 17, 2010,[5] and estimates are that final costs will be billions of dollars. What is interesting is that, despite the disaster, the United States Interior Department continued to grant new drilling permits and environmental waivers. The permits and waivers were authorized for work similar to the Deepwater Horizon, that is, at great depths in the western waters of the Gulf of Mexico.[6]

Why would the government and private organizations take these types of actions prior to fully understanding what caused the original explosion? One obvious answer is that the oil industry and associated governmental organizations are deaf to public opinion regarding the magnitude of environmental risk. But there are other reasons. Local and state governments have been pleading with the Interior Department to reopen the eastern Gulf of Mexico area for deep-water oil production. They are afraid of losing jobs and tax revenues. Their arguments have validity in that the longer the eastern area remains closed to exploration and production, the greater the likelihood specialized equipment will be moved elsewhere in the world. But what about the environmental damage that has been done? Many experts believe the control technology and organizational management systems need to catch up with the production technologies currently being used for safer deep-water exploration and production.

Admittedly, oil exploration is necessary to answer the world's demand for energy resources, even in challenging and dangerous locations such as deep water. However, these exploration and production activities must be conducted using best in class design, process management, and safety practices. Although the industry works very hard to improve its safety record, there have been a continuing number of major oil spills events around the world. Some of these caused loss of life, injuries, and widespread environmental damage. In fact, there was another oil spill in the western Gulf of Mexico on June 3, 2010, that released over 100 million gallons of crude oil into the gulf's waters.[7] There have also been at least 75 major oil spills around the world since 1967.[8]

Considering the enormous complexity and risk of the work activities necessary to explore and produce oil, it is not surprising that there have been many catastrophic events. The industry is an inherently dangerous one given the extreme environments and types of equipment used to explore and produce oil. As a result, the industry will always have a higher likelihood of failure. But more can be done to decrease this failure likelihood. As we create a framework for failure analysis, events such as Deepwater Horizon will be used to understand the underlying causal factors for unexpected and catastrophic failures and create preventative strategies.

Failure analysis of major software implementation projects also provides important lessons that can be applied to new product design and use. It's a commonly known fact that major software implementations sometimes fail, with severe consequences. Most of the impacts are financial, but people are also killed and injured because of software failures. A common causal factor is that teams fail to identify and manage project risks related to technology, scheduling, resources allocation, and similar factors. Recall, in the second chapter, we discussed how information that contradicts a team's beliefs is sometimes selectively filtered or dismissed. Throw in a few executives and key stakeholders who are influenced by previous experience and therefore have strong opinions or incentives for certain actions, and a project can spin out of control. The result is that a large information technology project can quickly disintegrate into disconnected work activities. The best way to prevent these situations is to follow good design and project management practices. In this context, there are right and wrong ways to design and deploy software.

A well-known software implementation failure occurred with an enterprise resource planning (ERP) implementation at FoxMeyer Drug, which at that time was the fifth-largest drug wholesaler within the United States. FoxMeyer Drug distributed pharmaceutical products and beauty aids to drugstores, hospitals, and health care facilities through 25 distribution centers. It had recently incorporated into its business strategy an ERP implementation to integrate its distribution systems. The ERP implementation strategy required that the software manage FoxMeyer Drug's distribution centers, customer service activities, marketing, order shipping, and handling as well as its inventory. Anderson Consulting was retained as the implementation consultant and SAP (Systemanalyse und Programmentwicklung) was selected to provide the ERP software. At that time, SAP had been widely used in manufacturing applications and Anderson Consulting had extensive experience implementing SAP systems worldwide. The initial ERP implementation costs were estimated at approximately $10–15 million with a projected annualized savings of approximately $40 million dollars per year.

This is a classic software implementation project gone wrong. No one died or was injured by this project. But the consequences of the resultant failure, according to a legal claim made by FoxMeyer Drug's bankruptcy trustee, was that the ERP implementation failure helped to bankrupt this $5 billion organization. The first indication that something was wrong was when the installed version of the new software could only process 10,000 transactions per day versus the legacy system, which processed upwards of 420,000 transactions. Also the transaction volume was expected to grow to 500,000 transactions per day.[9] Because of the transaction processing limitations, the ERP software was initially implemented in only a few of the newer distribution centers, which had lower daily transaction volumes, rather than in the majority of older and higher volume centers.

There were also other issues not directly related to the ERP software. These issues adversely impacted the implementation. They included inaccurate inventory records at the newer distribution centers and outdated and inaccurate customer order information. These later issues were thought to be the result of poor project management and planning by the implementation team, which included FoxMeyer Drug personnel. The total cost of the implementation ballooned to approximately $100 million and FoxMeyer Drug bankruptcy followed upon cash flow and related issues.

An analysis of the implementation failures concluded that several issues caused the ERP implementation failure. First, the original SAP software version was a poor choice because it only processed 10,000 daily transactions or orders rather than the required 500,000. Unfortunately, ERP software was implemented despite the advice of other consultants who said it was not a good choice for FoxMeyer Drug's business applications. There was also no risk analysis or contingency planning by the software implementation team and not all key stakeholders were consulted prior to or during the implementation of the software. These stakeholders included managers, workers, and various organizational functions such as accounting, distribution, sales, and marketing and purchasing. Instead, the project implementation team was dominated by consultants, information technology (IT) professionals, and only a few stakeholders.

Other issues associated with the project were that various work processes were not modified to reflect SAP's ERP system's software logic (which was known to be highly standardized at the time and requiring such process modifications), no small-scale tests were conducted to verify application feasibility, and users were not involved with deployment of the software. Implementation issues often occur in large-scale ERP implementations. If they do occur, the result is very high rework costs that typically exceed initial project budget estimates by 20 percent or more. However, in most situations, an organization's survival is not jeopardized.

An interesting footnote to the FoxMeyer Drug story is that after the bankruptcy several former FoxMeyer Drug distribution centers were purchased by McKesson, a much larger competitor to FoxMeyer Drug. McKesson used the same Arthur Anderson consultants, and with success. However, it is claimed that FoxMeyer Drug used a pre-3.0 version of SAP's ERP software, which had been constrained to process lower transaction volumes compared with the later 3.0 version, which processed 1.5 million daily transactions for McKesson.[10] Also, FoxMeyer Drug was simultaneously implementing a new warehouse management system and in addition brought on a major customer during its ERP implementation, which necessitated migrating to the new ERP system three months earlier than originally scheduled. FoxMeyer Drug was also short of experienced IT professionals. In combination, the consensus is that these many issues threw FoxMeyer Drug into bankruptcy. In retrospect, the issues associated with the software implementation were a combination of behavioral (FoxMeyer Drug executives), organizational (a failure to correctly implement operational systems), and technical (using a version of software that was transaction limited), and included a lack of process engineering and IT resources to support required workflow changes.

An analysis of major software failures is often relatively straightforward because lawsuits are filed to bring out facts regarding the causes for a failure. In contrast, complicated service and logistical systems such as those used for disaster relief efforts are more difficult to analyze because of the many interacting organizations and roles and responsibilities. Organizations must collaborate to manage natural disasters or their effects will become worse. As an example, the effects of Hurricane Katrina, were exacerbated by poor planning and management of its relief response (a subsequent disaster caused by people). What are the similarities and differences between failure analyses of very different catastrophic events such as natural disasters, major catastrophic events, technical failures, software or project failures, and other types?

First, an analysis of major software implementation failures often shows that organizations and their work teams, do not always objectively evaluate business needs, properly manage the associated project work, or estimate risks. Examples include a lack of standardized processes, ineffective management controls, interference with team work activities, having wrong team members (that is, members with the wrong skills), inadequate support from key stakeholders and customers, and poor communication of project requirements, activities, and other information.

Large-scale catastrophic events, either man-made or natural, share similar issues; but are worst because the root causes for failures are scattered across many disparate organizations and processes. These failures are seldom investigated to a level at which causal factors can be identified and solutions implemented to prevent future failures. In other words, we tend to learn more from technical or project failures than other types. Instead, we scapegoat when disasters occur. A consequence of this behavior is that the effects of these large-scale disasters are magnified.

Catastrophic product failures have similar issues. But, there are differences. As an example, some product failures are caused by using leading-edge technology in unknown application environments. These failures are difficult to predict in advance even under the best circumstances. However, once technical failures occur, solutions are often found and implemented based on their failure analysis. This is common practice in the aviation industry. In contrast to project and technical failures, unsafe use of products and services by people is more difficult to predict and control. This is especially true if products and services are poorly designed, and people are not trained to use them or they ignore instructions. Cognition errors and failure caused by fatigue are also difficult to control. Proper design methods will decrease the likelihood of these failures.

Useful tools and methods have been created to analyze or help prevent failures across very different industries. In combination, they provide a framework with flexibility regarding different approaches that can be taken to explain why things fail using a generic approach for the analysis of product and service failures. The analysis will be linked to technical, cognitive, and organizational causal factors to show similarities and differences between diverse catastrophic events. The goal is to create a general failure analysis framework that can be applied to disparate systems. Using this framework, we will show in later chapters that the unexpected and catastrophic events we read about usually have common causes, although their solutions will often be different. The major reasons for failure will be shown to be less technical than cognitive or organizational at individual, group, and organizational levels.

Table 5.1 shows seven basic steps commonly used for failure analysis. These include planning for failure, securing a failure site, gathering information, interviewing key actors, recreating an event sequence, doing a root cause analysis, and making recommendations. The tools and methods may differ by application, but the general approach is valid for all investigations.

Planning for failure is an important first step because events following an event unfold very rapidly. As an example, in some of the events discussed earlier in this book, organizations scrambled to control the public relations issues associated with an event while also investigating its causes for occurrence and working to manage and eliminate the effects on customers. The intent is not that organizations have, in advance, specific answers to explain the causes for a failure, although this would be very useful, but rather to quickly implement a set of well-thought-out and proven policies and procedures once an unexpected failure occurs. As an example, it was difficult to understand why BP had underestimated the risk of failure and did not have an effective contingency plan that could be quickly implemented if such an event occurred. Also, BP did not have control technology to prevent and stop oil leakage thousands of feet below the ocean's surface if a blowout preventer failed. It should be noted that BP is not alone. Its approach toward risk analysis is a cultural issue that plagues its industry. An overreliance on one piece of equipment given the risks has now been proven to be a poor strategy. Poor risk analysis and mitigation strategies also plague other organizations, both private and public, constituting one of the reasons catastrophic events occur or relief efforts are poor. Planning for serious failures should be a requisite for any organization.

Planning for a failure investigation should include definitions for roles and responsibilities of the actors who will be involved in the investigation. These include, by way of example, the people who should be immediately notified of an event, the people authorized to notify external organizations, as well as people responsible for the investigation and follow-up activities. There should also be policies and procedures in place to control all the activities associated with an investigation. People should also be periodically trained and certified to follow them.

Once a failure event occurs it is important to secure and control the site of the event for two reasons. First, it is important to protect material evidence to prevent it from being misplaced, lost, damaged, degraded, contaminated, stolen, or otherwise compromised by others. If evidence that is relevant to a failure investigation is not available for a root cause analysis, the causes contributing to an event may never be determined. In this context, evidence includes physical objects such as tools, machines, supplies, raw and finished materials, or products. A complete history of an event should also be created to show the movement and custody of evidence.

Second, it is important to obtain timely and accurate information from witnesses at the scene of an event. The information needs to be carefully collected, corroborated, and analyzed for consistency with other witnesses. This can be problematic. Recall our discussions of cognitive issues and the fact that people's perceptions and subsequent memories of events can be very unreliable regarding recollection and interpretation of facts. Most likely witnesses will get some of the relevant facts wrong. Also, as time passes people will increasingly confuse actual events with previous memories. This distorts their ability to accurately recall conditions associated with a failure event. Properly securing failure sites follows a standard set of activities regardless if an event is caused by an airplane accident, a bridge collapse, a failure to produce vaccines, an environmental catastrophe such as an oil spill, or other unexpected failures.

Once evidence has been identified and secured, investigators begin to make personal observations and map relative locations of actors (people, equipment, materials, and information systems), interview witnesses, and record the conditions. Personal observations and location mapping include identifying damaged equipment, and also structural elements such as a building's supporting structures (supports and frames and similar objects including materials if applicable to the analysis). Relevant damage associated with a technical failure would include identifying fracture and fatigue points, the types and locations of corrosion, any evidence of a lack of maintenance, scratches, dents, rips, tears, leaks, spills, and associated debris.

Relevant conditions at the time of the failure event include the time of day, week, and year, the weather, the amounts of light, noise, and cleanliness, as well as any external factors that may have stressed the system to its point of failure. Other important information includes the physical layout of a failure site that is, the relative locations of physical objects. This information can be documented using sketches, check sheets, and photographs. Information obtained such as sketches, maps, and similar aids should be calibrated and accurate relative to location, time and other relevant factors. Also, the names of witnesses and actors such as first responders to the failure site are recorded for subsequent interviews.

Witnesses are interviewed in the fourth step of a failure investigation. These people include first responders, victims, and other actors. The interviews should be done immediately after an event and in an objective manner to help collect evidence for the causes of failure. Interviewing requires asking the right people open-ended questions that are relevant to the investigation. Recall, people have biases that cloud objective analysis and their ability to make accurate decisions. The purpose of the interview is to identify the root causes of a failure event, not necessarily to place blame. The witness should speak uninterrupted without leading behavior by an interviewer such as words or actions that influence the interviewee's answers. It is also useful to repeat the answers back to the person being interviewed to ensure accuracy of the information. Unless there are mitigating circumstances for confidentiality, it is also a good practice to agree beforehand to share information with the interviewee.

An event timeline is created to show the sequence of events and relative positions of materials, equipment, key actors, and work activities leading up to the failure event. This requires an analysis of hazardous or unsafe conditions, personal behaviors, failures of equipment and structural components, material issues, and other breakdowns relevant to a root causes analysis. As an example, in Table 5.2, a recreation of a simple failure event is shown using the coffee example discussed earlier. The failure event is hot coffee spilling and burning a customer. Notice the event re-creation describes the materials, equipment, key actors, and overall conditions of the restaurant at the time of the event. This strategy enables an investigative team to compare notes, conduct second interviews with key witnesses, and perhaps to kick off supporting investigations to answer remaining questions. This information will be used to identify ways for preventing future failures within the restaurant.

As events unfolded, during the morning of the accident, notice the restaurant was very busy. The employees began their work by mixing coffee using a combination of materials, equipment, and a standardized mixing and brewing procedure. One theory that is the coffee was too hot, that is, its temperature exceeded an upper safety limit. Another theory is that the temperature of the coffee is right, but the customer may be fatigued or has been jostled by other customers, causing a spill. Notice there are also observational gaps in the event re-creation that require additional data collection and analysis. But this is a good start for investigating the failure event (customer is burned by hot coffee). If this had been a building failure then perhaps engineering analyses, testing reports, and different types of information would have been required for the investigation.

A root cause analysis is the sixth step of a failure analysis. It can take different forms. These depend on the specific product, service, structure, or system being analyzed to identify the causes for failure. In fact, when a building, product, or something else fails, root cause analysis can be very complex. It may require chemical and physical testing as well as sophisticated engineering analyses. As a general principle, root cause investigations have evolved in the past several decades from a reliance on blaming people toward an understanding that failures are the result of designs under stress by their application environments. The stresses and environments are of many types depending on the product or service.

It's recognized that people routinely make errors and mistakes that cause failures. In the absence of supporting systems including tools, methods, and information, the effects of such behavior are unavoidable. Recall, this failure is because of cognition and other effects. The justification for not blaming people is belief that almost anyone placed in similar circumstances would exhibit similar behaviors, and make similar errors or mistakes. But

Table 5.2
Event recreation—coffee example: *Customer is burned by hot coffee*

Time	Event	Materials	Equipment	Actors	Environment
8:00 AM	First shift starts work				Busy store with changing of shifts and many customers (twice normal demand).
8:10 AM		Coffee is mixed, water is added and pot is placed on heating plate.	Coffee pot Heating plate Thermometer	Associate in kitchen	Busy store with changing of shifts and many customers (twice normal demand).
8:30 AM	Customer order is taken at table			Associate at table Customer	Busy store with changing of shifts and many customers (twice normal demand).
8:35 AM	Coffee is poured into cup in kitchen	Coffee Cup		Associate at table Customer.	Busy store with changing of shifts and many customers (twice normal demand).
8:40 AM	Customer holding cup and drinking coffee	Coffee Cup		Customer	Busy store with changing of shifts and many customers (twice normal demand).
8:47 AM	Customer spills coffee			Customer	Customer fatigued.

this assumes people are consciously trying to follow procedures and policies and are not ignoring them.

The Microsoft *Encarta Dictionary* defines failure as, "Something that falls short of what is required or expected" or "a breakdown or decline in the performance of something, or an occasion when something stops working or stops working adequately." Another perspective of failure is when a product or service does not meet customer expectations regarding functions, features, and other attributes.

Failure analysis progressed from a single-event theory of failure causation to a domino theory wherein a series of events trigger a final failure. The domino theory has also been rendered obsolete because there is consensus that failures often have multiple causes that align to cause failure. In a single-event theory, a person involved in a failure event is assumed to be responsible for the failure. Subsequent corrective actions are focused on changing the behavior of the person. An inherent problem with this reasoning is that people tend to repeat similar errors. This makes preventing errors and mistakes very difficult to sustain over time if the focus is changing behavior alone. Although it is true the likelihood of errors can be reduced if people are well trained and provided with correct tools and methods, cognitive errors cannot be completely eliminated without design and process changes.

The domino theory of failure analysis implies failure events are the result of independent events. One causal event leads to another, eventually resulting in an overall failure. If the chain of causal events can be broken, then future failures will not occur. The single-event and domino theories of failure analysis do not drive to lower levels of a root cause analysis where effective controls can be implemented to prevent future failures.

The multiple cause theory is that causal events align to cause a failure. This theory considers failures to have resulted from a system's inherent complexity and contributing factors. These contributing factors are not in sequence like those of the domino theory. As a result, the alignment of causal events cannot be easily predicted in advance. As a result, all the possible ways causal events and failures could occur must be identified and preventive actions taken. This most recent theory of failure causation has enabled failure analyses to evolve to increasingly broader and more detailed investigations of causal events or factors. Some industries and organizations have done it better applying these concepts than others.

A failure investigation based on a multiple-cause theory moves through several levels of analysis. These levels proceed from failure analysis (e.g., actual property damage, personal injuries, or death) through an analysis of direct causes related to design and stressing factors, to lower-level analysis of causes. It should be noted that a multiple-cause approach has been followed in this book because events are discussed in a larger framework, that is, as a combination of technical, environmental, cognitive, organizational, and cultural factors. This is an important way to proceed through failure analysis. If only a first-level analysis is used to explain a failure event, then its underlying root causes and the required solutions to eliminate the causes cannot be identified to prevent similar events in the future.

As an example, suppose a customer spills coffee on his way out of a coffee shop. One approach is to blame the person for being clumsy. A second approach would be to post a sign to warn customers to be careful of spilling coffee. However, an analysis of root causes at a third level would focus a solution to ensure it works regardless of the restaurant's environment or the person drinking coffee. As an example, a tight lid could be placed on a cup of coffee before handing it to a customer. In addition to placing a lid on a coffee cup, perhaps a root cause analysis would show that cups sometimes slip out of a people's hands. A solution here might be to ensure disposable cups have rougher surfaces to aid when gripping them. Finally, it may be found that people cannot hold a cup of hot coffee for too long. A solution here would be to add an external liner to a cup so a person's hands are not burned if the temperature of the coffee is too high. These solution strategies recognize that if one person spills coffee, then others are likely to do the same. Also, these types of multiple causes are always working simultaneously. Modifying the design of a disposable cup and the process for handing a cup of coffee to a customer decreases the likelihood of failure in the form of spillage of the hot coffee by a customer.

Once a failure event has been well described, its direct causes are analyzed—a first-level analysis. In a second-level analysis, the original conditions causing failures are extrapolated backward in time based on observed damage and conditions at the time of failure. In these analyses, investigators analyze design attributes of a product or service versus the stresses that likely caused the failure. As a simple example, suppose a failed product was a long steel rod that was bent (deformed) by an applied stress or force, such as a weight. In these types of failures there are usually five factors or variables. These include the stress (force relative to time) that exceeded the steel's yield strength, the material properties of the steel, the bar's cross-sectional area, stress concentration points caused by sharp geometries, and contributing factors related to the environment such as corrosion. This type of failure analysis is relatively easy because the system has been well studied over several decades. It is a straightforward process to use this information to estimate the stress or force that deformed the steel rod. Simple failures such as these have been extensively studied and have well-known solutions. However, failure analysis becomes more complicated if the original conditions of an event cannot be reconstructed with certainty; failed objects are not available for examination or important information cannot be readily obtained from witnesses.

The causes for failure found using a second-level analysis are not the true root causes for a failure because countermeasures, solutions, or corrective actions cannot be applied to prevent future failures. As an example, seeing that an applied force exceeded the yield strength of a steel rod without collecting additional information such as cross-sectional area or material type will not enable estimation of its design strength or the applied stress that caused it to fail. If conditions of the system were typical, that is, the stresses will frequently reoccur, then the choice of the rod, that is, its cross-section or material, would need to be changed since this type of failure will continue to reoccur under similar stress. However, if the stress was atypical, then investigators need to identify different root causes and solutions to prevent future failures. As an example, perhaps the rod was weakened by corrosion. The root causes for the corrosion would need to be identified and eliminated to prevent future failures. This is a third-level analysis. Investigators must move past an obvious failure, identified at a first level, and a second-level cursory examination of a system's components such as design and stress factors, to find the specific root causes for a failure occurrence—a third-level analysis.

A root cause analysis focuses on the conditions associated with a failure event. It is also carefully expanded to incorporate newly discovered information. The goal is to work backward from a failure to successively identify its lower-level root causes until actionable solutions are found to eliminate them. There may also be several required solutions for a single root cause or one solution will sometimes eliminate several related root causes.

The sophistication of a failure analysis depends on the type of failure. Failures of electromechanical products such as airplanes and automobiles, structures such as buildings and bridges, or heavy machinery will require an engineering analysis. This is especially true if there has been loss of life, personal injury, or significant property or environmental damage. These analyses may also require extensive laboratory testing and analysis. In contrast, analysis of a simple process failure is often relatively easy and the sequence of contributing factors can often be quickly put together to identify the reasons for failure.

However, a failure analysis may become progressively more difficult when investigating psychological and organizational causes for failures. As an example, knowing that a steel rod failed under certain conditions identifies issues of design, maintenance, or a lack of understanding by, for example, operating environments. It may not be as easy to identify why a rod had a small cross-section, why operating conditions were not understood by users, or why maintenance was not properly done. In other words, a failure analysis targeted toward supporting service systems requires a more difficult in-depth investigation of people and behaviors as well as technical factors. Earlier topics, such as cognition, group dynamics, and culture, become very important for understanding unexpected and catastrophic failures in these situations.

Although there are many causes for failures, some common reasons, seen across many industries and organizations, include cost-cutting activities, a failure to identify customer requirements during design, and the tendency to ignore or override technical experts such as designers and operations people closest to potential failure conditions. Although there are many other contributing factors, these three factors, if present, can significantly degrade an organization's design, production, and maintenance processes.

The catastrophic events discussed in this book have very small technical contributions toward failures. As a result, our discussion of failure analysis must incorporate a more general perspective to explain failures of service and logistical systems as well as products. In other words, our discussion will not include complicated and specialized tools and methods (chemical, mechanical, physical, structural, or similar types of failure analysis methods). Instead, in addition to cognitive and organizational influences, we will discuss several generic analytical methods that can be used in combination with information and methods discussed in earlier chapters to identify causal factors for unexpected and catastrophic failures. These generic analytical methods include a 5-Why analysis, a cause and effect (C&E) diagram, a Pareto chart, and failure modes and effects analysis (FMEA). Recall the FMEA topic was discussed earlier in the context of identifying product and service failures using the coffee example to illustrate the concepts. Recent catastrophic events, such as the 2010 Deepwater Horizon event, the 2005 Hurricane Katrina, the Toyota failures, and many others will also be integrated into these discussions.

Returning to the coffee example, Figure 5.1 shows a simple root cause investigation using a method titled 5-Why Analysis. A 5-Why analysis begins with an event such as coffee that is too hot or cold. It then proceeds by asking why until a level in the analysis is reached where a specific action or actions can be taken to eliminate the causes of the problem. The first reason the coffee is too hot or cold (temperature variation) is that employees are rushed in the morning and do not measure its temperature. The second-level why is: why are employees rushed in the morning? The answer is that there are too few of them for the surge of incoming customers. Continuing with a third why question, we see that not enough employees have been hired or trained because the manager did not realize the restaurant needed more employees for that time of day. At the end of the analysis we arrive at the conclusion that there are no systems for measuring employee scheduling, process

	Coffee is too hot or cold.	
1.	Why is coffee too hot or cold?	Employees are rushed in the morning hours when there are many customers entering and leaving the store and do not measure temperature.
2.	Why are employees rushed in the morning?	There are not enough employees scheduled to work in the morning.
3.	Why are there too few employees scheduled in the morning?	Not enough employees have been hired and trained.
4.	Why haven't enough employees been hired and trained?	We did not know we needed more people.
5.	Why don't we know when we need more people?	We have no system to monitor employee scheduling, process performance (in this case, temperature), complaints, and similar process and customer information.

Employee training, scheduling, and measuring temperature

Note: Customer behavior and related factors were not captured by this 5-Why analysis

Figure 5.1   5-why analysis—coffee example: *Temperature variation*

performance (coffee temperature), or customer complaints. This simple root cause analysis, using the 5-Why method, is only a simple example. An actual root cause analysis could go in one of several directions depending on the conditions and factors contributing to a failure event.

Cause and effect (C&E) diagrams are useful for identifying cause and effect relationships. They are created by teams to identify and classify potential causes of a failure relative to an effect such as spilled coffee or coffee too hot or cold. Potential causes may also be identified using a 5-Why analysis and transferred to a C&E diagram. Alternatively, a C&E diagram may create a need for one or more 5-Why analyses. The C&E method helps a team classify causes into common categories (methods, people, materials, measurements, and machines, and other classification criteria). Once causes have been identified and classified, they can be prioritized for further analysis, managed using process controls, or their error conditions can be eliminated.

Prioritization uses information from previous testing, on-hand reports, previous or current analyses, and similar quantitative information to provide a focus for subsequent action. An example is shown using a Pareto chart in the lower right section of Figure 5.2 (temperature variation of

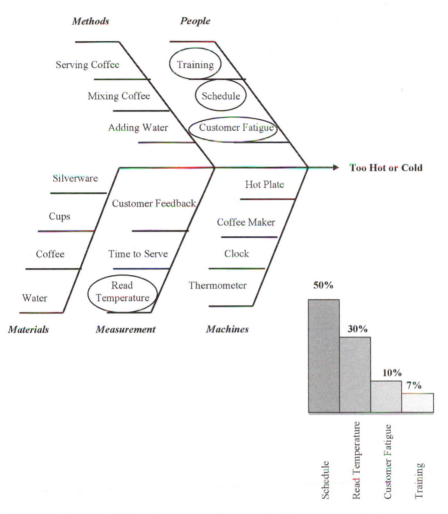

Figure 5.2   Cause and effect diagram—coffee example: *Temperature variation*

coffee) using the four causal factors identified in Figure 5.1 as major contributors to the effect or event of coffee being too hot or cold. These factors are employee training and scheduling, the methods used for reading temperature, and the thermometer used for the measurement. The relative contribution of each factor is also shown in the Pareto chart from highest to lowest effect (employee schedule contribution of 50%, reading temperature contribution of 30%, etc.).

The original failure event, in which hot coffee is spilled on a customer, can also be viewed from the perspective of James Reason's Swiss cheese model.[11] It has been applied to the coffee example using Figure 5.3. The

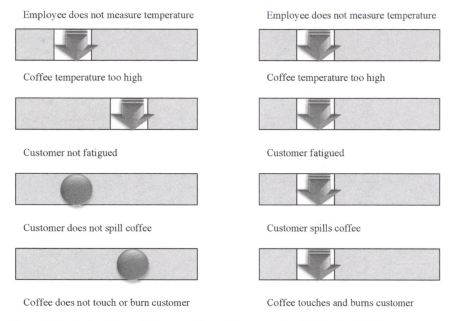

No Failure Occurrence   **Failure**

Employee does not measure temperature   Employee does not measure temperature

Coffee temperature too high   Coffee temperature too high

Customer not fatigued   Customer fatigued

Customer does not spill coffee   Customer spills coffee

Coffee does not touch or burn customer   Coffee touches and burns customer

Figure 5.3   Swiss cheese failure model—coffee example: *Spilling hot coffee*

concept is that several error-independent events or error conditions must line up for a failure to occur. This is a variation of the multiple-cause model. Each of these conditions has a likelihood of occurring. The goal is to decrease the likelihood these conditions actually occur by implementing design or process controls prior to their alignment and a subsequent failure such as spilled hot coffee. As an example, Figure 5.3 shows that several error conditions must occur for coffee to be spilled. A first error condition is that coffee temperature is not accurately measured by an employee. A second is that the coffee is too hot. This could occur for a variety of reasons that would also need to be investigated (not enough water for time allowed to boil, etc.).

Recall that the C&E analysis identified customer fatigue as a potential cause of spilling coffee. This information has been added to Figure 5.3 to show coffee must be both very hot (for various causes) and a customer must be fatigued to create error conditions to create a coffee spill.

The information gained from this overly simplified example can be used to create process controls for the restaurant's temperature measurements and other factors we can control because we cannot control customer fatigue or if they spill coffee because of physical coordination issues which are personal. In more advanced analyses, a more complicated set of error conditions would be used to describe and analyze this potential failure event. As an example, these conditions have an occurrence likelihood that can be used to focus preventive activities on likely events to reduce the overall potential for system failure.

Failure mode and effects analysis (FMEA) was described as a useful method for identifying how new products and services could fail, the causes for failure, and current controls or preventive measures. The FMEAs from previous versions of a new product or service are also useful for providing insight into likely types and causes for future failures. Although designers may not capture every type of potential failure mode and its cause, the methodology is an excellent way to collect information to create solutions and prevent failures.

After a failure event has been fully investigated, its accumulated information is summarized into a report. The report captures the causes for the event as well as preventive measures and recommendations that can be taken to avoid similar events in the future. This is the seventh step of a failure investigation. The summary report recreates the sequence of error conditions preceding an event; it documents interviews of witnesses and key actors and describes the root cause analysis. This accumulated information is used to create recommendations for improvements to help prevent future failures. Specific recommendations vary by type of failure and event.

A simultaneous occurrence of several error conditions that aligned contributed to the subsequent widespread environmental damage within the eastern region of the Gulf of Mexico in 2010. Figure 5.4 captures the commonly believed causes for the event. Note these are not the root causes for the explosion or the major environmental damage, but rather they are higher-level contributors to the event. Each of these contributors has numerous lower-level root causes. Also, some these contributing factors were lurking for many years before the event. These include minimal risk assessments by some of the key organizations associated with the event (including the United States government), no effective contingency planning for a major oil spill in deep ocean waters if controls did not work, and a lack of redundant control technologies if a major oil spill occurred in deep water and on-line control systems failed. Should these organizations have done a more effective risk analysis?

Interestingly, in a recent *Providence Journal* article, it was said that five new offshore drilling projects were approved by the Department of the Interior's Minerals Management Office. Some of them were approved in deep water and without having an environmental review even after the Deepwater Horizon event. At press time, the permits were waiting for the expiration

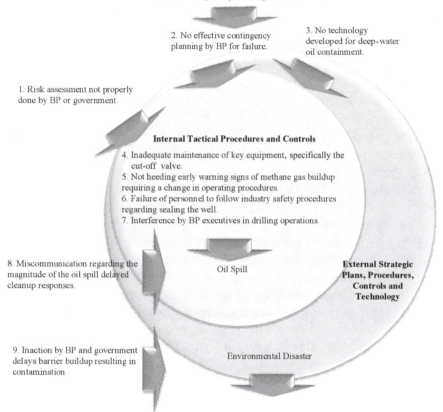

Figure 5.4   2010 Deepwater Horizon explosion and oil spill

of the recently enacted six-month deep-water drilling ban. The permitted organizations include Exxon Mobil, Chevron, Marathon Oil, and Rooster Petroleum (shallow water drilling permit).[12] Apparently, little has changed regarding requirements for environmental risk analyses, despite the known risks of drilling offshore and especially in deep water.

A recent article published by the *New York Times* also described the widespread environmental damage caused by oil exploration companies in Nigeria.[13] In the past 50 years, 546 million gallons of oil have been spilled in the region. In contrast, the Exxon *Valdez* spill was 10.8 million gallons of oil. Widespread water contamination as well as plant and animal kills have been the result. Some of the companies operating in the region included Shell Oil, Exxon Mobil, and Chevron.[14] The lack of environmental compliance by oil and gas companies is apparently quite common in many parts of the world.

Organizational cultures are often lulled into complacency by weak regulatory environments. This complacency contributes to the likelihood of a catastrophic event occurring. If there is weak regulations in inherently dangerous industries, catastrophic events are likely. Weak regulations lead to poor operational practices. Poor internal operations contributed to the 2010 Deepwater Horizon explosion. Some included inadequate maintenance (especially of the blowout preventer), not paying attention to early warning signs regarding methane gas, a general failure of BP and its contractors Halliburton and Transocean to effectively cement the well, and decisions made by BP executives on-site on the drilling rig the day of the tragedy. These factors and the relative contribution of each organization to the disaster must be sorted out in the coming years. It is true, these organizations, and BP in particular, have extensive safety procedures and employee training programs, but what is it about this event that enabled a few people to make decisions that apparently violated commonly accepted industry best practices? Were the causes limited to a few people or organizational? Currently, we suspect there were personal, organizational, as well as technical causes for the explosion and subsequent environmental disaster. Once these error conditions were created, the likelihood of failure (e.g. an explosion, oil spill, and widespread environmental damage) occurred. The result was that 11 people were killed, others injured, and extensive environmental damage done in the eastern Gulf of Mexico.

The magnitude of the environmental damage significantly increased because BP and various agencies of the United States government could not rapidly deploy the correct combinations of technologies, equipment, and people. As a result, the oil slowly spread into the Gulf of Mexico and to its surrounding coastal region. Time was lost. Complicating the relief efforts was continuing underreporting of the amount of oil spilling into the Gulf of Mexico by BP and the governmental agencies. Only after severe public criticism did the United States government formally request more accurate estimates of the oil flow rate. Several months later the amounts around which there is much consensus are still being disputed by BP.

So why do the things we trust fail catastrophically and cause loss of life and injuries as well as property and environmental damage? Typical analyses of these types of failure events is usually confined to isolated accidents related to failures of construction such as bridges, dams, and similar man-made structures or if airplanes crash and machines unexpectedly fail. However, failures are caused by a combination of factors, including human, organizational, technical, and natural. Some of the most catastrophic events are either caused by nature or are man-made. Relative to the former, it is difficult to predict an earthquake, fire, or other natural disaster. But, people know there is a likelihood of risk and should plan accordingly. Earthquakes, in particular, are an example where buildings could be made safer. The recent major damage and loss of life in Haiti is an example where poor building construction resulted in more than 200,000 deaths. Similar building collapses have recently occurred in China and other countries because of earthquakes and poor building construction practices. However, Chile did not suffer a large number of deaths even in a more powerful earthquake than Haiti, because its buildings were better built than those of Haiti. Tornados are another example where homes should be built with shelters to protect people rather than built on slabs or worse in trailer parks.

Unfortunately, the future portends even worse tragedies because of poor planning and a failure to mitigate risks. As an example, as the world's population increases, more people will inhabit marginal areas. Experts agree that ocean levels will increase, leading to flooding and displacement of people in low-lying areas. However, poorer people around the world have little choice but to endure these adverse conditions considering their economic and political conditions. They could be helped, but there is little will by nations to do so. In contrast, people (including some in the United States) purposely build in low-lying areas and ignore risks of flooding. This was the situation in New Orleans and it still is. In fact, many coastal states within the United States continue to support construction in areas that have a high risk of hurricanes, earthquakes, and flooding. The people supporting this construction argue that people have a right to live where they want. But the reality is, not only are the people building in marginal areas damaging surrounding ecosystems, but they also want others living in other areas to subsidize their risky behavior.

Many of the world's megacities are built on earthquake-prone fault zones. Countries have little choice where they build cities since the cities have existed in these locations for hundreds of years. But building construction should be modified to reflect physical realty regarding the likelihood of earthquakes. If not, then future earthquakes will continue to create catastrophic damage and loss of life. Then there are many such examples showing a willful disregard for the application of technology, physics, governmental laws, and regulations as well as good practices, which also contribute to likelihood of future catastrophic damage.

The energy industry provides a long list of such catastrophic failures. The most notable recent example is the recent Gulf of Mexico oil spill. The United States government, BP, and other organizations are culpable to various degrees for this event. A second event was the recent financial crisis in which the financial industry squandered the wealth of millions of people. What do these two events have in common? The answer is a willful disregard of risks and a lack of personal accountability. Unfortunately, incentives in many industries usually favor and promote risky and dangerous behavior because people are seldom held accountable for their actions or punished. We know how to prevent these failures, but most people choose expediency. Unfortunately, as the world becomes more complicated, interconnected, and resource-competitive, ignoring science, technology, and facts will make these catastrophic events worse.

In the last chapter we discussed organizational culture and how it influenced the ways work is done within organizations. Before proceeding to the next chapter, we need to discuss the importance of safety subculture and its relationship to failure analysis within the context of organizational culture. A safety culture espouses organizational values focused on reducing risk from work operations, investigating failure events using correct tools and methods, and promoting continuous improvement of safe operations within an organization.

Safe operations depend on several principles. These include the use of simple and standard operations that have been mistake proofed the transparency of organizational information as it relates to risk, and the formal control of work operations. It is also necessary that organizational leaders believe employee health and safety are important. A basic requirement is that products and services be designed for safe usage. Also, there is an assumption they can be safely maintained, disposed, or recycled. Although there are no guarantees, safety subcultures reduce the likelihood of failure, but cannot completely eliminate it.

I have known organizations that pay much attention to safety. Lids must be on hot coffee cups to prevent burning people with hot coffee, extension cords are required to be taped to the floor to prevent tripping, and no running is allowed in work areas to avoid injuries. There are also safety moments, routinely held before meetings, where a person tells a group about a recently observed hazardous condition to share best practices. I consulted with an organization in the Midwestern region of the United States that used these types of methods to promote safe work practices. Safety moments included advice for visitors to drive slowly because of roaming deer or slippery or icy roads. These are good practices, but are not a substitute for the effective and safe design of products and services or systematically identifying and eliminating error conditions.

A heavy reliance on a safety subculture is in itself not enough. Employees continually make poor decisions that increase risks. The result is that sometimes people are killed or injured, or there is property damage. Failure analysis helps but only if cognitive, cultural, and organizational factors are considered as well as technical causes. Blaming employees for accidents and disciplining, demoting, or terminating them is not helpful. Unless an accident is caused by intentional acts of employees, the blame is with the organization because it controls all resources for managing and eliminating risks.

In earlier chapters, cognitive and organizational influences for failure events were discussed relative to decisions people make when designing, doing work, or using products and services. From a different perspective, it should be apparent that when managers, key stakeholders, and employees make risky decisions, things can go very wrong. Poor decisions could be caused by willful intent, ignorance, or error. It is generally true employees tend to follow safe practices if trained to do so; but some will not. Executives and managers can be particularly problematic in this regard because of their power relative to other employees. In fact, some well-known CEOs have sociopathic traits that affect their behavior. How many coworkers, managers, and executives have you known who have little empathy for others, who lie, cheat, and abuse people through insults and manipulative behaviors, and who crave control over others? You most likely brushed these encounters off as a personality conflict or management style. The assumption was these were good people who simply disagreed with you, who were stressed or had a few faults, but who also had admirable personality traits.

However, an interesting article written by Alan Deutschman appeared in *Fast Company*. It was titled, "Is Your Boss a Psychopath?"[15] It discussed examples wherein famous CEOs, tested for personality traits, scored moderately or severely psychopathic. In fact, their scores were characteristic of criminals, killers, and other social deviates. A corroborating fact is that approximately 1 percent of the United States population is highly psychotic or cold-blooded in relating to others. Higher percentages of people show various levels of psychopathic behaviors. We encounter psychopaths frequently. Sometimes they are coworkers, managers, key stakeholders, suppliers, or customers. Unfortunately, there is a long list of other behavioral issues that affect decision making by people.

This fact must be considered when creating a safety subculture. Not everyone will want to participate. Others may interfere with safe operations. If they are powerful, their actions can negate safety systems regardless of the systems' usefulness or effectiveness. Unfortunately, organizational sanctions for preventing managers and executives from engaging in such behavior are often weak. Legal sanctions around the world are also very weak in this regard. In fact, lack of accountability is common if considered within the context of catastrophic events. This is why a safety subculture, even if very well designed, can sometimes be easily sabotaged to the detriment of an organization and society.

There are several ways organizations deploy safety subcultures. Some simply use slogans, newsletters, and exhortations that employees to do better. In the absence of stronger preventive actions, these methods are ineffective. Other organizations carefully design processes by simplifying, standardizing, and mistake proofing work operations to prevent red flag and error conditions. These latter actions are more likely to prevent errors and mistakes than slogans. Measuring accident and injury incident rates is also popular and necessary. But without effective actions to identify and eliminate root causes for high incident rates, recurrences are likely. An organization claiming to be safety centered should invest time and resources to ensure things are done right. Safety subcultures reflect organizational and cultural behaviors regarding how work is done. They also reflect the attitudes, beliefs, and competencies of employees.

A first step for creating a safety subculture requires understanding industry standards and applicable laws and regulations. These have been designed for specific industries and work processes based on best judgments of industry experts and available technologies. Organizations that go against accepted industry practices are especially egregious because failures are likely to occur. Failures arising from such behaviors are also more severe because they involve basic work processes necessary to design and produce products and series. As an example, failures to correctly inspect oil pipelines and equipment, control systems in a nuclear facility, or equipment lockouts come to mind. Inspection of pipelines is necessary because they corrode if exposed to extreme weather and other conditions. Nuclear facilities rely on complicated control systems to regulate the flow of fluids and move materials. Lockouts are required for equipment maintenance of dangerous machines that could injure or kill people if not properly shut down. The inspection and periodic testing of these systems to industry standards is necessary to maintain safe operations.

Let's review lockout systems in more detail. Accidents caused by dangerous equipment, which must be shut down and locked before maintenance work can be performed, occur quite frequently. As an example, according to a National Institute for Occupational Safety and Health (NIOSH) report, "No detailed national data are available on the number of workers killed each year by contact with uncontrolled hazardous energy. However, during the period 1982–1997, NIOSH investigated 1,281 fatal events as part of their FACE Program. Of these, 152 involved installation, maintenance, service, or repair tasks on or near machines, equipment, processes, or systems. Because the FACE program was active in only 20 States between 1982 and 1997, these fatalities represent only a portion of the U.S. workers who were killed by contact with uncontrolled hazardous energy. . . . Review of these 152 events suggests that three related factors contributed to these fatalities: Failure to completely de-energize, isolate, block, and/or dissipate the energy source (82% of the events, or 124 of 152); Failure to lock out and tag out energy control devices and isolation points after de-energization (11% of the events, or 17 of 152); Failure to verify that the energy source was de-energized before beginning work (7% of the events, or 11 of 152)."[16]

Effective lockout systems require a strong safety subculture as well as a complete understanding of their electromechanical and human systems and how they interact with each other. However, lockouts are only one type of safety methodology. It should be noted there are many different methods and procedures depending on the type of equipment.

There are also different types of maintenance and operating procedures required by standards used in various industries to ensure safe operations. To the extent basic standards are not used or are circumvented, much insight can be gained regarding an organization's safety subculture. Recall the April 25, 1986, Chernobyl Reactor 4 accident. Safety systems had been disabled by management and workers several hours before the tragic accident.

In addition to creating basic safety systems based on industry standards, laws, and regulations, organizations also need management systems to track safety performance to targets. Integral to these management systems should be an application of effective failure analysis as well as continuous improvement. Also important are risk analyses and actions, which focus organizational resources to improve documentation and maintenance systems, training, the elimination of red flag conditions, process simplification, standardization and mistake proofing, and effective communications. These strategies help reduce hazardous risks. However, supporting systems are also necessary to ensure a safety subculture can flourish. Examples include leadership commitment, employee involvement and empowerment, effective change management, training in correct procedures, providing the right tools and equipment, and other resources.

Organizations wanting to prevent unexpected failures must also create systems for hazard identification as well as risk assessment and management. Some of this information is available from industry associations or governmental sources. Hazard identification begins with preparing a hazard inventory to identify hazards an organization will likely encounter. This requires listing major hazards and their impact. As an example, some industries such as oil and gas have many hazardous operations and working conditions. Oil exploration occurs in some of the most hostile environments on earth. These types of hazardous conditions are unavoidable considering how oil, gas, and their components are produced and moved through complicated machinery and systems. This implies fires and explosions are likely to be encountered within these systems if contributing error conditions align to create an accident. However, these are only a few of the many potential hazards that need to be evaluated within industries such as oil and gas. There are also secondary effects of primary hazards. If a fire occurred, people could suffer smoke inhalation, be burned, or be killed by explosive impact.

Machinery is another potential operational hazard. People can be crushed, cut, stabbed, and harmed in many other ways depending on the specific types of equipment being used. Each has its specific hazards. Fortunately, with the correct engineering, mistake proofing, and controls, the likelihood of failures can be reduced. Then there are other types of industry specific r hazards. These include radiation, biological agents, chemicals, and electrocution, to name a few.

Once major hazards and their impacts are identified, risk analyses are used to determine the likelihood (frequency) and impact or effect of each hazard on people, property, and the environment. Occurrence frequency varies by industry, organization, and hazard. Typical frequencies range from days to many years. As an example, hazards occurring in manufacturing operations may occur in days or hours. In contrast, major natural disasters such as earthquakes occur in high-activity regions of the world perhaps every couple of hundred years. But if 20 major cities across the world are located in such regions, then a major earthquake is expected to strike a major city every 10 years. In other words, naturally caused catastrophic events are analyzed differently relative to their type and likelihood. Consequences also vary from minor to major relative to the effects on people, property, and the environment. Using this information, current control technologies are identified and analyzed for their effectiveness regarding hazards and their various failure modes or types. Each industry has its own hazard list and control strategies. But a good question is, "Have they performed a rigorous hazard and risk analysis?"

In previous chapters we discussed risk from a project management perspective. Recall there were several types of project management risks. These included scheduling, cost, technology, product performance, market demand, supply, and capacity, as well as laws and regulatory risks. Risk, from a failure analysis perspective, is defined as the likelihood (occurrence probability) that a particular failure type (mode) will occur under certain conditions, and its impact (effect). Recall that we have discussed risk elements in the context of failure mode and effects analysis (FMEA). An FMEA uses estimated or known risk levels to help focus process controls and improvements. As an example, if a product could kill someone by failing in several ways, it would be useful to know the likelihood of each of the ways, that is, failure types or modes. Failure types or modes also have occurrence probabilities. Finally, the inherent ability to detect abnormal process conditions can be estimated to create a risk prioritization number (RPN). Recall, the RPN is the multiplicand of severity, occurrence of the failure type, and its detection likelihood ratings. This makes an FMEA a useful method for improving products and services.

The information used to create an FMEA is gathered using historical information of failure types. An example would be information such as the probability a person is injured or dies in an accident if they drive a distance of, say, 10,000 miles, as well as the reasons for the accident. There are other mitigating factors that may also be useful for such an investigation. These include time of day and week and location (e.g., rural or city). In a manufacturing facility, safety engineers will have tables of information showing the likelihood of injury or death for different types of processes containing equipment and work operations of various types. In addition, they will have a record of historical performance for their facility to guide decisions regarding where to focus their safety efforts.

This accumulated information is also useful if investigating failures. An investigative team would be well positioned to do analysis work if this type of information is available (FMEAs, risk analyses of specific processes, and industry safety standards and recommendations). If failures occur, basic safety principles have most likely been violated if a system was well designed. Safety systems, across different industries, will also most likely have unique types of failures with differing effects on people, animals, and property. A safety management system will usually be on a firm basis if employees rigorously follow procedures promoting safe work methods. Unfortunately, although some organizations do this, others do not.

On December 29, 2009, a Nigerian man, Mr. Farouk Abdulmutallab, age 23, flew from Yemen to Nigeria and eventually toward Detroit, Michigan, in the United States. As the airplane approached the city of Detroit, reports were made by passengers and crew members that Mr. Abdulmutallab was seen trying to detonate a high-explosive device in mid-air. The high explosive was found hidden in his underwear. In the investigation of the incident, it was found Mr. Abdulmutallab had a valid United States passport as well as a two-year visa that allowed him to visit the United States. In the months and years prior to the event he was also known to have been radicalized. Complaints were also made by his father and others to U.S. officials, but were ignored.[17] One response from U.S. officials after the incident was to install very intrusive full-body scanners and pat-downs of passengers. Was this a proper response to the security threat? Is it fact based? Will it make people safer?

First, the United States government has assured its citizens and visitors to the country that the scanners are safe. Precautions have also been taken to ensure passenger privacy. Interestingly, discrepancies with these statements have been found. First, it has been reported this type of scanner will not detect the specific high explosive carried by Mr. Abdulmutallab. Second, the security of these types of scans or pictures of passengers have also ready been compromised in other situations.

Complicating the discussion of the usefulness of these scanners for preventing similar incidents are rumors that a major reason for their purchase was the pressure of lobbyists who worked with political leaders to sell the equipment to the Transportation Security Authority (TSA). In an article written by Mail Online, Tory Member of Parliament Ben Wallace, who had helped design the machines, stated they would not have detected the high explosive Mr. Abdulmutallab carried on December 29. In fact the machines cannot detect chemicals or light plastics. Only an X-ray machine can detect such materials.[18] The scans are also not necessarily secure. As an example, an article written by Mr. Wilson Rothman discussed the fact that more than 35,000 naked body images were stored by the U.S. Marshall's office in Orlando. Under the Freedom of Information Act, one hundred of these pictures were released to the public.[19]

These security methods depend on visual inspection of passengers and human judgment. We know both are subject to error induced by cognitive and group influences. As a consultant, I know the accuracy of visual inspection is not 100 percent. Also, an article that appeared in *USA Today* placed the failure of visual inspection at several U.S. airports between 24 percent and 41 percent.[20] This is a typical response to failure events and especially if there are political consequences to effective action. What's the answer? Do other countries have better airport security systems?

According to an article by Helene Cooper in the *New York Times,* Israeli screening is very intrusive.[21] It requires gathering passenger information in advance and aggressive interviewing methods conducted by highly skilled interviewers. However, Israel also has only two airports and approximately 50 flights per day. Most likely their security systems would not be cost-effective for a country such as the United States, which has thousands of flight each day and numerous airports. The answer lies, in part, in the continual application of security methods based on factual analysis of historical failures and threats and the application of effective solutions. Politics complicates these situations and makes us less safe in the end. Organizational cultures are also political and produce similar issues.

SUMMARY

In earlier chapters, red flag and error conditions were discussed with the advice they must be eliminated or mistakes (failures) are likely to occur. Good design is an important way to help ensure this elimination occurs. It's not an easy task. There are cognitive, group, and organizational dependencies. This chapter discussed a generalized approach for failure analysis that is applicable for analysis of products, services, and systems, including logistics. Logistical systems are important because catastrophic events are often made worse by ineffective relief responses.

This generalized approach used a seven-step method that included planning for failures, securing a failure site, gathering information, interviewing key actors, recreating the failure event sequence, completing a root cause analysis, and making recommendations. The specific tools and methods will differ by application, but the general approach is valid. The discussion of failure analysis methods also progressed from a single-event theory of failure causation to the domino theory, wherein a series of sequential events triggers a final failure, and then to a multiple-cause model when error conditions align to cause a failure. The importance of creating a safety subculture was also discussed within the context of organizational culture. A safety subculture should espouse organizational values focused on reducing risk from work operations, investigating failure events using correct tools and methods, and promoting continuous improvement of safe operations within an organization.

In later chapters we will see that this is all sometimes easier said than done. Almost every organization does such work. However, the problem is that their analyses are done relative to currently expected hazards and risks. Unusual events are seldom considered by such analyses. We will discuss ways to avoid this limited approach to hazard and risk analysis.

NOTES

1. "A Failure of Initiative: Final Report of the Select Bipartisan Committee to Investigate the Preparation for and Response to Hurricane Katrina," report by the Select Bipartisan Committee to Investigate the Preparation for and Response to Hurricane Katrina, February 15, 2006 (Washington, DC: US Government Printing Office, 2006), www.gpo.gov.

2. Jamie Colby, "FOX Facts: Hurricane Katrina Damage," FOX News, August 29, 2006, http://www.foxnews.com/story/0,2933,210970,00.html.

3. "A Failure of Initiative," Preface, ix.

4. United States Army Corp of Engineers, Louisiana Coast Protection & Restoration (LACPR) home page, "Hot Topics" discussion of the LACPR report on Hurricane Katrina, http://www.lacpr.usace.army.mil/, retrieved August 9, 2009.

5. "A Failure of Initiative," Conclusion, 359.

6. Christine Hall, "BP's Gulf Oil Spill Cleanup Costs Nearly Double," *Houston Business Journal,* May 18, 2010.

7. Ian Urbina, "NYT: Despite Moratorium, Drilling Projects Continue; Records Show At Least 7 New Permits for Drilling, 5 Environmental," *New York Times,* May 24, 2010, www.msnbc.com.

8. Infoplease, "Oil Spills and Disasters," http://www.infoplease.com/ipa/A0001451.html.

9. Peter Key, "SAP Hit with a $500M Suit," *Philadelphia Business Journal,* October 30, 1998.

10. Peter Buxbaum, "Lawsuit against an ERP Consulting Firm Could Signal More Litigation for the Industry," *TechRepublic,* August 24, 2001.

11. James Reason, *The Human Contribution: Unsafe Acts, Accidents and Heroic Recoveries* (Burlington, VT: Ashgate, 2008), 102.

12. Shashank Bengali, "Approvals Flowing for Drilling Plans," *Providence Journal,* June 19, 2010.

13. Adam Nossiter, "Niger Delta: Where Oil Spills Are No Longer News: Region Has Endured the Equivalent of Exxon Valdez Spill Every Year for 50 Years," *New York Times,* June 17, 2010, msnbc.com.

14. Xeni Jardin, "More Oil Spilled in Nigeria Every Year than Has Been Lost in the Gulf of Mexico," Monday, June 14, 2010, http://www.boingboing.net/2010/06/14/more-oil-spilled-in.html.

15. Alan Deutschman, "Is Your Boss a Psychopath?" *Fast Company,* December 19, 2007, http://www.fastcompany.com/magazine/96/open_boss.html?page=0%2C4.

16. NIOSH Alert, *Preventing Worker Deaths from Uncontrolled Release of Electrical, Mechanical, and Other Types of Hazardous Energy* (Cincinnati, OH: National Institute for Occupational Safety and Health Publications Dissemination, 1999), Publication No. 99–110.

17. "US Jet Plot Suspect 'Was in Yemen in December,'" BBC, December 29, 2009, http://news.bbc.co.uk/2/hi/8433410.stm.

18. Mail Online, "Body Scanner Wouldn't Have Foiled Syringe Bomber, Says MP Who Worked on New Machines," *Sunday Reporter,* January 3, 2010, http://www.dailymail.co.uk/news/article-1240193/Body-scanner-wouldnt-foiled-syringe-bomber-says-MP-worked-new-machines.html.

19. Wilson Rothman, "Leaked U.S. Marshal Body Scan Images Revealed: Evidence Shows Scanners Definitely Are Capable of Storing and Transmitting Pictures," MSNBC News, November 16, 2010, http://www.msnbc.msn.com/id/40218074/ns/technology_and_science-security.

20. Blake Morrison, "Airport Security Failures Persist," July 1, 2002, *USA Today,* http://www.usatoday.com/travel/news/2002/2002-07-01-airport-security.htm.

21. Helene Cooper, "TSA Alternatives: Israeli Airport Screening Methods Suggested for U.S. by Some," *New York Times,* November 22, 2010, http://www.cleveland.com/world/index.ssf/2010/11/tsa_alternatives_israeli_airpo.html.

Chapter 6

CATASTROPHIC FAILURES HAVE COMMON CAUSES

Insanity is doing the same thing over and over, but expecting different results.

—Albert Einstein

As I pulled into the BP service station this week, I saw its Helios logo. Helios is a personification of the sun in Greek mythology. It also symbolizes both the origin of current fossil fuels, primarily as former plant materials, as well as eco-friendly replacements such as wind and solar power. Its green and yellow coloring symbolizes both these renewable energy sources as well as BP's goal to supply energy in a responsible manner. It's an inspiring logo and one I have become fond of over time. As I fueled my car, I reflected on BP and recalled the many wonderful people I had met and worked with over several years. I know the recent Gulf of Mexico oil spill has caused them great pain because the employees of BP have worked very hard to create a safety culture. The disconnection between what they strove for and stark reality has been a true test of their corporate culture.

BP's green and yellow Helios logo truly reflects its goals of becoming a leading-edge energy producer. Yet it stands in stark contrast to the reality of several recent BP catastrophic events, including the 2010 Gulf of Mexico oil spill. In the time I spent with BP I know its culture is very serious about the safety of its people and I saw that safety culture continuously in words and action at every level of the organization. Its teams of safety experts travel to every corner of BP's vast enterprise to help prevent failures from occurring. As a result of these experiences, it was not my intention to include BP as one of the 40-plus catastrophic events discussed in this book, but the 2010 spill cannot be ignored, for it holds many lessons.

First, it shows what can go wrong even when an organization works very hard to prevent failure. It's also an example to other organizations that safety programs are not enough to prevent catastrophic failure. Risk analysis, mitigation, and recovery planning are also essential as well as several other components. Ensuring a safe working environment is difficult. It requires serious thought and actions. The 2010 Gulf of Mexico event also shows that lax government oversight does no one any good, including the organizations being regulated. If BP would do a cost-benefit analysis now, I wonder what different decisions it would make regarding risk analysis and mitigation? Proper and just regulations based on facts are the best defense against organizational, group, and individual decisions contributing to errors.

But the most important lesson from the BP accident is that we as a society, collectively, regardless of political persuasion, tend to avoid responsibility for the complex and dangerous machines and systems we create. We also respond poorly to such events. We have lazy attitudes regarding proper failure investigation and effective actions to prevent future recurrence of events or the effective coordination of relief responses. As an example, recall the sensationalism and vilification of Mr. Hayward, BP's CEO, in the aftermath of the 2010 oil spill, by the very people responsible for lax regulation and oversight. Prior to the event, Mr. Hayward was regarded as an excellent leader. Knee-jerk responses to the disaster, especially within the United States, do little good to anyone. No one person was responsible for the 2010 Gulf of Mexico disaster. In fact, its many underlying causes were all too common. In this chapter, we analyze this catastrophic event, with others, to demonstrate the commonality and differences of causation, root cause analyses, and solutions of these events. The goal is to demonstrate that although recurrence risks can be mitigated, some industries such as oil and gas production have inherently higher risks and impact than other industries. This is not an excuse for failure, but only a realization that when failure occurs in these industries, its impact will be very damaging.

The logical conclusion is this: for inherently dangerous industries, we need to become more serious with respect to preventing and responding to catastrophic failure. In other words, safety programs are not enough. Organizations like BP, because of recent events, will most likely significantly improve their failure prevention and response systems in the coming decades. At least they will within the United States. This can only be done by properly analyzing the root causes for failures so as to understand them from social psychological perspectives (e.g. cognitive), group dynamics, and organizational, ethical, as well as technical perspectives. So in the coming years I will continue to visit my BP service station, purchase its products, and continue to reflect on the meaning of its Helios logo. I will also do the same regarding Toyota, Ford, and other organizations that I have been associated with over the past decades, but whose products have sometimes unexpectedly and catastrophically failed.

The initial goal of this book was to understand the causes of technical failures. Typical examples of such failures are aircraft accidents, product failures causing injuries and death, and others having a technical basis for failure. However, the focus began to change when it became clear that the most catastrophic events were not necessarily technical failures. As a result, research for the book changed to include several well-known catastrophic events. Examples include Hurricane Katrina in 2005, the 2010 Haiti earthquake, the recent 2010 BP Gulf of Mexico oil spill, and many others.

The goal became one of finding linkages and common causes of the reasons for failure and the impact on life and property. In this context, a catastrophic event was evaluated from two perspectives. First, could it have been prevented? Some events could have been prevented, but, others (such as natural disasters) could not. Second, if an event occurred, was additional damage created by poor planning or poor responses to its aftermath (inadequate relief efforts)? The 2010 Haiti earthquake comes to mind as an example. It could not have been predicted with certainty, but the building infrastructure was poor and the relief efforts strained. These conditions either directly or indirectly caused more than 200,000 deaths.

Surprisingly, technology played a small part in most disasters. Actually, if it had been properly utilized, technology may have helped prevent injuries, death, and extensive property damage. In fact, cognitive processes and organizational dynamics, including ethics, are major contributors to unexpected and catastrophic events. There is also commonality between products and major service system failures. Unlike isolated technical failures, such as aircraft accidents, investigated by experts to find their root causes, the major events associated with service systems were only partially investigated and their root causes seldom identified or fully understood. Over the past several decades, the result of ineffective root cause analysis and resolution has been a continuing series of unnecessary catastrophic events.

The societal impact in terms of injuries, deaths, and property damage caused by service or logistical system failures are orders of magnitude greater than for isolated technical failures such as an aircraft accident. In total, these facts suggest that society should focus on understanding the root causes for service and logistical failures. These systems are often broken. Lives can be saved and property not lost when major catastrophic events occur. Also, the proper use of technology may have prevented several catastrophic events. The New Orleans levee breach and the collapse of the I-35W Mississippi River Bridge in Minnesota are examples where technology applied in advance would have helped prevent these failures. However, to say that systems fail because of nonapplication of technology misses the point that humans make the decisions regarding technology application. The reasons why people fail to act or act inappropriately take us down to a next level of root cause analysis and away from the most obvious causes for failure. These root causes are organizational dysfunctions, group dynamics, and cognition issues at an individual level.

Information discussed in previous chapters will be used to integrate the concepts and make sense of these events. The discussion will focus on how technical issues of design, the application environments, cognitive issues, group and organizational dynamics, and ethics cause failures and hinder their resolution. Technical issues include identifying and understanding interrelationships between design functions and features in the context of the application environments that stress them. Application environments consist of major factors related to people, methods, materials, measurements, machines, and direct environmental factors related to stressors such as temperature, vibration, chemical, physical, and similar factors.

Failures also occur if people misuse products and services. There are reasons for misuse including poor design, ignorance, and errors of judgment or action. Relative to service and logistical systems, to the extent there is one best method to do work, incorrect methods may be inadvertently used or the correct method may be incorrectly applied. Unknown to most people, measurement errors are also very common if they are wrong for the purpose, incorrectly applied, or results are misinterpreted by a machine or person. Designers also make assumptions regarding a design's useful life relative to the materials, components, and their geometry. Poor materials and component geometries will cause rapid failure even under normal usage conditions. There are also external contributing factors. These include temperature, vibration, chemical, physical, and similar stressing factors external to a design. In service systems, stressing factors include demand, capacity, and supply constraints integrated within logistical and informational systems. Every product and service system is constrained and under varying levels of stress regarding its functions and features as well as its availability.

Information regarding cognitive factors, discussed in earlier chapters, will be used to analyze the catastrophic events discussed in this chapter. Recall, cognitive factors included attitudes (opinions and beliefs), behaviors, information filtering, and self-concept (comparisons with others or to standards). Other cognitive factors include issues of self-esteem, cognitive dissonance (inconsistencies between personal actions and beliefs), and social influence (influence of group size, beliefs, and status on individual behavior). Information regarding informal and formal groups will also be used in our analyses. Informal and formal groups are influenced by rules and norms as well as the behavior and interpersonal relationships that people within a group use to influence each other and differentiate themselves from other groups. They also control interpersonal relationships, that is, interpersonal attraction, by the ways in which people interact both positively and negatively with each other. Organizational factors influence the desire of people to associate. These factors include organizational structure, transparency, communication, and ethics.

More than 40 unexpected and catastrophic events were researched for this book. They are summarized in Table 6.1 and include intentional injuries, accidents, construction failures, environmental and food contamination, as well as failures of health care, information technology, mechanical and electrical design, natural disasters, and laws and regulations. Although these events represent a non–randomly selected sample, their diversity and combined magnitude relative to injuries, deaths, and property damage enables useful information to be gained from an analysis. How were these events selected? Some of them are classic historical failures caused by natural events, but their negative impact became magnified through poor relief response. Some events such as the 2010 Gulf of Mexico oil spill and the 2010 Haiti earthquake occurred while this book was being written. Other events were selected because of their significant impact on societies around the world.

Individually, the 40-plus events may appear at first to have been unexpected, in terms of injuries, deaths, and property damage. We will examine the events and show that some of them could have been predicted with high confidence. Others such as natural disasters (e.g., earthquakes) could only be predicted with a probability or not at all. However, resultant injuries, deaths, and property damage could have been significantly mitigated by better planning or relief responses. The balance of the events could have been predicted to varying degrees. As an example, isolated airline accidents are very difficult to predict unless chronic causal factors exist such as pilot training and certification, maintenance, and similar issues.

Several events associated with failures of law and regulations are also discussed and analyzed. As an example, the recent 2009 financial crisis almost sent the world into another great depression. A recurrence of this crisis is not impossible well into 2010. Enormous wealth has been lost and unemployment remains high more than two years after the event. However, the crisis was not completely unexpected given the preceding loose regulatory environment and high financial leveraging of several economic sectors within and outside the United States. But, as we now know, people routinely ignore or distort information they do not want to agree with. There are several reasons for doing this, but cognitive dissonance is one reason. Recall, it

Table 6.1

Examples of Unexpected and Catastrophic Failures

Major Failure Incidents by Type	Expenses	Total Deaths	Percentage of Expenses	Percentage of Deaths
Intentional injuries		**1,618,800**	**0.00%**	**8.59%**
Intentional injuries including war and violence		1,618,800	0.00%	8.59%
2010 Haiti earthquake	—	230,000	0.00%	1.22%
Accidents		**3,876,000**	**0.00%**	**20.56%**
Unintentional injuries		3,876,000	0.00%	20.56%
Construction failures	**$1,794,000,000**	**4,069**	**0.27%**	**0.02%**
I-35W Mississippi River Bridge (Minnesota)	$294,000,000	13	0.04%	0.00%
April 25, 1986, Chernobyl's Reactor 4 disaster	$1,000,000,000	4,056	0.15%	0.02%
Denver Int'l Airport baggage system delay	$500,000,000	—	0.07%	0.00%
Environmental poisoning	**$76,000,000,000**	**27,542**	**11.26%**	**0.15%**
BP Gulf of Mexico Oil Spill 2010	$50,000,000,000	11	7.41%	0.00%
Environmental poisoning CDC 2006 (Use as average annual representative)	$26,000,000,000	27,531	3.85%	0.15%
Health and safety: food contamination	**$35,000,000,000**	**5,000**	**5.18%**	**0.03%**
Food contamination 1996–1998 CDCP, Average Annual	$35,000,000,000	5,000	5.18%	0.03%
Health care system failures	**—**	**13,016,695**	**0.00%**	**69.06%**
SARS in Asia 2003			0.00%	0.00%
Production problems with the H1N1 swine flu virus	—	15,921	0.00%	0.08%
Infectious and parasitic diseases		13,000,000	0.00%	68.97%
Information technology failures	**$1,437,400,000**	**23**	**0.21%**	**0.00%**
Mariner I Space Probe failure, July 28, 1962	$80,000,000	—	0.01%	0.00%

(*continued*)

Major Failure Incidents by Type	Expenses	Total Deaths	Percentage of Expenses	Percentage of Deaths
National Cancer Institute, Panama City miscalculation of radiation dosage, November 2000	—	23	0.00%	0.00%
AMR reservation system for Budget's hotel and car bookings	$109,000,000	—	0.02%	0.00%
Conversion to new order entry system from Baan Co. at Snap-On	—	—	0.00%	0.00%
Anderson SAP ERP issues for FoxMeyer	$1,000,000,000	—	0.15%	0.00%
Greyhound Bus trips reservation and bus dispatch system issues	$61,400,000	—	0.01%	0.00%
Hershey Foods, IBM issues, SAP Manugistics	—	—	0.00%	0.00%
Norfolk Southern integration issues, Consolidated Rail	$80,000,000	—	0.01%	0.00%
Oxford health plans billing processing, UNIX and Oracle	$78,000,000	—	0.01%	0.00%
Grainger SAP issues	$23,000,000	—	0.00%	0.00%
Trivalley Growers Oracle ERP integration	$6,000,000	—	0.00%	0.00%
Mechanical and electrical design failures	**$9,000,000,000**	**498**	**1.33%**	**0.00%**
Pitot tube failures on Airbus planes, Air France A430-300 (F-GLZL), Air France A340-300 (F-GLZN), and possibly Air France Flight 447 as well as other planes, 2009	—	228	0.00%	0.00%
Continental Connection Flight 3407 near Buffalo	—	49	0.00%	0.00%
Toyota 2010 recall	$2,000,000,000	34	0.30%	0.00%
Ford cruise switch control fires, late 1990s	—	13	0.00%	0.00%

(*continued*)

Table 6.1 *(continued)*

Major Failure Incidents by Type	Expenses	Total Deaths	Percentage of Expenses	Percentage of Deaths
Boeing Dreamliner delays	$4,000,000,000	—	0.59%	0.00%
Ford/Firestone tire issues 2001	$3,000,000,000	174	0.44%	0.00%
Natural disaster	**$221,000,000,000**	**300,544**	**32.73%**	**1.59%**
2010 Haiti earthquake	—	230,000	0.00%	1.22%
Hurricane Katrina (New Orleans)	$100,000,000,000	1,300	14.81%	0.01%
2008 Sichuan earthquake	$115,000,000,000	69,181	17.03%	0.37%
1989 San Francisco earthquake	$6,000,000,000	63	0.89%	0.00%
Regulatory failures	**$315,670,000,000**	**—**	**46.76%**	**0.00%**
SEC regulatory issues— Madoff pyramid scheme	$65,000,000,000	—	9.63%	0.00%
Fannie/ Freddie mortgage issues	$250,670,000,000	—	37.13%	0.00%
Software Viruses	**$15,255,000,000**	**—**	**2.26%**	**0.00%**
The Love Bug 2000	$8,750,000,000	—	1.30%	0.00%
Code Red 2001	$2,600,000,000	—	0.39%	0.00%
SirCam 2001	$1,150,000,000	—	0.17%	0.00%
Melissa 1999	$1,100,000,000	—	0.16%	0.00%
Explorer 1999	$1,020,000,000	—	0.15%	0.00%
Nimda 2001	$635,000,000	—	0.09%	0.00%
Grand Total	**$675,156,400,000**	**18,849,171**	**100.00%**	**100.00%**

occurs if a situation differs from one a person expects (e.g., disconfirming evidence). The simple fact is that people don't like to be wrong relative to an expectation, which in this situation was becoming wealthier. Cognitive research shows people will create elaborate ways to lie to themselves or deceive others to meet personal expectations. One of the major contributing factors to the recent financial crisis was that people thought they could purchase expensive homes without equity with low income levels. The house of cards eventually collapsed with devastating effects. There were several contributing causes including lax regulations, a lack of personal responsibility, and systematic greed.

The sample of case studies presented in this book, while not representative of all catastrophic events, is relevant because it also comprises a very diverse sample representing many major current events. However, it is not representative because the event selection process was biased in favor of notable events as opposed to selecting them at random, in a statistical sense. But the patterns associated with the causes of failure are so significant that several conclusions can certainly be made from an analysis. As an example, the magnitude of the financial losses and human deaths shown in Table 6.1 is staggering. The associated events represent more than 18 million deaths and $675 billion dollars in property damage. Interestingly, many of the deaths occur annually. They are caused by health care failures, accidents, and injures. Let's examine the summarized tables to identify some of the major causes for the events. The information shown in Tables 6.1, 6.2, and 6.3 are either annual (e.g., repeating each year) or isolated events. A particularly disturbing statistic is calculated annually by the World Health Organization (WHO). Approximately 13 million people die from infectious or parasitic diseases each year.[1] Perhaps not all of the deaths are preventable, but the question remains, "How many of them could have been prevented if the resources were made available to people around the world?"

Ironically, we are both mesmerized and terrified by the infrequent but dramatic loss of life caused by airplane accidents, but remain indifferent to an average of 35,000 people dying each day from preventable infectious or parasitic diseases. Many of these people are children. To put the number in perspective, estimating the capacity of an airplane at approximately 200 people, the number of deaths by infectious or parasitic diseases is equivalent to 175 airplane accidents each day. If these deaths were caused by dramatic events such as that of an aircraft accident, the root causes would be quickly found and eliminated. The reason a horrific airplane accident is quickly and thoroughly investigated is that the people who are impacted have the resources to do investigative and preventive work. There is public and regulatory pressure to do so.

Earthquake destruction is another interesting analysis. Although earthquakes cannot be predicted with certainty, most injuries and deaths are caused by substandard construction practices and poor relief efforts. Many of the injuries and deaths caused by earthquakes are preventable. Compare the effects of the 2010 higher-magnitude earthquake that occurred in Chile to the lower-magnitude 2010 Haiti earthquake. Approximately 300 people died in Chile because of the higher-quality building infrastructure versus more than 200,000 in Haiti, where the major causes of death involved collapsed buildings.

The story becomes more dramatic if the percentages of deaths and expenses or costs are analyzed across the 40 events. In Table 6.2, the failure events are categorized by failure type, the underlying reasons, and estimated percentages of total. The failure types include intentional injuries,

Table 6.2
Major causes for different failure types

Major Type of Failure	Expenses	Total Deaths	Percentage of Expenses	Percentage of Deaths
Intentional injuries	—	1,618,800	0.00%	8.59%
Organizational issues	—	1,618,800	0.00%	8.59%
Accidents	—	**3,876,000**	**0.00%**	**20.56%**
Cognitive issues	—	3,876,000	0.00%	20.56%
Construction failures	**$1,794,000,000**	**4,069**	**0.27%**	**0.02%**
Cognitive and organizational issues	$294,000,000	13	0.04%	0.00%
Structural design and cognitive issues	$1,000,000,000	4,056	0.15%	0.02%
Technical design issues	$500,000,000	—	0.07%	0.00%
Environmental poisoning	**$76,000,000,000**	**27,542**	**11.26%**	**0.15%**
Organizational issues	$76,000,000,000	27,542	11.26%	0.15%
Health and safety: food contamination	**$35,000,000,000**	**5,000**	**5.18%**	**0.03%**
Organizational issues	$35,000,000,000	5,000	5.18%	0.03%
Health care system failures	—	**13,016,695**	**0.00%**	**69.06%**
Organizational issues	—	13,016,695	0.00%	69.06%
Information technology failures	**$1,437,400,000**	**23**	**0.21%**	**0.00%**
Organizational issues	$1,357,400,000	—	0.20%	0.00%
Technical design issues	$80,000,000	23	0.01%	0.00%
Mechanical and electrical design failures	**$9,000,000,000**	**498**	**1.33%**	**0.00%**
Cognitive and organizational issues	—	49	0.00%	0.00%
Technical design and organizational issues	$5,000,000,000	221	0.74%	0.00%
Technical design issues	$4,000,000,000	228	0.59%	0.00%
Natural disaster	**$221,000,000,000**	**300,544**	**32.73%**	**1.59%**
Structural design issues (deaths)	—	230,000	0.00%	1.22%
Structural design and organizational issues	$100,000,000,000	1,300	14.81%	0.01%
Structural design (expenses)	$121,000,000,000	69,244	17.92%	0.37%
Regulatory failures	**$315,670,000,000**	—	**46.76%**	**0.00%**

(*continued*)

Major Type of Failure	Expenses	Total Deaths	Percentage of Expenses	Percentage of Deaths
Organizational issues	$315,670,000,000	—	46.76%	0.00%
Software Viruses	$15,255,000,000	—	2.26%	0.00%
Cognitive issues	$14,235,000,000	—	2.11%	0.00%
Technical and organizational issues	$1,020,000,000	—	0.15%	0.00%
Grand Total	$675,156,400,000	18,849,171	100.00%	100.00%

Table 6.3
Major causes for unexpected and catastrophic failures

Major Causes of Failure	Expenses	Total Deaths	Percentage of Expenses	Percentage of Deaths
Cognitive and organizational issues	$294,000,000	62	0.04%	0.00%
Cognitive issues	$14,235,000,000	3,876,000	2.11%	20.56%
Organizational issues	$ 428,027,400,000	14,668,037	63.40%	77.82%
Structural design and cognitive issues	$1,000,000,000	4,056	0.15%	0.02%
Structural design and organizational issues	$100,000,000,000	1,300	14.81%	0.01%
Structural design issues	$121,000,000,000	299,244	17.92%	1.59%
Technical and organizational issues	$1,020,000,000	—	0.15%	0.00%
Technical design and organizational issues	$5,000,000,000	221	0.74%	0.00%
Technical design issues	$ 4,580,000,000	251	0.68%	0.00%
Grand Total	675,156,400,000	18,849,171	100.00%	100.00%

accidents, construction failures, and several others. The reasons for failure are also summarized and include organizational issues associated with policies and procedures, human errors associated with cognition, and technical issues associated with poor design, technology, and application environments. Many of these events were caused by combinations of causal factors. The label "Major Causes of Failure" used in Tables 6.2 and 6.3 shows these combinations.

In summary, environmental damage, natural disasters, and regulatory failures represent approximately 80 percent of all expenses. From a different perspective, accidents and health care system failures account for approximately 90 percent of total deaths. Much of the financial loss and many of the deaths were preventable to varying degrees. The financial impact from natural disasters is not entirely unexpected because the effects of the events could often have been mitigated to a larger extent. As an example, Haiti lies on top of an active earthquake fault that will periodically produce earthquakes having a high magnitude, but people do not recognize and act on this fact for several reasons. It is a well-known fact that Haiti's building infrastructure was of poor quality and could not withstand a major earthquake. The poor quality is the result of inadequate resources, but also political issues over many years (that is, organizational reasons). Complicating the situation is the reality that the countries surrounding Haiti have poor disaster planning (organizational factors).

The recent environmental damage caused by the Deepwater Horizon explosion in the eastern Gulf of Mexico should not have been unexpected. The oil and gas industry has fought regulatory oversight for many years. BP and its partners failed to create an effective disaster recovery plan or to develop redundant deep-water technologies that would be used if a major spill did occur in deep water (cognitive dissonance and organizational factors). The recent financial crisis was caused, in part, because governmental and private organizations failed to properly regulate the industry (again, cognitive dissonance and organizational factors).

In summary, catastrophic effects from these and other major events are not unexpected. But of course they are not expected by the people within these organizations. This is because the people within an organization are part of inherently complex systems that insulate them from information regarding the entire end-to-end system they work within. No one really understands how complicated systems work or their dynamic behavior. Groupthink is also often in play (e.g., it can't happen here, or, why us?). Complicating the situation are cognitive issues such as cognitive dissonance. To the people within these systems, catastrophic events are really unexpected. This is why the right types of regulatory oversight and additional methods are necessary to prevent these major failures. Unfortunately, the regulatory agencies themselves are subject to the same issues and can often become more of a problem than a solution. However, tools and methods exist to help overcome internal organizational biases regarding risk identification and mitigation as well as organizational responses to catastrophic events.

Failures of health care systems are caused, in part, by organizational issues, logistical system breakdowns, and resource constraints. These create chronic problems around the world. Millions of lives could be saved every year if we prevented or mitigated their effects. Unfortunately, sufficient preventive measures are not taken with the result that this chronic situation repeats every year. There are several reasons. People far away are invisible. Relief agencies have limited resources. There are also cultural, religious, and political barriers that sometimes need to be overcome prior to providing relief, such as local wars. The overall result is a failure to adequately respond to these types of chronic and non-dramatic catastrophic events.

People are also injured or killed after natural disasters occur. This is often because logistical systems are minimal or nonexistent. A chronic failure to fix these logistical systems guarantees the severity of major events will become increasingly greater because population densities will continue to increase in high-risk areas. Complicating these situations is that resources are becoming increasingly constrained in an environmentally challenged world. The expected result is that more people will be injured or killed if disasters occur. What should organizations do?

Unfortunately, some solutions will be difficult to implement. Countries around the world and individuals within these countries are competing for resources. Most likely this competition will increase over time. Contributing to an already difficult situation, political and other organizations continue to obscure the real causes for catastrophic events by failing to identify causal factors (that is, root causes). This is seen as a continuing failure to properly regulate some industries within the United States and around the world. These issues will most likely continue to occur. However, through the right regulations, the application of technology, the improvement of work, and upgraded organizational processes, we can help prevent or mitigate events caused by people or organizations. Also, although we cannot prevent a natural disaster from occurring, we can improve our preparation and relief responses. Many of the unexpected and catastrophic events occurring around us can be better managed.

Table 6.3 attributes approximately 98 percent of deaths and financial losses associated with catastrophic events to cognitive and organizational issues. It is true that horrific events such as airline accidents often monopolize the news; but they are minor events relative to their effects if compared to more serious ones. Also, their causes are usually combinations of human error, technology, or design. In other words, we need to begin moving toward an analysis of the contributions of social psychological factors to failure. Technical influences are important, but their effects are smaller.

Table 6.4 classifies catastrophic events into four categories. These are isolated events related to technology, events caused by poor project management, events having chronic causal factors, and major events including natural disasters. The events within each of the four categories were analyzed to identify root causes and strategies for implementing solutions.

Table 6.4
Why aren't solutions always implemented?

Failure Group	Root Causes Identified?	Solutions Implemented?	Major Issues	Some Examples
Isolated technical failures	Yes	Yes	Difficult to identify failures in advance	• I-35W Mississippi River Bridge (Minnesota) • April 25, 1986, Chernobyl Reactor 4 disaster • Denver Int'l Airport baggage system delay • 2009 Pitot tube failures on Airbus planes, Air France A430-300 (F-GLZL), Air France A340-300 (F-GLZN), and possibly Air France Flight 447, as well as other planes. • Toyota 2010 recall • Ford cruise switch control fires (late 1990s) • 2001 Ford/Firestone tire failures • and others
Isolated project failures	Yes	Sometimes	One-off projects, people-dependent, and subject to interference by stakeholders. Failures often reoccur.	• AMR reservation system for Budget's hotel and car bookings • Conversion to new order entry system from Baan Co. at Snap-On • Anderson SAP ERP issues for FoxMeyer • Greyhound Bus trips reservation and bus dispatch system issues • Hershey Foods IBM issues, SAP Manugistics • Norfolk Southern integration issues, Consolidated Rail • Oxford health plans billing processing, UNIX and Oracle • Grainger SAP issues • Trivalley Growers Oracle ERP integration • and others

Chronic issues	Yes	Only partially and with good results on an isolated basis.	Lack of priority and resources commitment, political instability, cultural and religious barriers to solutions.	• Food contamination 1996–1998 • 2003 SARS in Asia • Production problems with the H1N1 swine flu virus • Infectious and parasitic diseases worldwide • and others
Major events and natural disasters	Not for the actual natural event. But yes for the damage, death, and responses.	No, except for narrowly focused technical issues.	Political scapegoats; no failure analysis, root cause analysis, or process improvement training. Problems continue to occur in different major disaster contexts.	• 2005 Hurricane Katrina (New Orleans) • 2008 Sichuan earthquake • 1989 San Francisco earthquake • 2010 Haiti earthquake • 2010 Deepwater Horizon GoM oil spill • and others.

Isolated technical failures were often unexpected and catastrophic. Examples include the collapse of the I-35W Mississippi River bridge in Minnesota, the 1986 Chernobyl Reactor 4 disaster, the Denver International Airport baggage system delay, pitot tube failures on Airbus planes, the 2010 Toyota recalls, the Ford cruise switch control fires in the late 1990s, and the Ford versus Firestone tire failures in 2001. Although these were isolated technical failures, the causal factors resulted from human error at individual, group, and organizational levels. As an example, Ford and Firestone exchanged accusations of blame in 2001 for tire failures on Ford Explorers. Each organization accused the other of negligence. Ford said Firestone's tires separated at high speeds. Firestone accused Ford of designing the Explorer in a way that increased its center of gravity and made it more likely to roll over at high speeds if tires failed. There were also accusations that Ford's engineers recommended inflating the tires to a lower pressure to decrease the vehicles' center of gravity. Firestone claimed lower tire pressures increased heat buildup in its tires and increased the likelihood they would fail under normal driving conditions.

Recall, from the first chapter, a tire is a composite of several pieces of rubber and steel inserts that are compressed together under high heat and pressure to form a single composite tire. A tire can quickly break apart if stressed by heat beyond its strength. Organizational politics, group dynamics, and various cognitive issues ensured that investigation of the causal factors for this event would be difficult at best. Eventually, Ford and Firestone parted ways. Ford eventually contacted with another tire supplier and the failures disappeared.

This event is an example where technical issues escalated and dragged on, resulting in additional injuries, deaths, and financial losses. It didn't have to be this way. If the engineers and executives involved with these events had worked together objectively to identify the root causes for the failures, the effects could have been mitigated much earlier. Technical issues are difficult enough; interference by organizations, groups, key stakeholders, and individuals only obscures and delays effective failure analysis. As an example, once the root causes of technical failures listed in Table 6.4 were identified, solutions were found. However, the reasons for delay are common. They include a failure to quickly acknowledge errors because of insufficient information (a good reason), conflicts of interpretation, and organizational and legal considerations (bad reasons). Contrast the behaviors of the automotive industry with the aviation industry to see the different approaches for preventing and investigating causal factors to reduce the effects from an unexpected failure event. Attitudes and behaviors of the people tend to become internalized and characterize certain industries. One possible explanation is differing levels of regulatory control between the automotive and aviation industries.

The category containing project management failures is typical of complex software projects that depend on judgments and knowledge of many people for success. Examples of major events analyzed within this category include the AMR reservation system, the FoxMeyer SAP implementation, and other major enterprise-wide software and hardware implementations. In these failure events, the root cause investigations were well done, predominantly because they were subject to litigation to assign personal and organizational blame. However, solutions to these types of events are not easily transferrable to future projects because root causes are often nontechnical and associated with organizational, group, or individual behaviors.

In these projects, issues of attitude and behavior lurk beneath the surface of the implementation teams and key stakeholders. All the cognitive and group issues discussed in earlier chapters can come into play. However, the situation continues to improve. Over the past several decades, effective project management methods and best practices for software design have been created to help manage these types of projects. There has also been success in spite of human dependencies. Examples include improving communications by gathering customer requirements in advance, properly managing projects using tollgate reviews with customers and key stakeholders, and using many of the project management methods discussed in the first chapter.

The events contained in the third category are chronic. They are particularly troubling because the causal factors preventing a solution have a technical basis and solutions are often known, but not implemented. Typical examples include food contamination in the United States, vaccine production problems, and disease and deaths caused by infectious and parasitic diseases across the world. In the latter situation, many of these deaths are preventable if resources were made available to the United Nations and worldwide relief organizations and efficiently used by local governments. The unfortunate truth is these problems will become worse as the world's population density increases, resources become scarcer, environmental damage accelerates, and populations of people are dislocated. Although the causes are known, solutions are often poorly implemented. The reasons are many. Lurking below the surface of these catastrophic events are often political and economic instabilities, resource constraints, and organizational inefficiencies at global and local levels.

The last category includes several well-known major events and natural disasters. Examples include the 2005 Hurricane Katrina response, the 2008 Sichuan earthquake, the 1989 San Francisco earthquake, and the 2010 Haiti earthquake. The root causes of these events can be considered from three perspectives. First, the actual timing of the events could not be predicted with certainty (day and hour). However the impact if an event occurred could be predicted with a high degree of certainty. As an example, for the 2010 Haiti earthquake, the resultant damage was not unexpected based on its poor infrastructure quality and population density. The incremental damage relative to injuries and deaths should also have not been unexpected given the lack of relief planning for the region. So, although the specific timing of an event's occurrence cannot be predicted, its contributing factors, which cause injury, death, and damage, can be predicted.

The situation becomes problematic if analyses of relief efforts are considered. Again looking at the recent Haiti earthquake, at press time, people are still living in tents; any remaining building infrastructure remains unreinforced(hopefully future building infrastructure will be upgraded and reinforced), and the countries surrounding Haiti have not modified relief planning and systems for future disasters. Disasters are likely to occur in the region. A major contributor to unnecessary injuries and deaths in Haiti was the low quality of logistical and relief coordination systems surrounding Haiti. Haiti itself must plan for these events and its neighbors should do the same. So why is there a continual lack of preparation between countries in the region regarding providing basic humanitarian aid?

The 2005 Hurricane Katrina event and the recent 2010 Deepwater Horizon Gulf of Mexico explosion have several similar characteristics. The exact timing of the events was not predictable, but a future event was expected. Also, after both events, major damage occurred either because of a general lack of effective risk and contingency planning or a poor relief response. As an example, Katrina reached a category 5 hurricane before its intensity fell to a category 3 as it made landfall. A category 5 hurricane was expected to occur eventually in the Gulf of Mexico region. However, after decades of knowing the limitations of the levees, authorities did not modify their infrastructures to withstand such an event. The residents of New Orleans also lived in low-lying areas that people knew would become quickly flooded if New Orleans's levees failed. There was little or no response planning or communication before the event or in its aftermath. People were encouraged to take appropriate action only as the catastrophic event occurred.

The 2010 Deepwater Horizon event had similar characteristics. Drilling in deep water is dangerous. But BP and its partners failed to develop control technology to match their operational technology or to develop realistic risk and contingency plans. The event's causal factors are mostly known. There was also political interference at local, state, and national levels. However, there is also increasing pressure to continue deep-water drilling despite limited technological solutions for managing future accidents. What's the answer?

One answer is that the oil and gas industry must itself create its control systems, both technical and human. Its technology is too specialized for outsiders to be of much use. Higher operational cost is also an issue. Higher exploration and manufacturing costs have political consequences because of the industry's size and reach. Cost pressures create political pressure to keep exploring and producing oil and gas regardless of risks. Also in play are ingrained attitudes and behaviors by all stakeholders including politicians, the workers involved, organizations in the industry, the government, and the people who use oil and gas (you and me).

There is a long list of catastrophic environmental events caused by the oil and gas industry. This implies there will be others in the future and most likely of similar magnitude and effect. Some people do not believe another catastrophe will occur. But history is not on their side. If we consider potential risk and likelihood of recurrence, we should also consider that experts have said Deepwater Horizon employees violated industry best practices. This occurs frequently in many industries. It also occurred in 2005 at BP's Texas City refinery. This was discussed by Andrew Hopkins in his now prophetic book titled *A Failure to Learn,* wherein he discussed BP's Texas Oil refinery explosion as an event caused by cognitive and organizational issues.[2] The book was prophetic because, since its publication, other BP failures such as Alaska pipeline leaks, the 2010 Deepwater Horizon explosion, and repeated safety violations have occurred. It's a long list. However, it should also be remembered that other organizations in the oil and gas industry have similar issues to varying degree. According to Hopkins, one major failure often portends future ones if root causes are not identified and effective solutions implemented to prevent recurrences. This is especially true if the underlying reasons for failure are human and organizational rather than technical. But a question remains: How do we prevent and manage catastrophic events around the world and in different industries?

Isolated technical failures can occur in design, production, distribution, and use by customers. As we now know, there are many reasons such as requirements poorly translated and the use of poor design and production practices. There are several factors that exacerbate these types of issues. Complexity is a major cause for technical failures. A second occurs when there are mismatches between customer expectations and a design's functions and features. Mismatches result in misuse by customers and end users. Isolated technological failures are often caused by technology constraints, but, they are sometimes the result of poor decisions regarding design or execution.

Technology failures also occur if designers do not understand application environments in which products and services are used. This is seldom their fault. Application environments can be very extreme and their effects simply not known, especially for products incorporating new technology. Designers are usually very experienced with previously known application environments and stresses; but unexpected technical failures seldom occur in these applications. Rather they are caused by new application environments in which stresses are unexpected and cause sudden failure. Examples include the collapse of a bridge due to corrosion or the breakup of an aircraft high above the surface of the earth in severe weather because of mechanical forces. In these hostile environments, physical structures are mechanically stressed by tensional, compressive, and shearing forces until they break apart.

Service systems, that fail should be similarly analyzed to prevent future failures. In these systems the expected demand on a system must be known over extended periods of time and conditions to create sufficient capacity to maintain service levels. Demand patterns vary by hour, day, week, month, and year depending on the type of industry. As an example, a call center answers incoming customer calls and provides information. Staffing levels must be matched to ensure calls are answered within an agreed-upon service level time and the correct information is provided to customers. Low operational cost is also a goal. The types of incoming calls, the skills of available agents, changing demand patterns and other factors must all be understood to design and operate these service systems, or failures are likely to occur.

More effective work can always be done by designers; they unfortunately cannot anticipate every failure type. Designers translate customer and business (stakeholder) requirements into specifications describing features, functions, forms, and aesthetic appearance. Although the design process is usually straightforward, it is always prone to error; there are many factors that can derail it. In addition to technological and application factors, others include individual and team dysfunctions, and organizational interference. However, we also know design teams sometimes fool themselves and make false assumptions and decisions. It can happen anywhere within a design process: gathering customer requirements, testing and analysis, selecting design alternatives, and other activities. Even if a design team is on track and is making the right decisions, interference by a few people can create situations in which poor decisions are made. Lost sales may be one result, or the consequences could be more severe. Some of the events discussed in earlier chapters demonstrated how failures can result from a deterioration of a design process.

Cognitive issues also affect isolated technical failures because they influence activities related to design, production, distribution, and use of products and services. As an example, cognitive dissonance will cause people to resort to clever ways to reduce dissonance. They will resort to lying and misleading others to maintain feelings of comfort. They even lie to themselves consciously or unconsciously by filtering information or selectively recalling memories. To the extent this behavior is not controlled within design teams through project management and facilitative methods, it has negative effects on the design of reliable products and services. Cognitive issues also impact how consumers evaluate, use, and misuse products and services. Even designs that are superior in many ways may fail in certain circumstances when designers do not consider cognitive factors.

It is very difficult, even impossible, for individuals to do work if not supported by their organization or if key stakeholders interfere with work activities. Unfortunately, these are common occurrences in many organizations. In contrast, there exist what are called high-reliability organizations. These organizations have extraordinary safety records in very dangerous work environments. An important characteristic of these organizations is that decision making responsibility is diffused and assigned at an appropriate local organizational level. This assigned level has timely situational information, understands its meaning, and knows the required correct actions. There is no interference by powerful stakeholders in its daily work activities. Instead, decisions are made by people best qualified and who are closest to the work. In contrast, for some of the major disasters discussed in this book, there were examples of interference by key stakeholders either in the design process, how the system operated, or when responding in the aftermath of an event.

Organizational structure and culture exert major influences on how products and services are designed and supported. Some organizations have effective cultures while others do not. Several of the events discussed in this book show people were not held responsible for decisions that caused others injury, death, or financial hardship. There is a general lack of accountability that is common to catastrophic events. Few people are jailed, punished, or forced to make restitution for errors and mistakes. In fact, the larger the damage, the less likely people are held individually responsible. Imagine if a gunman went into a store and killed people; there would be swift justice. However, such is not the situation in industrial accidents where responsibility is diffused. There is little incentive, other than personal ethics, to do better. Personal ethics used to be enough incentive, but are no longer.

It is also surprising that even if an organization knows there may be situations in which products and services fail, risk analyses and contingency planning are often not done. Why don't they do planning and risk analysis? The reasons are many. There is a genuine belief, by individuals and groups, that failures cannot occur. Another reason is organizational complexity. It overwhelms people who are already very busy working. There are also ethical lapses within organizations.

Also, some organizations do not want to spend money or allocate time to conduct risk analyses or contingency planning. Interestingly the results of an initial cost-benefit analysis quickly change after an unexpected and catastrophic event occurs. Organizations believe circumstances today will likely reflect those in the future, so risk planning and mitigation are not useful. However, absent such analyses and planning, failures are likely to occur. There are also likely to be breakdowns in logistical systems. These affect relief responses. If an organization slowly or ineffectively reacts to an event (e.g., a poor relief response), the amount of personal and property damage increases. The 2005 Hurricane Katrina, the 2010 Haiti earthquake, and the 2010 Deepwater Horizon Gulf of Mexico explosion events quickly come to mind.

As technology supporting the design, production, distribution, and use of products and services continuously evolves, organizations need to create control and management systems to predict, mitigate, and eliminate failures. There are many examples where these activities currently occur in very different industries. First consider that as buildings were built higher and higher, fire prevention and mitigation technology also changed to either extinguish fires at higher elevations or increase the capabilities of responders to work at higher elevations. Also, computer security continually evolves by creating forensic tools and methods to prevent, detect, or eliminate security vulnerabilities as technology becomes more sophisticated.

In contrast, recent events in the eastern Gulf of Mexico showed the technology for sealing wells did not keep pace with the drilling technology created for use in deep water. This is an industry problem. Interestingly, BP quickly created rudimentary control technology such as well capping within 90 days rather than 30 years after the explosion and oil spill. The conclusion is that the technology necessary for failure prevention or mitigation, that is, control technologies, must keep pace with production technology. This is especially important when it is used in dangerous application environments having a potential to cause widespread injuries, deaths, and property damage. In service systems, analogues include the communications and logistical systems used to respond to and manage disasters, that is, relief resources and systems. This helps create effective solutions as well as risk mitigation and response plans.

Table 6.4 analyzes the 40 events relative to root cause analyses. Surprisingly, the larger and more damaging an event, the less likely its root causes are fully investigated to levels where solutions can be identified to manage future events. As an example, isolated technical events such as aircraft accidents are typically analyzed by experts to identity the cause of failure.

The information is incorporated into regulatory and operational systems to prevent future failures. A very methodical process is followed in such situations. In contrast, catastrophic events caused by project management errors and mistakes that are influenced by human judgment and prone to interventions by people and groups (e.g., key stakeholders) continue to occur. Although people, organizations, and systems continually change, the same mistakes are made, but by different people and in different circumstances. Root cause analyses are often not completed unless there are legal issues. Legal issues force an objective investigation of why a system failed because there are claimed damages such as injuries, deaths, or financial loss. However, the people change, and the result is that similar failures reoccur, but in different organizations and projects.

As catastrophic events become larger in scale and more complex (e.g., chronic issues and natural disasters), the likelihood of effective root cause analyses diminishes. Solutions for eliminating chronic issues are often known. But there are resource and other constraints that prevent them from being implemented. There are also issues from group and organizational perspectives. Cultural, political, and religious differences sometimes hinder the implementations of solutions. Natural events share some of these characteristics, but because of their widespread impact they are influenced by many groups. One reason is the complexity of the events, but also organizational, cultural, and political interference quickly force out logical debate and methodological studies of causal factors. Another issue is that causal studies are made only at higher levels, and not in sufficient detail to identify root causes or solutions to prevent and manage similar events in the future.

Although major events and natural disasters occur in different forms (floods, hurricanes, environmental contamination), they have common characteristics relative to extent of damage, political influences, causal analyses, and solutions. They are also likely to reoccur in the future, but with location and timing unknown. Although natural disasters cannot be predicted with certainty, relief systems such as logistics and communications should be designed to manage responses to these events to reduce damage. Historically, major relief efforts have been ad hoc and depended on publicity. The 2010 Haiti earthquake and 2005 Hurricane Katrina responses come to mind. Unfortunately, analyses of poor relief responses are seldom driven to a root cause level. Nor are solutions implemented to prepare for future events. As a result, they are likely to occur in one form or another.

Two interesting articles were recently published by the *Providence Journal*. One described the 2010 Pakistan flooding, which caused the dislocation of more than one 1 million people. In the first article, it was reported that relief efforts were managed by the United Nations, the Pakistani Army, and local and international agencies.[3] The relief response was well done given the sudden flooding over only 30 days and the difficult geography of the region. But according to a second article in the *Providence Journal,* more than 8 million people are still in dire need of help.[4] The article complained Americans were giving little aid to the Pakistani relief effort. A few observations can be made regarding the activities associated with this relief response. First, there are usually many organizations involved in these types of relief efforts. As a result, unnecessary complexity is created that strains communication and logistical systems. Second, there is an overreliance on private donations, especially from Western economies, and from the United States in particular. Logistical, communication, and management systems supporting relief efforts should be more simply designed and standardized; fewer organizations should be directly involved and resources should be regionally staged for emergencies. These systems shouldn't be operated hat-in-hand and begging for resources and coordination. People are dying.

In an analysis of the many events discussed in this book, common underlying contributors to the damage caused by their aftermath emerge. These contributing factors have been discussed one by one in previous chapters. Most likely my list is not exhaustive. But, for now, they suffice for organizing what superficially appear to be different catastrophic events. The 13 factors shown in Table 6.5, if present, increase the likelihood of similar future catastrophic events occurring within an organization or its industry (near-miss analogy). They are associated with an organization's previous failures, not creating risk analyses or contingency planning, regulatory laxness, the use of dangerous equipment, dangerous application environments, complex systems, highly manual or people-dependent processes, a significant potential for financial loss or loss of life if failures occur, numerous people who could potentially be impacted across large regions, political sensitivity to failures, the application technology is ahead of control technology, relief efforts are dependent on complicated logistical systems and scarce resources, and root cause analysis and mitigation have historically not been effectively done. Let's discuss these 13 factors to show why they are relevant for risk analysis. The method uses a simple rating scale, between 0 and 13. The likelihood percentages are calculated as a percentage of the total number (13) of potential factors. A simple comparison was made with respect to a small number of events. Some interesting insights can be gained using this method.

A major theme of this book is that organizational culture has a dramatic impact on the attitudes and behaviors of individuals and groups. Some cultures have a higher likelihood of having a major failure event than others. This is why culture in the context of previous failures has been chosen a recurrence factor. Experiments have repeatedly shown people will modify

Table 6.5
Risk recurrence analysis

Risk Recurrence Factor	2010 Toyota Recall	Anderson SAP ERP issues for FoxMeyer	2009 Continental Flight 3407 Near Buffalo	2010 Haiti Earthquake	2005 Hurricane Katrina	2009 SEC Failures	2010 Deepwater Horizon GoM Oil Spill
1. Organizational and cultural issues resulted in significant previous failures	N	Y	Y	N	N	Y	Y
2. A lack of risk analysis and contingency planning	Y	Y	N	Y	Y	Y	Y
3. Regulatory laxness	N	N	Y	Y	Y	Y	Y
4. Dangerous equipment	Y	N	Y	N	N	N	Y
5. Dangerous application environment	Y	N	Y	Y	Y	N	Y
6. Complex systems	N	Y	Y	Y	Y	Y	Y
7. People dependent or cognition issues	N	Y	Y	Y	Y	Y	Y
8. Significant potential financial loss or loss of life if failure occurs	Y	Y	Y	Y	Y	Y	Y
9. Would impact many people across latge geography	Y	Y	N	Y	Y	Y	Y
10. Politically sensitive	Y	N	N	Y	Y	Y	Y
11. Application technology ahead of control technology	N	N	N	N	N	Y	Y

(continued)

Table 6.5 (*continued*)

Risk Recurrence Factor	2010 Toyota Recall	Anderson SAP ERP issues for FoxMeyer	2009 Continental Flight 3407 Near Buffalo	2010 Haiti Earthquake	2005 Hurricane Katrina	2009 SEC Failures	2010 Deepwater Horizon GoM Oil Spill
12. Dependent on complicated logistical systems and resources for failure mitigation	N	N	N	Y	Y	Y	Y
13. Poor root cause analysis and mitigation	N	N	N	Y	Y	Y	N
Score(0-13)	**6**	**6**	**7**	**10**	**10**	**11**	**12**
% Recurrence	46%	46%	54%	77%	77%	85%	92%
Recurrence likelihood	**MED**	**MED**	**MED**	**HIGH**	**HIGH**	**HIGH**	**HIGH**

Risk recurrence classification: 0–4 low (0%–37%); 5–8 medium (38%–68%); 9–13 high (69%–100%)

and engage in very destructive behaviors based on group expectations and demands. This fact has important relevance for explaining certain types of failures. An organization may have a very proactive safety culture, good policies, and well-established procedures to enforce ethical and safe conduct amongst its employees. But at a local level a small group of employees or even strong-willed individuals may decide to violate policies and procedures for a number of reasons. Some violations are intentional acts of misconduct or even willful sabotage.

Cognitive and sensory errors are always present. They dull our minds and obfuscate our thoughts. In these situations, people subconsciously readjust their opinions to better reflect either personal attitudes or biases of their work group. They convince themselves that the things they believe and do are correct. Typical statements reflecting these beliefs include, "The procedure doesn't reflect what we need to do," and "It's not risky to violate this procedure because the likelihood of a failure is low." Unexpected and catastrophic events based on these false beliefs and resultant behaviors are common. The 1986 Chernobyl and 2005 Texas City explosions are two examples. In both events, workers at a local level convinced themselves that violating safety procedures would not cause failure. The situation becomes more complicated when executives and managers make modifications to established policies and procedures. This was a contributor to the 2010 Deepwater Horizon explosion.

There are no easy answers. But organizations should be vigilant. As an example, no one person should be able to easily change established policies without being required to undergo a review and approval by independent parties. This is a basis for auditing and safety systems management. When organizations violate these control strategies, failures are more likely to occur. A policy of no exceptions should be applied unless exceptions are approved through formal reviews. However, these reviews should be simple, standardized, and mistake proofed; otherwise, the sixth reoccurrence factor, complex systems, becomes operative. This discussion assumes an organization has written policies and procedures regarding how its products and services are designed, produced, distributed, and used. Unfortunately, some organizations do not.

The likelihood of failure also increases if risk analyses and contingency planning have not been done. The likelihood for failure will be higher in these situations. This is why it is a second risk recurrence factor. If a risk analysis has been properly done, weak points within a system will be identified. Potential failures will be prevented from occurring or their impact will be mitigated to varying degrees. Risk analyses are usually completed for the design of products and services or logistical systems, but not always. This is also a cultural issue. There are many excuses for not completing them. However, the result is a poor understanding of the ways in which products and services may fail. The likelihood of failures will be higher for these systems.

Figure 1.1 listed several common risks that should be considered by design teams. These included scheduling, cost, technology, performance, market demand, supply and capacity, and legal and regulatory environmental risks. Also, recall the failure mode and effects analysis (FMEA). It is one of several methods used by design teams as well as other groups within organizations to identify ways in which their products, services, and logistical systems fail. Process maps and analytical methods are also useful for analyzing current operations and historical information respectively. Risk analyses are especially important for designing and managing complex systems that have many places where failures occur. The more such systems depend on manual operations, the greater the likelihood for errors. This is because policies and procedures can be ignored or misinterpreted by employees. An up-front analysis using process maps, FMEAs, and similar methods can help identify potential risks and ways to eliminate or reduce their impact. Organizations should also analyze causal factors (root causes) for failures to identify effective solutions if it experienced previous catastrophic event. This strategy will help prevent recurrences.

Once a risk has been identified, contingency planning is used to identify ways to prevent and manage it. Contingency planning requires that people be trained to understand the actions required for monitoring risks before failures occur as well as the specific activities necessary to eliminate, mitigate, and manage the effects of risk. Many of the catastrophic events discussed in this book had a high likelihood of occurrence. However, subsequent damage, relative to life and property, was greatly magnified because there were no effective contingency plans in existence during relief efforts.

A lack of effective regulatory oversight is the third risk recurrence factor. An analysis of the many events discussed in this book shows poor regulatory oversight is a major contributor to failure. This is true across diverse industries as well as different types of products and services. Regulations are dependent on political decisions regarding specifics and extent. As a result they range from nonexistent to ineffective to effective. Some regulations may even be damaging, and create problems or unintended consequences. If there are no external rules and regulations to help balance competing interests of organizations and community stakeholders, then the likelihood of failure or its effects will be higher. There are many examples where organizations design and manufacture unsafe products such as vehicles that catch on fire, or where the organizations provide faulty services, commit financial frauds, or pass internal costs to a community, for example, via improper disposal of hazardous wastes. There are many others.

The damage caused by organizations acting only in self-interest is seen by even a cursory examination of the catastrophic events discussed in this book. Without regulatory oversight people are injured, die, and lose property. But, at another extreme, excessive regulations introduce complexity, which creates confusion. Complexity contributes to failures since there are many handoffs from one organization or operation to another or one person to another. The result is confusion of how things are done. Only in retrospect do we see not enough regulations or the wrong types of laws and regulations.

Political influences and outright interference are contributors to regulatory issues. They also influence how failure investigations are done. As an example, typical behavior patterns in the aftermath of a catastrophic event are first public outrage, then political wrangling over who is to blame, and finally public investigations by elected politicians having little understanding of the technical issues surrounding an event and who are beholden to special interests. Some, but not all, of these public forums are confusing. They also yield little information for the causes of failure. Solutions are seldom put into place or are weak. This is especially true for logistical systems related to relief responses. The result is a continuing series of major failures whose effects are magnified beyond what should occur. Hurricane Katrina comes to mind.

Good regulations are an essential feature for making product and services safer. It's not hard to see why this is true. Serious issues occur if, despite a catastrophic failure, governmental and private organizations fail to investigate reasons (root causes) at a level where effective actions in the form of regulation, law, or process improvements should be taken to prevent a recurrence. However, even if there are good regulations in place, they may be ignored or weakly enforced. The recent issues within the financial and housing industries are examples.

A third article recently published in the *Providence Journal* discussed a situation in which an Iowa egg farmer repeatedly violated Iowa's environmental laws. He was labeled a "habitual violator."[5] The article was precipitated by a massive egg recall upon discovery of salmonella contamination. The mode of transmission is from rodent droppings to chicken ovaries and into eggs. Several hundred million eggs have been recalled. The major organization involved was Wright Country Egg. It has paid millions of dollars in fines for willful violations of law. But, what will happen if people die? If these chronic violations of law continue to occur, catastrophic failures should be also expected to recur. Iowa's regulators took action, but the system was not effective for protecting the general public. Maybe the laws and regulations should be stricter?

It's interesting to see businesses continually fight regulations of any type. Effective regulations, if fair and evenly enforced by agencies, help protect the reputations and financial interests of organizations being regulated as well as the general public. As an example, several major organizations have been destroyed in recent years. Examples that quickly come to mind include Arthur Anderson, Enron, WorldCom, Sunbeam, and Global Crossing, to name a few. There are many others. An analogy for these industries would be parents not enforcing children to do homework and the children thinking they are better off. The consequences of things left undone or poorly done catch up with people and organizations. A lack of effective regulatory oversight should be a red flag that bad things will eventually happen. This is why it is chosen a recurrence factor.

Some industries are inherently more dangerous. What is a dangerous application environment? Examples include exposures to extremes of temperature, elevation, radiation, light, noise, vibration, chemicals, and similar stressing factors. In some extreme environments people must be protected with safety equipment to prevent injury or death. A person working in an office is exposed to hazards such as power cords on the floor, bumping into other people, tripping, , and similar hazards. In contrast, people working 100 miles out in the ocean, drilling for oil and using complicated and powerful equipment under adverse environmental conditions seven days a week and 12 hours a day, are exposed to much more dangerous working conditions. It is true the level of safety awareness is significantly increased under such adverse conditions, but given the potential for loss of life, injuries, property damage, and environmental contamination from accidents, even a very small occurrence likelihood will over time result in a catastrophic event.

It is generally not known that there are thousands of oil fields around the world. Each contains numerous oil wells. These wells are usually connected to larger production by a facility designed to separate water and contaminates from the oil. The large number of wells increases the likelihood of a failure. There is also a large number of metal-producing mines in the world. The number is estimated at 2,500.[6] There are also thousands of smaller mines. Mining is also an industry where working conditions are inherently hazardous. As a result, although not analyzed in Table 6.5, mining organizations would have many of the same recurrence factors as organizations operating within the oil and gas industry. As an example, the inevitable result of operating within hazardous conditions is that there have been 10 major mining disasters in the United States alone in the past 20 years.[7] Almost every week there are stories of other mining disasters around the world. The conclusion is that some industries are inherently more dangerous than others and technologies have limitations.

Interestingly, oil and gas or mining are not the most dangerous occupations for workers. A listing of the most dangerous occupations shows loggers and fisherman to have the highest fatality rates amongst all occupations. They have approximately 70–100 deaths per 100,000 workers. Although these occupations have higher death rates than others, because they employ less people, they have less total number of deaths each year. In contrast, truck driving has a low death rate, but because there are many truckers, several hundred people die each year. In contrast, airline accidents kill only a few hundred people annually.[8] People also die through falls, assaults, and violence (especially women), fires, falling objects, and many other ways in the United States and across the world. However, there is a variety of root causes associated with these lower incident rate events. This makes it difficult to lower the rates. The practical interpretation is that recurrence risk for dangerous working environments that can injure and kill people or cause significant damage is higher. People become confused when comparing rates and total deaths. Numbers aren't always what they appear.

The types of equipment used in an industry also influence the likelihood of failure because they injure or kill people if not properly maintained or if misused. Property damage or environmental contamination may also occur. This is why it is a risk recurrence factor. Even the best-designed equipment used under optimum conditions may fail because of manufacturing flaws and stress overloading. Also, well-maintained equipment has a finite useful life. The likelihood of unexpected and catastrophic failure increases if maintenance is poor or workers don't follow instructions.

Injuries and deaths associated with electromechanical equipment are common. This includes equipment used in our homes and offices. In fact, we are surrounded by dangerous equipment that can quickly injure or kill us. Consider a lawnmower. Its blade speed is several thousand revolutions per minute. This calculates to a few hundred miles per hour. The rotational speed makes it a very powerful and dangerous piece of equipment. As an example, in 2006 there were 133 deaths from lawnmower accidents.[9] Approximately 77,000 people were treated for injuries related to lawnmowers in 2006. These injuries included lacerations and lost body parts. The lawnmower is a very dangerous device. People do not understand its power. But how many times have parents forced young children to mow grass without proper training or protective equipment? The situation becomes more serious when larger, more powerful, and more complicated equipment is operated in environments where a single failure can injure and kill hundreds or even thousands of people. This type of event occurred several decades ago.

In the early morning hours of December 3 in 1984, a cloud of methyl isocyanate (MIC) traveled slowly from a Union Carbide plant in Bhopal, Madhya Pradesh, India, into the adjacent town. This chemical, MIC, is an intermediate used in the production of various carbamate pesticides. It is highly toxic. There are differing theories for the causes of the exothermic reactions that ruptured Tank 610 at the plant, which was filled with more than 40 tons of MIC. It is a generally accepted fact that the exothermic explosion was caused when water entered the tank, increasing its temperature and pressure and resulting in the release of MIC through emergency venting.[10] As the deadly gas travelled into the town, thousands of people were quickly killed and thousands more were killed over time because of exposure to MIC. Tens of thousands of serious injuries also occurred over the ensuing months and years, as reported by the Indian government.

In retrospect, it can be seen that several recurrence factors listed in Table 6.5 were present prior to the accident. The organizational culture within the chemical plant punished workers for complaining of safety violations; also there had been many repeated safety violations found through audits. The effect of failure, if it occurred, was expected to be catastrophic, and there were many manual operations dependent on employee training, skills, perceptions, and behaviors. The resulting catastrophic event should not have been unexpected if the many recurrence risk factors had been identified and if plans were created to prevent or mitigate failure occurrence. Although this event exhibited several risk recurrence factors, our intent is to discuss the equipment within the plant at the time of the accident to illustrate why dangerous equipment is a risk recurrence factor.

A chemical plant is a system consisting of many integrated subsystems. These contain different types of specialized equipment that must be operated carefully by well-trained people. The specific types of equipment vary by industry. A chemical plant is designed to produce either chemical precursors or final products. It should be noted that a final product is a relative term in that one facility's final product may become another's raw material (precursor material). From an outsider's perspective, a chemical plant can be considered in its entirety a machine. The difference between a simple machine and a chemical plant are the many complicated manual operations necessary to maintain and operate equipment, insert materials, perform maintenance, and control its operations. To do this, sophisticated control systems and equipment are used, employees need to be well trained, and contingency or reaction plans must be created describing procedures to be taken if things fail. Information must be freely shared, especially when things go wrong.

At the time water entered the tank, the exothermic reaction quickly raised the tank's temperature and pressure to release MIC through emergency venting; at the time, safety systems were not properly functioning. Critical valves were also not operational and pipes were corroded because of poor maintenance. Employee training and safety systems were also in disarray.

Many of the recurrence factors listed in Table 6.5 were active prior to and during the accident.

The local facility management, that is, the organizational culture, exacerbated these recurrence risks. After the accident, Union Carbide paid only some several hundred million dollars to compensate the thousands of Bhopal victims and their families and the Union Carbide Executives were not punished. As an example, its chief executive officer, Mr. Warren Anderson, left India when he was released on bail on December 7, 1984.[11] In 1992, he was declared a fugitive of culpable homicide by a Bhopal court for failing to appear in person. Whether he is guilty or innocent for contributing to the poor maintenance and operating at the plant will not be known because he never appeared at a trial where the truth would have been determined by an Indian court of law. However, in retrospect, it is obvious there was little incentive for the organization to have done better.

Decisions regarding equipment design, maintenance, and use are directly controlled by executive decisions. The disaster that occurred at the Union Carbide plant in Bhopal, Madhya Pradesh, India, is only one of many examples where executives make very poor decisions that have catastrophic consequences. A deeper analysis by Dan Kurzman in his book titled *A Killing Wind: Inside Union Carbide and the Bhopal Catastrophe* mentions that teams of safety experts from Union Carbide's Danbury, Connecticut, office warned of a possible reaction in the methyl isocyanate tank and that regulation by Indian authorities was poor due in part to conflicts of interest.[12] The culpability of their American business partner, Union Carbide, is still not clear. However, dangerous equipment, especially when not well maintained or operated properly, is a major cause for catastrophic failures.

Complex systems have many places where failures can occur. To the extent these systems depend on manual operations, there is a greater likelihood of errors and mistakes. Policies and procedures can also be ignored or misinterpreted. A working environment becomes dangerous if poorly trained people, dangerous equipment, dangerous materials, and other high-risk objects interact. It is particularly dangerous if the risk factors combine (e.g., dangerous equipment operated in dangerous working environments using complicated work procedures while interpreting ambiguous information).

It is obvious that the more components there are in a system, the greater the likelihood it will fail, assuming no redundancies. As an example, if a system has a component with an expected failure of 5 percent over 1,000 hours of use and two such components are placed in sequence (series, that is, they are independent), the likelihood of failure increases to approximately 10 percent.[13] However, complicated systems have more than two components as well as different types. They are combinations of machines, people, materials, information technology, and other factors that have risks.

Complexity also prevents people from fully understanding how a system works. The result is people only partially know its functions and features. There are several reasons. First, a system's components may be geographically dispersed. One example is a design process scattered across the world. One group may gather customer requirements, another may create designs, and a third group may sell the product or service. Management systems and controls are created to manage these complex group interactions, but few are perfect. Second, a system usually consists of different advanced technologies. Each technology may require specialized knowledge and training to use. Third, underlying modeling assumptions that are used to create and manage a system may not be generally known except to the original designers. In these situations, no one person may know everything. Making matters worse, the original designers may not have correctly modeled the system or not analyzed all usage conditions or component interactions. In other words, their assumptions may have been wrong.

Component interactions are unusual observed effects when factors occur in combination. A simple example of an interaction between several components is the heat produced from an exothermic reaction that depends on certain unique combinations such as levels of temperature, pressure, and a catalyst. Only certain combinations of these components or factors will cause an exothermic reaction. Call monitoring operations is another example where interactions occur between several components. One important measurement of such systems is the average time to answer customer calls and provide accurate information. This is also called the average handling time (AHT). It is a known when system capacity, that is, staffing and skill levels are properly matched to incoming call volumes, AHT is relatively constant. But when incoming call volumes approach the capacity of the system, waiting time increases nonlinearly. The average waiting time (AHT) is calculated using queuing models of the system. An untrained person cannot know how such a system functions unless the person is trained and provided tools. For this reason, call monitoring centers visually display real-time metrics that are easily seen and interpreted. In the background supporting these systems are information technology systems that manage and balance incoming and outgoing demand across a call center system by automatically transferring calls from one facility to another anywhere in the world using queuing models.

Complex systems of many types are also often patched over time to create new features and functions. Software code is an example where hundreds or even millions of lines of code are routinely added to existing software code (patched) to create functionality or features, or to fix issues called software bugs. In combination, these software coding modifications increase the likelihood things will go wrong because absent design redundancy, everything must work together. Complex systems have issues, but, throw in human error such as the effects of cognitive factors described earlier and it is easy to understand why complexity is a major contributor to catastrophic events.

We know human cognitive limitations cause errors and failures. Processes depending on manual operations such as people doing work tasks, audits, inspection, and similar activities must be considered riskier than automated processes in that they have higher recurrence risks than well-designed automated systems. Automated machines such as those helping assemble automobiles using robots are examples where low variation of work tasks can be achieved at levels humans cannot perform. Prior to using robots, welding, painting, and assembly operations took longer, were more costly, and had higher defect levels. A review of the many events shown in Tables 6.3 and 6.4 shows many of them were caused in part by cognition errors. In fact, Table 6.3 shows catastrophic events often occur because several recurrence risks act in combination with cognitive error.

The potential magnitude of an event is another recurrence risk. Events having a potential to cause significantly higher numbers of injuries, deaths, or greater financial loss or environmental damage increase the likelihood an event will be catastrophic. Contrasting examples include losing power to a home versus to a city, or a person making a wrong bank deposit versus a major financial fraud of hundreds of millions of dollars. If the consequences of failure are severe, then preventive actions must be taken to decrease its occurrence risk. The greater the magnitude or effect, the greater the need to identify preventive measures to ensure that a failure does not occur, that it can be detected if it should occur, and that its impact can be managed. In other words, an event's overall effect or impact should be considered when analyzing its recurrence risk. Interestingly, some catastrophic events have low profile, such as the millions of annual deaths from infectious and parasitic disease around the world, but a great effect on people. They quietly kill people around the world year after year. Only their cumulative impact is noticed.

The ninth recurrence risk evaluates if people are impacted across large geographical areas. Several types of effects occur if the effect is widespread. The relief response may be poorly coordinated; the result is people may be injured or die and property damage will be more expensive to repair. Interdependencies and political influences are also operative if many people are affected over large geographical areas. Political pressure is also often exerted to take action regardless of facts. Sometimes actions are taken and found later to be very wrong. As an example, the 2005 Hurricane Katrina event impacted a large geographical area, causing a temporary collapse of relief efforts. Exacerbating the relief efforts was political bickering between local, state, and national governmental agencies.

It is also more difficult and expensive to identify causal factors for failure because investigations need to be done over large areas and with many groups. Sometimes these governmental investigations are useful, such as the Army Corps of Engineering Hurricane Katrina report. But often they result in little further action after an initial flurry of investigative activities, which are often politically motivated by public pressure. This is especially true if the government itself is to blame for causing a failure or has poorly responded to an event. Environmental contamination by the United States military and its contractors comes to mind. But these types of issues can be effectively addressed when agencies and the public focus on the right things. The Defense Environmental Restoration Program (DERP) is an example.

According to a report by the United States Government Accountability Office (GAO), "Under the Defense Environmental Restoration Program (DERP), the Department of Defense (DOD) is responsible for cleaning up about 5,400 sites on military bases that have been closed under the Base Realignment and Closure (BRAC) process, as well as 21,500 sites on active bases and over 4,700 formerly used defense sites (FUDS), properties that DOD owned or controlled and transferred to other parties prior to October 1986. The cleanup of contaminants, such as hazardous chemicals or unexploded ordnance, at BRAC bases has been an impediment to the timely transfer of these properties to parties who can put them to new uses."[14] It takes time and political consensus, but the process for correcting governmental failures works, albeit very slowly.

Events affecting many people over wide geographical areas are by nature often politically sensitive. But other events whose effect would otherwise be relatively minor may be politically sensitive too. This is why political sensitivity is identified as a recurrence risk. Political sensitivity is included as a 10th recurrence risk because politics does little to improve a poor situation unless its root causes are identified and solutions implemented. Unfortunately, the situation is very often that the wrong things get fixed, or the right ones get fixed, but in the wrong ways. With differing competing political interests, it is challenging to get all the right things done well.

In leading-edge products such as electronics, defense systems, aerospace, and similar applications, technology is new. Despite the use of best methods, failure rates are inherently higher than products manufactured for many years. As an example, the yields of silicon wafers used for manufacturing electronic circuits are low although the frequency and types of failures can be predicted through testing. There are unavoidable situations where technology is pushing the limits of understanding and skill. Depending on the situation, this may become a problem if potential damage from failures is severe. The 11th recurrence risk is if control technology is not designed and developed with production technology. If technology is not the limitation, these situations often occur in weak regulatory environments. The 2010 Deepwater Horizon Gulf of Mexico oil spill is a classic example where production technology was deployed, without creating effective control technologies. Only after months of agonizing widespread environmental damage from oil spillage did BP and its partners become able to design effective capping tools and methods to stop the high-pressure flow of oil into the water. These tools and methods should have been developed prior to conducting the deep-water drilling. The government should not have allowed deep-water drilling without the development of corresponding control technologies. To the extent control technologies do not exist in an industry, the recurrence likelihood of a failure is higher. This is why it is chosen a recurrence risk factor.

The 12th recurrence risk does not cause a catastrophic event, but to the extent an event is widespread, poor logistical relief responses result in higher injuries and deaths than would have occurred otherwise. We saw the aftermath of a poor relief response during the 2005 Hurricane Katrina, the 2010 Haiti earthquake, and similar events. If regional logistical systems for disaster relief around the world are not upgraded or are properly designed, then future effects from unexpected and catastrophic events will become worse than previous events of similar nature because population densities are increasing. Relief and logistical systems provide materials such as food, water, medicine and clothing, police and medical services, and communications to help manage the aftermath from a major disaster. These systems' importance for preventing injuries and deaths are obvious. But there are issues.

In a recent news article report, fraud was found by auditors of the Global Fund. The fund supports AIDs treatments, tuberculosis (TB) treatments, and malaria prevention activities in 150 countries. Several countries and charitable trusts support the work. There have been more than $25 billion committed to the fund and it spent approximately $10 billion since 2002. According to its website it has helped millions of people.[15] Approximately 2 million people die from TB and 1 million from malaria each year.

Recently, the fund's inspector general's office discovered fraud in several of the audited countries.[16] The audits have not been extensive, so these initial findings are disturbing. The estimates of fraud ranged between 30 and 67 percent. The countries were Mauritania, Zambia, Mali, and Djibouti. However, since approximately 50 percent of the money is spent through the United Nations Development Fund, which has not allowed external audits of the donated monies the full extent of fraud is not known.

It would be easy to conclude that the fund is a failure and withhold donations. In fact, several countries are considering this action. But shouldn't the causal factors for fraud be first identified? As an example, the management of the fund is solid. Its own auditors discovered and reported the fraud. Also, the nations mentioned have taken action against the perpetrators of the fraud. As an example, 15 people were arrested in Mali. The fund helps people around the world maintain their health. It is an important organization.

The operations associated with donating the money can certainly be improved to prevent misuse of funds. However, the United Nations will need to create transparency. The audits should also be expanded. There is significant financial incentive for doing these things.

However, more disturbing are reports that diseases such as malaria are becoming resistant to medical drugs. As an example, a recent news article reported that the malaria parasites in Cambodia are becoming resistant to Artemisinin (qinghaosu), the primary antimalaria drug.[17] Artemisinin remains in the body for three days. As a result it is used in combination with lumefantrine, which lasts seven days.[18] In combination they are effective for killing the parasite, Plasmodium falciparum malaria. Tuberculosis and AIDs are also becoming resistant to current treatment methods.[19] People are already dying. However, solutions are pushing the limits of science.

The final recurrence risk considered how well an organization investigates failures by correctly identifying causal factors and solutions. An analogy is identifying and removing near misses, that is, their error conditions. To let known risk languish without investigation and solution is a clear sign that organizations are likely to have other failures. If the causal or root factors of a catastrophic event are known, solutions can be created to prevent or manage future events and relief responses. However, there are limitations relative to the occurrence of natural and some major disasters. They cannot be predicted with certainty.

Figure 6.1 provides a useful summarization for this chapter. It provides guidance for helping prevent and manage unexpected and catastrophic failures. Ideally, a standardized approach for analyzing and managing risk should be created by an organization to reflect industry best practices. This work requires multidisciplinary teams facilitated by neutral third parties, that is, outside consultants rather than employees. In the last chapter of this book, we will discuss several methods for doing this work. At the very least, organizations should be using available tools and methods. Some of these include process maps, FMEAs, and analytical tools and methods used in their industry for identifying, analyzing, and reducing risks. It is also essential to understand customer requirements and intended application environments prior to designing products and services. This requires the application of the correct technical knowledge. It also requires understanding the influence of cognitive influences on a design process and how customers use products and services. Things are sometimes missed when creating new designs, but more can be done.

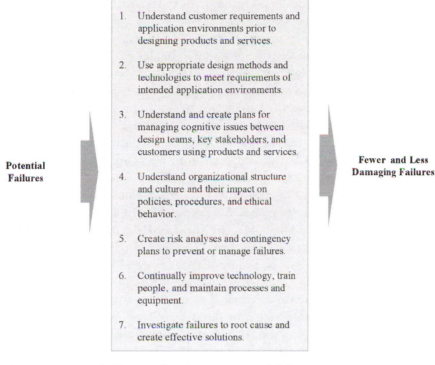

Potential Failures

Fewer and Less Damaging Failures

1. Understand customer requirements and application environments prior to designing products and services.

2. Use appropriate design methods and technologies to meet requirements of intended application environments.

3. Understand and create plans for managing cognitive issues between design teams, key stakeholders, and customers using products and services.

4. Understand organizational structure and culture and their impact on policies, procedures, and ethical behavior.

5. Create risk analyses and contingency plans to prevent or manage failures.

6. Continually improve technology, train people, and maintain processes and equipment.

7. Investigate failures to root cause and create effective solutions.

Figure 6.1   A standard approach reduces unexpected failure

To the extent organizations create risk analyses and contingency plans to prevent or manage failures, the likelihood of failures will be lower. Some industries can go further than others. In inherently dangerous industries, this work will be more difficult than in inherently safer ones. But the stakes are higher. For this reason, efforts should be very rigorous. The continuous improvement of technology, training of people, and maintenance of processes and equipment should always be a priority. Effective root cause analyses should also be done. Different catastrophic events will also require modifications to these recommendations. However, in combination, this approach to risk reduction will result in fewer and less damaging events.

SUMMARY

This chapter discussed several catastrophic events related to failures of products, services, and logistics that represented very diverse industries and applications. They were analyzed by type of failure (intentional injuries, accidents, construction failures, environmental poisoning, etc.) and the causes for failure. The summarized results are shown in Table 6.1 relative to expenses (costs), deaths, and percentages of total. Higher-level causal factors including structural and technological designs as well as cognitive and organizational issues were superimposed on the events to show technical issues were minor if compared with the effects of cognition and organizational influences. This discussion centered on Tables 6.2 and 6.3.

Causal factors for isolated technical failures were usually well determined because events were analyzed using standardized failure analysis methods. However, because they were often caused by unique combinations of error conditions, they were difficult to predict in advance. Most of these isolated events resulted in few deaths, injuries, or economic damage. They included the I-35W Mississippi River Bridge (Minnesota) collapse, the April 25, 1986, Chernobyl Reactor 4 disaster, the Denver International Airport baggage system delays, the 2009 pitot tube failures on Airbus planes, Air France A430-300 (F-GLZL) planes, Air France A340-300 (F-GLZN) planes, and possibly Air France Flight 447, the Toyota 2010 recall, the Ford cruise switch control fires in the late 1990s, and the 2001 Ford/ Firestone tire failures. Some of these events had more than one causal factor. An example is the Chernobyl reactor disaster, which failed through a combination of technical, cognitive, and organizational errors.

Isolated project failures were shown to be different. Their causal factors were cognitive and organizational. The most significant events resulted in large financial losses. Causal factors were identified because of lawsuits and their effects were usually economic. The frequency of these types of project failures has been reduced in the past several decades because of project management and improvements of software as well as organizational policies and procedures. However, they still occur because of dependence on individuals and teams. Examples included the AMR reservation system for Budget's hotel and car bookings, the conversion to new order entry system from Baan Co. at Snap-On, the Anderson SAP ERP issues for FoxMeyer, the Greyhound Bus trips reservation and bus dispatch system issues, the Hershey Foods IBM issues with SAP Manugistics, the Norfolk Southern integration issues with Consolidated Rail, the Oxford health plans billing processing with UNIX and Oracle, the Grainger SAP issues, and the Trivalley Growers Oracle ERP integration issues.

Chronic failures are particularly disturbing because they cause millions of deaths each year around the world. Also, causal factors and solutions are known, but only partially implemented and on an isolated basis. The reasons are a general lack of prioritization of resources as well as economic, political, cultural, and religious barriers. Examples include chronic food contamination issues 1996–1998, the 2003 SARS epidemic in Asia, production problems with the H1N1 swine flu virus, and infectious and parasitic diseases worldwide. As population densities increase, unless action is taken, failures of food safety and ineffectiveness and misdistribution of vaccines and medicines will continue to cause widespread injuries and deaths around the world.

The last category included major events and natural disasters. There are three variants of these events: naturally caused such as the 2010 Haiti earthquake, human-caused such as the 2010 Deepwater Horizon Gulf of Mexico oil spill, and disaster made worse by people such as the 2005 Hurricane Katrina (New Orleans). Natural disasters cannot be precisely predicted by location or time. But since they occur frequently around the world, there should be contingency planning of relief response efforts rather than an ad-hoc strategy after an event occurs. A causal factor analysis can be focused in only two areas. These are event preparation and relief responses. As an example, preparing for an earthquake should include reinforcing building structures, making recommendations for how to behave if an earthquake strikes, and creating plans for how relief efforts would be implemented when needed. Unfortunately the root cause analyses of damage, death, and poor responses for these events are narrowly focused on technical issues. There is also often political scapegoating with no detailed failure analysis or subsequent system and process improvements. As a result, worldwide damage from a lack of preparation continues to occur. Examples include the 2005 Hurricane Katrina (New Orleans), the 2008 Sichuan earthquake, the 1989 San Francisco earthquake, the 2010 Haiti earthquake, and the 2010 Deepwater Horizon Gulf of Mexico oil spill.

A final discussion of this chapter is focused on identifying risk recurrence factors to show why catastrophic events occur. These factors are shown in Table 6.5. The analysis shows many catastrophic events should not be unexpected because they have several risk recurrence factors. The more factors they have, the greater the likelihood a major catastrophic event will occur. Some industries naturally have higher recurrence ratings than others because their operations are inherently dangerous. But it will be shown in the last chapter that much more can be done to reduce recurrence risks even in dangerous industries.

This chapter ended by continuing earlier discussions for creating standardized approaches for reducing failures. A summarization was shown in Figure 6.1. In the final chapter, we will discuss how removal of risk recurrence factors decreases an organization's risk of having a major catastrophic event, but not necessarily to zero. In other words, some industries are simply more risky than others. We will also attempt to answer the question of how much improvement is possible given constraints on an organization's industry. Finally, several methods will be introduced and discussed to help organizations reduce or better manage risks.

NOTES

1. World Health Organization, *The World Health Report 2004: Changing History,* ISBN 92 4 156265 X (NLM Classi?cation: WA 540.1). Copies of this publication can be ordered from Bookorders@who.int, and http://www.who.int/whr/2004/en/.

2. Andrew Hopkins, *Failure to Learn: The BP Texas City Refinery Disaster,* 1st ed. (NSW, Australia: CCH/Wolters Kluwer, 2008).

3. Shakil Adil, "The Levee Breaches Force Nearly 1 Million to Flee," Associated Press, Pakistan, published in the *Providence Journal,* August 28, 2010.

4. David Crary, "Americans Give Little to Pakistan," Associated Press, published in the *Providence Journal,* August 28, 2010.

5. Ryan J. Foley, "Iowa Egg farmer Expanded Empire Despite Violations," Associated Press, *Providence Journal,* August 28, 2010.

6. "Mining Explained," *Mining Journal Online,* http://www.mining-journal.com/knowledge/Mining-Explained.

7. United States Department of Labor, Mine Safety and Health Organization, "Chronology of Recent Major Mining Accidents in the United States," http://www.msha.gov/DisasterHistory/disasterchronology.asp.

8. Kim Khan, "The 10 Most Dangerous Jobs in America," *MSN Money,* October 14, 2003, http://moneycentral.msn.com/content/invest/extra/p63405.asp.

9. Trevor Butterworth and Jenna Krall, "The Risks of Lawn Mowing: What Happens When You Take a Set of Sharp Blades and Spin Them at 160 mph across a Lawn?" *Stats Articles 2007,* (Washington, DC: George Mason University), http://stats.org/stories/2007/risks_of_lawn_mowing_july17_07.htm.

10. "Bhopal Disaster Spurs U.S. Industry, Legislative Action," *The United States Chemical and Safety Hazard Board,* July 29, 1999, http://users.khbo.be/lodew/CSB%20-%20Bhopal%20Disaster%20Spurs%20U_S_%20Industry,%20Legislative%20Action.htm.

11. "Bhopal Tragedy: Who is Warren Anderson?" New Delhi, NDTV Correspondent, June 7, 2010, http://www.ndtv.com/news/india/bhopal-tragedy-who-is-warren-anderson-30302.php.

12. Dan Kurzman, *A Killing Wind: Inside Union Carbide and the Bhopal Catastrophe* (New York: McGraw-Hill, 1987).

13. David K. Lloyd and Myron Lipow, *Reliability: Management, Methods and Mathematics,* 2nd ed. (Milwaukee, WI: American Society for Quality Control, 1984), 222.

14. *Environmental Contamination: Information on the Funding and Cleanup Status of Defense Sites,* GAO-10-547T (Washington, DC: US Government Accountability Office, March 17, 2010), http://www.gao.gov/products/GAO-10-547T.

15. The Global Fund to Fight Aids, Tuberculosis and Malaria homepage , n.d., http://www.theglobalfund.org/en/.

16. John Heilprin, "Fraud Plagues Global Health Fund Backed by Bono, Others," Associated Press; MSNBC.com, January 23, 2011, http://www.msnbc.msn.com/id/41221202/ns/health-health_care/.

17. Ian Williams, "The Race to Contain Drug-Resistant Malaria," NBC News, January 22, 2011, http://worldblog.msnbc.msn.com/_news/2011/01/22/5825008-the-race-to-contain-drug-resistant-malaria-?utm_source=twitterfeed&utm_medium=twitter.

18. Jordan Lite, "What Is Artemisinin?" *Scientific American,* December 23, 2008, http://www.scientificamerican.com/article.cfm?id=artemisinin-coartem-malaria-novartis.

19. "Drug-Resistant Tuberculosis Found in U.S.: Misuse of Drugs has Caused Once-Curable Diseases to Rapidly Mutate into Aggressive, Resistant Strains Worldwide," Associated Press, December 28, 2009, http://www.cbsnews.com/stories/2009/12/28/health/main6029752.shtml.

Chapter 7

RETHINKING UNEXPECTED CONSEQUENCES

Never make forecasts, especially about the future.

—Samuel Goldwyn

The island of Haiti lies on the Enriquillo-Plantain Garden Fault System. A fault system builds up energy beneath the earth's surface at the juncture of locked tectonic plates, creating increasingly higher mechanical stresses over time. If the cumulative stress becomes great enough, the friction holding the plates together cannot prevent the pent-up forces from moving them past each other. During plate movement, energy is quickly released by raising, lowering, or twisting the earth over great distances. Familiar objects are shaken and moved from their original positions.

At 4:15 P.M. local time, late in the afternoon on January 12, 2010, buildings began to crumble and collapse in the capital city of Port-au-Prince in Haiti. This catastrophic event was caused by a magnitude 7.0 earthquake. Its epicenter was located 16 miles west of Port-au-Prince. In the ensuing days, more than 200,000 people died and 300,000 were injured. Another 1 million became homeless.[1] The 2010 Haiti earthquake is but one of several earthquakes in the country's recent history.

There are similar fault lines across the earth at the junctures where tectonic plates collide. These plate collisions appear in several forms. They slowly move over and under each other, slip against each other, or directly collide to form mountain ranges. Interestingly, the average incident rate or number of major earthquakes each year has not significantly increased in the past 200 years. However, the world's population has increased by more than 10-fold during the same 200 years.[2] As a result, one reason for catastrophic property damage, deaths, and injuries when an earthquake occurs is that cities have grown considerably larger, and many of them are located on fault lines where seismic activity is greatest. Exacerbating the catastrophic effects from these natural disasters is the location of many such cities in poorer regions of the world, where building construction is marginal.

The force of an earthquake's shock wave causes damage, but if coupled with marginal building construction, the resultant damage becomes especially severe. Recent events have borne out this terrible fact. The result is that we can expect to see significantly greater damage from earthquakes and other natural disasters in the future. In fact, according to a recent report by the United Nations International Strategy for Disaster Reduction, earthquakes caused some of the deadliest disasters in the past decade.[3] The news brief stated more than 60 percent of people killed in natural disasters died from earthquakes. The brief went on to state that "3,852 disasters killed more than 780,000 people over the past ten years, affected more than 2,000,000,000 others and cost a minimum of $960,000,000,000." The natural disasters were classified as earthquakes (60%), storms (22%), extreme temperatures (11%), and others (7%). The number of people killed by earthquakes was about 468,000 people over 10 years. These people died from collapsing buildings, being hit by objects, and drowning in tsunamis.

Geologists have also noticed earthquakes are causing more damage than in previous centuries. In fact, they now differentiate between *major* versus *significant* earthquakes; when a major earthquake occurs in a heavily populated area it is significant. As a result the number of significant earthquakes is increasing as the number of megacities in earthquake-prone areas increases. Examples of some of these megacities were discussed by Joel Achenbach in an article quoting Roger Bilham of the University of Colorado. They include, "Tokyo, Istanbul, Tehran, Mexico City, New Delhi, Kathmandu. . . . Los Angeles, San Francisco, Dhaka, Jakarta, Karachi, Manila, Cairo, Osaka, Lima and Bogota."[4] One interesting point of the article was that if a major earthquake hits any of the 25 highest-risk cities, at the probability of being hit about once every 250 years, than we can expect one significant earthquake event every 10 years in one of these cities.

Several factors exacerbate property damage, loss of life, and injuries from earthquakes. These include location of megacities in seismically active areas, poor building design, a high density of people within buildings, no warning systems, and poor relief responses. A major recommendation from agencies familiar with earthquakes is that economic development be better managed by enforcing earthquake-proof building codes and regulations, ensuring key infrastructures including hospitals and public safety systems are resistant to earthquakes, creating an enhanced capacity for search and rescue, as well as increasing public awareness of earthquake risks and behaviors to be followed after an event. Although we should be working to reinforce our building infrastructure in earthquake-prone areas, we are not. As a result, the world is quickly becoming a riskier place in which to live.

It is not a generally well-known fact, but approximately 57 million people die each year across the world from all causes.[5] Over 10 years the number is 570 million people. In a similar time period of 10 years, approximately 780,000 people die from earthquakes and other natural disasters, so on average about 0.13 percent of all deaths, in a given year, are caused by unexpected and catastrophic events (natural disasters). In contrast, most people die from unintentional injuries (6.8%), intentional injuries including war and violence (2.84%), or infectious and parasitic diseases (23%).[6]

People across the world face a life-or-death existence every day. The causes for their deaths and injuries are not interesting compared to those of a major earthquake, natural disaster, or a plane accident, so they get little notice. But, their number of deaths is much higher.

The result is large numbers of people continue to get sick and die every year from inaction. As an example, in a typical year approximately 13 million people will die of infectious and parasitic diseases compared with 78,000 from earthquakes, storms, extreme temperatures, and other natural disasters. Sadly, some of these diseases are preventable or curable. However, these events receive little public attention because catastrophic events easily capture people's interests; they are newsworthy and receive attention out of proportion to other more serious events with lower profiles. This doesn't imply we should not prepare for and respond to natural disasters, but only that the cumulative numbers of deaths and injuries associated with infectious diseases are higher. A more balanced response is needed. Preventive and managing strategies should be developed for all major catastrophic events causing loss of property, death, or injuries; but those causing greater damage should have a higher priority. Understandably, there are many competing demands for time and resources. These decisions are not easy to make.

An analysis of the many events discussed in this book shows that with an exception for technical and cognitive failures, which require specific solutions and have a relatively low impact on society, many man-made or natural disasters are not as unexpected as they first appear. This is the reason the chapter is titled, "Rethinking Unexpected Consequences." It may be a surprise when they occur, but better preparations can be made prior to their occurrence. As an example, enforcing correct building laws and regulations would go a long way toward preventing or mitigating the detrimental impacts of unexpected and catastrophic events.

Let's review some examples. Hurricane Katrina's property damage could have been prevented by correctly building and maintaining New Orleans's levee system and managing the relief responses. The solutions to prevent flooding of New Orleans and the potential effects of flooding were known in advance. Things could have been different at many levels in the hurricane's aftermath. Many other major events can be analyzed with similar conclusions.

The United States knows natural disasters will likely occur within its borders year to year. It has local, state, and national agencies to help prevent some events from occurring and to effectively manage them if they do occur. The results are often very good, but not always. Despite creation of the Federal Emergency Management Agency (FEMA), disaster planning remains challenging. The 2005 Hurricane Katrina response is an example. Most recently the Deepwater Horizon Gulf of Mexico explosion, which caused widespread environmental contamination, also showed a pattern of regulatory failure by the United States Interior Department. The private organizations involved (BP and others) did not have effective contingency plans and apparently did not follow all industry safety procedures. Complicating the situation, relief efforts were initially chaotic, confusing, and heavily influenced by public pundits and politicians. In fact, local and state politicians wanted to immediately resume deep-water drilling despite the fact control technologies, contingency plans, and organizational policies and procedures were risky.

If societies across the world continue to ignore basic principles of science, the adverse effects relative to loss of life, injuries, and property damage will become much worse. The world is becoming a very crowded place where reverberations from one catastrophic incident immediately impact many other people. We need to do better. In this chapter several new concepts will also be introduced to help us rethink the unexpected consequences associated with major events. We will create a framework to examine the many topics presented in earlier chapters and integrate them with these new concepts. This will help us frame potentially risky situations in ways they can be analyzed, prevented, and better managed in the future. The goal is to reduce risks.

Although hindsight may be perfect, it is useless for preventing future events unless causal factors can be identified and eliminated from future designs and processes. We need to create predictive models of various sorts for different types of failures. Unfortunately, while quantitative models are useful, they are lacking when attempting to predict uncertain future events such as natural disasters and major events. Our focus will be to introduce and discuss useful qualitative methods to help us understand future outcomes and threats in the context of coordinating infrastructures and emergency responses.

Some people have difficulty creating models because they do not like quantification of causes and effects. One consequence is they may accept information without critically thinking of its source, meaning, or consequences. A second issue is that people may not evaluate outcomes in terms of more than one causal factor when often two, three, or more outcomes would better represent a system. They also often prefer an estimate of a single number, that is, a point estimate, although a range would be more useful. Finally, there is an overreliance on quantitative models, which depend on historical information that may be erroneous or not relevant for predicting future events.

In contrast, mental models and similar modeling constructs are often good approaches for estimating the types of unlikely events and their characteristics. There are several variants of such models. One approach uses expert opinions of several people familiar with a situation and its complexities (experts). Many times experts can help create useful estimates of future outcomes. There are also facilitative tools and methods that help ensure, given available information, that these opinions are efficiently obtained from experts. The practical result is, although we may not be able to estimate timing of a future event with certainty, we may be able to estimate potential outcomes over a range of possible scenarios. As we begin to rethink our approaches to predicting and managing catastrophic events we will find it useful to discuss better ways to describe them. An effective method is scenario planning.

Shell Oil Company, a worldwide energy producer, has used scenario planning for decades. Scenario planning is a structured process for creating mental models to understand potential future events. It differs from forecasting in that a forecast will predict an event with an occurrence probability whereas scenario planning creates several possible future events. Its usefulness is facilitating risk analyses and helping create contingency plans if an event occurs. Some relevant applications for an energy producer such as Shell Oil Company would be evaluating the effects of natural disasters on oil producing and refining operations, considering disruption of oil supplies by major political events, or analyzing the effects of unexpected capacity constraints leading to increases of oil prices.

Unlike a heavy reliance on mathematical models, scenario planning is a holistic approach for understanding possible future events.

Shell used it successfully and has refined the methodology over several decades. An acronym, TINA, has been created to describe Shell's methodology. TINA represents two concepts. First, it stands for "There is no alternative." In this context, the phrase implies alternative scenarios exist, but they have not been previously considered. Some reasons usually include time and resource constraints. Also, TINA stands for the four basic steps of the methodology: tackle it yourself, isolate uncertainties, name it, and act on it.[7] In addition to Shell Oil's use of the methodology, scenario planning methods are now well known to many other organizations. There are also many case studies showing its usefulness in diverse applications.

When creating scenarios, it is important to properly facilitate planning sessions using neutral third parties. This helps ensure a planning group does not become biased. Properly facilitated scenarios identify drivers likely to transform a current system into a different one, a potential future state. As an example, higher population growth is expected to drive higher resource usage. Higher resource usage would then be expected to increase prices and create competitive conflict unless political and technical solutions are found to neutralize the future higher usage levels. These types of analyses help a team identify several possible scenarios. Scenarios are created by modifying assumptions related to factors causing change and by also considering differing outcomes. The goal is to identify risks, the major drivers of a scenario, and its outcomes to create contingency plans. These plans help mitigate the effects of expected outcomes from a scenario.

As an example, higher rainfalls drive potential flooding in certain terrains. Although an exact amount of rain cannot be predicted with certainty, a range of possible amounts can be predicted. This enables the creation of several scenarios showing the impact of different amounts of rain and relevant factors such as time of year, population density, and location as well as other factors to describe the effects of flooding. This analysis is used to create a range of potential flooding conditions for planning. Scenarios should also focus on extremes as well as expected outcomes. In other words, don't create scenarios only for expected outcomes, but rather the unexpected ones. Using this information, contingency plans can be created to respond to each scenario's drivers and outcomes both expected and unexpected. Examples of well-known drivers include higher population levels, cycles of boom and bust (especially economic ones), supply and demand relationships, the occurrence of natural disasters, political conflicts, likely technological developments, and similar major events.

In summary, there are several other considerations for creating useful scenarios. First create a broad range of potential outcomes, especially those that are not expected to occur. Create both the worst and best case scenarios representing significant risks and benefits. Don't examine minor changes to a current state because these are usually captured by conventional planning activities. Also, don't throw away useful scenarios. Rather, do the hard work of completely analyzing each of them. Prioritization must also be used to manage team resources. This scenario-planning strategy will avoid being forced to create response plans during a crisis. Also, identify all the known drivers of a particular scenario, and their effect on outcomes of interest.

This will increase the likelihood that essential leading indicators necessary to predict future events are captured for analysis. Finally, use neutral facilitators and experts to ensure the group is diverse in its thinking, experience, and perspectives. An advantage of scenario planning is that an organization will be able to more quickly manage its response to unexpected catastrophic events.

However, it is often difficult to convince organizations to consider alternative future scenarios that significantly diverge from ones currently identified by planning teams. There are several reasons why not just any group of employees should be involved in these activities. First, there is little interest in doing the work by most executives, managers, and employees. As a result, scenario planning activities have little priority with most organizations. Either people don't have time to do them or even if they are authorized to do the work, they simply don't expend the effort necessary to understand the fundamentals of the methodology. In other words, they are too busy or don't care. There are also practical reasons for not wanting to create scenarios. Organizations don't want to be on the record as knowing of alternative scenarios, which if they occur expose an organization to poor publicity, lawsuits, or financial losses. We live in a world in which recorded information can be easily obtained for use in lawsuits. There is also an element of ignorance at play. Finally, it is difficult to facilitate scenario planning activities because useful results require up-front research of all situational factors such as driver, outputs, and system, and of current state conditions including their magnitudes, interrelationships, and relative importance. Few organizations have this expertise.

Interestingly, scenario planning could have helped several organizations involved in the recent financial crisis avoid heavy financial losses. Several recent financial bubbles burst over the past several decades, which resulted in market collapses. In the usual buildup before a financial collapse successful organizations create contingency plans to help manage responses prior and during a crisis to protect their financial interests. They analyze extremes rather than only expected outcomes. As an example, some financial organizations actually profit when financial bubbles collapse.

Recently, scenario planning has been integrated with the Delphi methodology for helping predict uncertain events. The Delphi method brings experts together anonymously to ask their opinions regarding drivers, outputs, and relevant conditions of different scenarios. The experts also estimate the likelihood of future events. Since the responses are anonymous, there is little interference by one expert with opinions of others. Using this approach, as each analysis is completed, the results are reported, the group assimilates the information, and then it moves to the next topic. A scenario evolves over time in an iterative manner from these discussions.

The integration of the Delphi methodology, scenario analysis, and contingency planning and sensitivity analysis recently coalesced into a combined methodology called morphological analysis.[8] This method identifies relationships between relevant factors, and analyzes their effects over a range of potential scenarios. The drivers and outcomes of each scenario are identified and contingency planning is applied to the outcomes. An example would be planning for the aftermath of an earthquake. A major factor would be the magnitude of the earthquake since it is correlated to expected damage, given a known building infrastructure. Contingency plans would be created for low, medium, and high magnitude earthquakes as well as assumptions regarding population density, time of day, and building quality. If the scenario was being used to create a medical response system, the availability of medical personnel, facilities, equipment, and supplies would be important factors for consideration in various scenarios and would also drive expected outcomes.

On September 18, 2008, during the recent economic crisis, money market accounts within the United States were being depleted by an unknown source. According to Congressman Paul Kanjorski, who claimed he received the information from Mr. Bernanke of the Federal Reserve and Mr. Paulson of the Treasury Department, approximately $500 billion was withdrawn in just a few hours that morning. Estimates were that over $5.5 trillion would have been withdrawn from money market accounts by early afternoon unless action was immediately taken by the Federal Reserve Banks. Estimates are, the United States economy would have collapsed if the electronic funds transfer operations had not been closed.[9] September had already been a devastating month for the world's financial markets. In rapid succession more than a million homes were in foreclosure, Fannie Mae and Freddie were seized by the U.S. government, and Lehman Brothers collapsed. However, the U.S. congress took several successful actions to stabilize the economy, although the subsequent recovery has been very slow even two years after the crisis began.

Not every organization lost money during the recent crisis. Several prominent financiers understood market dynamics and bet against a continuing rise in real estate prices, company stocks, stock funds, and similar financial products. Examples include John Paulson, Andrew Lahde, and others. These people had correct mental models of the economic landscape and used this knowledge to fair advantage. Scenario planning would have helped other organizations create their own successful mental models.

Microsoft's *Encarta Dictionary* defines a model as "a simplified version of something complex used in analyzing and solving problems or making predictions." We use models, that is, simplified versions of reality, to help understand where to focus attention on important factors that drive outputs or outcomes of interest. Models are also used in a variety of forms and practical applications.

Many years ago, I was a senior research engineer working in a process industry. The work required creating models of various types. First, we would translate customer needs and requirements by using simple mathematical models to create laboratory samples. Computer models and laboratory samples were analyzed to study correlations between the physical characteristics of the laboratory samples and customer requirements. This information was used to design experiments for the larger machines. The experiments themselves were simplifications of the production system's inherent complexity and required varying just three of four machine settings or factor levels. Eventually, the samples were tested by the customer to verify requirements were correctly mapped to their product's functions and features.

This modeling simplification strategy saved time and money. At other times, when working in different industries, drawings and simple analyses were sufficient for improving process efficiency. There are many types of useful models for simplifying complicated systems. Examples include conceptual, physical, virtual, and mathematical models. To the extent organizations effectively use them to create scenarios, they can help reduce exposure to several types of risk.[10]

In a previous book titled *Operational Excellence* I describe simple steps useful for building models. The basic concepts are easily applicable to scenario planning and analyses of complicated systems.[11] The key steps include selecting the right people and modeling strategy, developing modeling rules and constraints, and using analytical tests for determining statistical significance and consistency. Although models of various types are proving increasingly useful for predicting losses from natural disasters, they need to be used more often to help prevent catastrophic failures.[12] Creating scenarios is useful when trying to understand future events that occur with low frequency or whose effects are expected to be significant.

In Figure 7.1, 10 steps are shown for creating scenarios. The complexity of their associated activities varies depending on a specific scenario. Some scenarios are relativity simple whereas others are complicated because they rely on collection and analysis of historical information. Complicated scenarios include those relying on econometric modeling applications and extensive data analysis. The first step is bringing together people familiar with the drivers, outcomes, and other relevant aspects of a perceived problem or issue. The problem should be clearly described. If necessary it should also be modified by a team before proceeding with brainstorming activities to provide focus.

Problem Statement

- Using the team's problem statement, create a list of relevant issues.
- Organize issues and risks into common groups, which are scenarios.
- Agree to prioritization rules for the scenarios, that is, which ones will be analyzed first. There are several useful prioritization methods such as Analytical Hierarchy Process (AHP, a Pugh Matrix or simple voting).
- Rewrite the problem statement for the highest-priority scenario.
- Do a SWOT analysis for the highest-priority scenario.
- Identify drivers (factors) of the scenario's outputs.
- Evaluate the scenarios in terms of known issues and relevant risks such as scheduling, costs, technologies, product performance, market demand, supply and capacity, laws and the regulatory environment, politics, and other factors. Assign probabilities (degree of uncertainty) to risks that have occurred or will occur.
- Check for extreme outcomes and disequilibrium, verify timeframes, and verify relational consistencies and additional players such as stakeholders.
- Attempt to quantify using regression and similar methods.
- Create contingency or crisis management plans.

Figure 7.1 Creating scenarios

As a team's discussions and analyses evolve, the problem's description can be successfully modified. Eventually, the problem will be summarized as a clear problem statement. A problem statement describes scenarios in terms conveying historical performance, the likelihood of future occurrence, current or future effects on an organization or system, and supplemental information, to help focus a team within constraints and boundaries of its problem statement. As an example, a scenario could be focused on an analysis of one region of the United States for one type of natural disaster as opposed to the world. It is also important a problem statement does not contain solutions or anything that biases a team's discussions and analyses. Let's apply scenario planning to help understand a 2010 gasoline explosion that caused death and destruction near San Francisco, California.

As people drive automobiles through cities of the United States, they have reasonable expectations to be safe if traffic laws are obeyed and weather conditions are good. So our eyes are fixed on traffic ahead; but we remain alert and guarded to sudden or immediate danger. We seldom consider dangers that may lie just below the surface of the roads on which we drive to doctor's appointments, to work, or to social events, or that our children use to ride school buses every day cross the many roads within the United States. What is not commonly known is that beneath some of the roads we travel, while we are oblivious, are forces that if unleashed can unexpectedly and catastrophically cause death or injury and massive destruction of property.

If an earthquake occurs, buildings may collapse, electrical transmission lines and wires may fall, and there may be other types of damage. However, a natural gas explosion is different in both its impact and destruction. This was the recent situation in San Bruno, California, on September 9, 2010. This community is located near San Francisco, a city that is no stranger to the destructive forces of nature. Earlier in the 20th century, the 1906 San Francisco earthquake twisted and destroyed the gas lines beneath the city, causing fires. Ironically, the city of San Bruno saw its greatest growth after the San Francisco 1906 earthquake and subsequent fires. Crisscrossing the city of San Bruno is a myriad of water and sewer lines as well natural gas transmission lines. Around the time of the 2010 explosion and fire, there was much construction work in the city installing and repairing underground infrastructure.

Over the many years that preceded the 2010 explosion, frequent rainstorms left the ground saturated with water. Natural gas pipelines are made of thick-walled steel, which slowly corrodes. The walls become thinner over time as they lose mass because of oxidation (rusting). As the thickness of the pipelines is reduced, their strength or ability to contain the highly pressurized natural gas decreases. As a result, the margin of safety declines. Also, damage to a pipeline, such as a crack, lowers its inherent strength in several ways. Cracks or surface gouges may decrease the wall thickness of a pipeline or concentrate the forces of the pressurized natural gas at the surface of the crack. This concentration effect is called a point-of-stress concentration. Depending on the geometry of the crack, the forces may be multiplied by up to 100 times their initial level. Exacerbating the situation is that within a pipeline network, natural gas flows under high pressure and will explode if it is ignited by an energy source such as a spark caused by surface friction.

Unfortunately, on September 9, 2010, a chain of causal events aligned to cause an enormous natural gas pipeline explosion. It killed seven people, six went missing, and 37 homes were destroyed. The pipeline was buried just three feet below the surface in a residential area. There are more than 300,000 miles of gas transmission lines throughout the United States and there were 63 explosions in 2008 alone. Also, thousands of gas leaks are detected and repaired each year.

Although the natural gas distribution system's safety record is very good compared to other energy distribution systems, it requires manual work to maintain its safety record.[13] Examples include inspections, repairs, and responding to reports of natural gas leaks. A review of major catastrophic events shows systems depending on manual intervention and human judgment are prone to failure. Scenario planning would be very useful for systems such as natural gas pipelines prone to catastrophic failure. As a result, we will use a natural gas pipeline system to illustrate how a simple scenario could be created for a hypothetical example.

The initial problem description could be constructed as, "In the past twelve months there have been 1,000 leaks in our natural gas pipeline transmission system, but no deaths, injuries, or property damage. Also, maintenance costs have increased by 20 percent to $1 million per 100 miles of pipeline." A team would be formed around this problem description. It would consist of people supplying the process, those who do the work within the process, various stakeholders and perhaps consultants acting as proxies for customers, and regulators or public safety officials. Other experts may also include construction, safety, and materials engineers and the people who design, maintain, and repair a pipeline system.

The issues associated with the problem description are identified by the team using the method shown in Figure 7.2. First, the team participates in an interactive brainstorming exercise. It is asked to write issues and place them on a wall. After everyone has finished writing issues, the issues are organized into logical categories. These may include key drivers or inputs

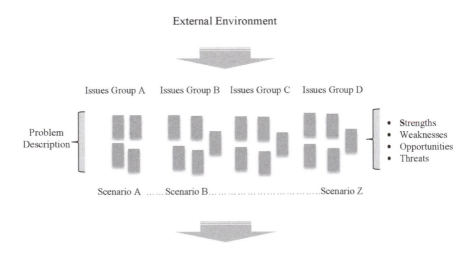

Figure 7.2   Create scenarios from external to internal environments

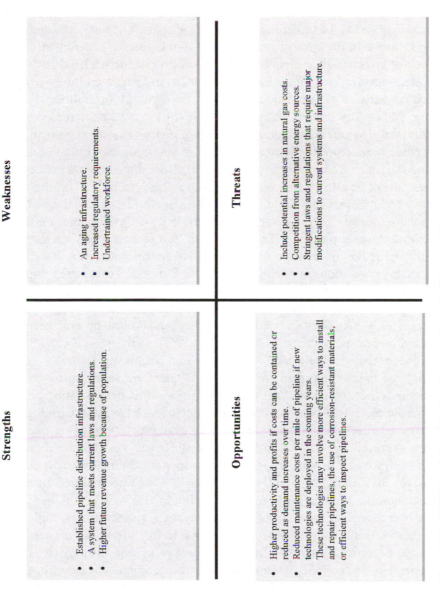

Strengths

- Established pipeline distribution infrastructure.
- A system that meets current laws and regulations.
- Higher future revenue growth because of population.

Weaknesses

- An aging infrastructure.
- Increased regulatory requirements.
- Undertrained workforce.

Opportunities

- Higher productivity and profits if costs can be contained or reduced as demand increases over time.
- Reduced maintenance costs per mile of pipeline if new technologies are deployed in the coming years.
- These technologies may involve more efficient ways to install and repair pipelines, the use of corrosion-resistant materials, or efficient ways to inspect pipelines.

Threats

- Include potential increases in natural gas costs.
- Competition from alternative energy sources.
- Stringent laws and regulations that require major modifications to current systems and infrastructure.

Figure 7.3   SWOT analysis applied to the natural gas pipeline example

into the scenario, expected outcomes, and relevant factors such as location of pipelines, status of installed infrastructure, regulatory requirements, customer demand, stakeholders, and other factors consistent with the problem description.

Once potential issues are identified, they are analyzed, using a SWOT analysis. SWOT is an acronym for strengths, weaknesses, opportunities, and threats. In the current example shown in Figure 7.3, current strengths include an established pipeline distribution (infrastructure), a distribution system meeting current laws and regulations, and expected future revenue growth because of population increases and demand for additional housing. Weaknesses include an aging pipeline infrastructure, increased future regulatory requirements, and an undertrained workforce. Opportunities include higher productivity and profits if costs can be contained or reduced as demand increases over time, and also reduced maintenance costs per mile of pipeline if new technologies are deployed in the coming years. New technologies may yield more efficient methods to install and repair pipelines, create corrosion-resistant materials, or develop more efficient ways to inspect pipelines. Threats include future cost increases for natural gas, higher competition from alternative energy sources, and stringent laws and regulations requiring major modifications to the current pipeline distribution systems. Once all issues have been analyzed using a SWOT analysis and brainstorming, several scenarios are created corresponding to strengths, weaknesses, opportunities, or threats. Follow-up brainstorming activities may be required to expand the SWOT analysis.

One scenario is selected for analysis. The remaining scenarios will be analyzed based on a team's prioritization. There are several prioritization methods that can be used depending on the specific prioritization criteria. One approach is to consider a scenario's occurrence likelihood, timing, and expected effect on an organization. As an example, in Figure 7.4, Scenario A is expected to occur prior to Scenario B. Scenario A is focused on current infrastructure whereas Scenario B is focused on major disruptions of supply. This implies that although Scenario A will be analyzed first, it is also important to analyze Scenario B. It should also receive a higher priority over time. The outcomes from Scenario A (capacity, for example) will directly affect the inputs of Scenario B, that is, the infrastructure necessary to satisfy future demand. Relationships between scenarios may also be independent or dependent. If independent, the outcomes of Scenario A have no impact on inputs into B. If dependent, then outcomes of Scenario A have an effect or impact on the inputs into Scenario B.

Let's identify major drivers of the natural gas pipeline's outcomes. These drivers are also called causal factors or independent variables. The outcomes are also called effects or dependent variables. Suppose the scenario

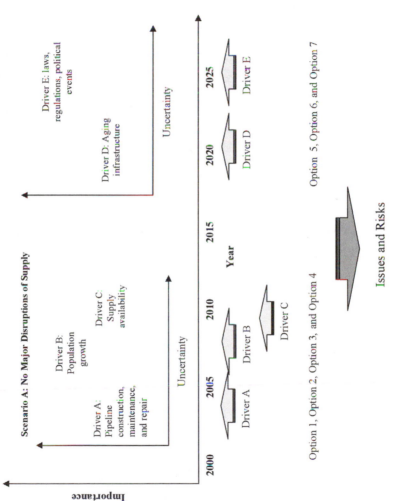

Figure 7.4 Scenarios are created based on a SWOT analysis

is being created to answer the question, "If population density increases, do we have capacity, that is, sufficient pipeline infrastructure and natural gas supplies to meet expected demand with 99.9 percent probability for the next 10 years, that is, meet this required service level in the future?" The drivers for this scenario are expected population growth, current and future pipeline capacity, current and future availability, and cost of natural gas. These variables are all important for meeting current and future demand. There are also others such as an unexpected restriction of supply, a pipeline explosion that interrupts capacity, new laws and regulations that control where future pipelines can be located, or an aging pipeline infrastructure with respect to its vulnerability to corrosion and environmental stresses such as earthquakes. Some of these variables, system conditions, and outcomes are dependent on lower-level variables. Once all variables, at every level of the system, have been identified using all available information including brainstorming, they are classified into issues or risks.

Issues are certain to occur. They often include increases of material and labor costs, regulations that will take effect at a future date, contracts set to expire, and similar certain future events. In contrast, risks have not and may never occur. They have a likelihood or probability of occurrence. In earlier chapters we discussed several types of project risks. These included scheduling, cost, technology, product performance, market demand, supply or system capacity, laws and regulations, politics, and others.

A simple example of risk analysis is shown in Table 7.1, in which each risk level is calculated using estimates of risk likelihood and impact.

Table 7.1
Calculating Risk Levels

Risks	Likelihood of Occurring	Impact Severity	Risk Level
Scheduling risk (pipeline construction, maintenance, and repairs)	25%	6	1.5
Cost risks (supply, labor, materials)	30%	7	2.1
Market demand risks (population growth, alternative energy sources).	10%	8	0.8
Law and regulatory risks	10%	5	0.5
Competitive risks	10%	5	0.5
Technological risks (ability to use new materials and methods)	5%	5	0.25
Natural disasters such as earthquakes, disease and epidemics, acts of terrorism, wars and conflicts, conditions of extreme weather, and technological accidents	1%	10	1.0

Scenarios are also useful for identifying extreme and unlikely outcomes. In the current pipeline example, the current demand growth rates could be simply extrapolated into the future. But a more useful approach would be to evaluate wide extremes of expected demand and its drivers. This is done by asking questions such as, "What will happen if demand decreases by 50 percent because of alternative energy sources?" or "What would happen if demand increases 100 percent, 200 percent, or higher?" In other words, it is important to check for system disequilibria. Some other considerations, when creating scenarios, are to verify time frames, relational consistencies, and impacts to customers, suppliers, and stakeholders. In some scenario planning analyses, quantitative models must be created using experts. The information gained during scenario planning and analysis is used to create contingency plans to manage known issues and eliminate or mitigate risks.

In January 2010, after the Haitian earthquake, two C-130 planes almost collided over the city of Port-au-Prince because of high aircraft density.[14] Many nations wanted to help the Haitians, but the initial relief response overwhelmed the country because it was poorly coordinated. Complicating the situation was heavy damage to the capital's port by the earthquake. The port was needed to offload relief supplies, but it was not available. Scenario planning would likely have identified this situation as a potential limitation of future relief efforts.

The United States sent troops and supplies including aircraft carriers to Haiti. France sent ships; Canada, Cuba, Brazil, and Italy each sent over 1,000 medical and other personnel.[15] Asian countries such as China and Japan as well as Australia also provided help. Many other nations such as Israel, the European Union, countries of the Americas, as well as organizations and individuals also made significant donations to help Haiti. In fact, the total donated amount exceeded $3.8 billion. The list of donors is very long. This is not unusual; countries in conflict with each other often work together if a natural disaster occurs.

Unfortunately, major events occur quite often. There is usually confusion during the first few days or weeks of a major event. Relief efforts can also be haphazard. An example is the recent flooding in Pakistan, where millions of people became homeless because the widespread flooding overwhelmed relief efforts. Why wait before creating relief coordination plans for disasters certain to occur somewhere in a region? Why not coordinate, in advance, regionally and across the world? Scenario planning is a useful approach for coordinating analyses necessary for these types of future coordination efforts.

An advantage of scenario planning is it helps organizations overcome issues associated with individual cognitive dysfunctions and organizational dysfunctions caused by group attitudes and behavior. In earlier chapters, it was shown that cognitive dissonance, in particular, is a major contributor of error conditions and mistakes. This makes it a very important influencer of individual, group, and organizational behaviors. Because we know it exists, effective actions can be taken to reduce its influence by eliminating barriers to communication and the suppression of diverse viewpoints. Scenario planning helps organizations detect weak signals difficult to notice because people have mental models. Recall that mental models filter information dissonant to accepted attitude and beliefs. Without scenario planning and similar interactive activities, viewpoints and perspectives that contradict established organizational policies and opinions will be eliminated from discussions and analyses. The long-term effect may be major failures if external conditions change. Absent scenario planning or creation of a contingency plan, it is difficult for an organization to quickly adapt to external conditions, including catastrophic events. This is because changes can be sudden and violent. The practical results will be relief efforts that are ineffective or make bad situations worse.

Contingency plans can be created once scenarios have been created and drivers, situational factors, and outcomes identified. Plans vary by scenario and expected outcomes. Some outcomes are desirable (e.g., high sales or customer satisfaction). Others are undesirable (e.g., a major industrial accident causing widespread environmental damage). Depending on the types of outcomes envisioned, plans must be created to prevent or accelerate and manage their effects. It is also desirable to identify early warning signs to help decision makers become aware a scenario is beginning to occur. In other words, it is useful to recognize otherwise weak signals as they become stronger once the pieces of a particular scenario begin to fall into place and begin to create a previously identified pattern explored in scenarios.

Nepal, or as it is called officially, the Federal Democratic Republic of Nepal, is located between China and India high in the Himalayan mountains. It geography is mountainous and contains eight of the world's tallest mountains. It is also no stranger to devastating earthquakes. It has had several in the past century in which thousands of people died. Earlier this year, the *Huffington Post* asked a question in an article titled, "Catastrophic Earthquakes: Will Nepal Be Next?"[16] The "next" was in reference to the 2010 Haitian earthquake a few months earlier. Recall that a major contributor to the horrific number of Haitian deaths was poor building infrastructure that collapsed and crushed more than 200,000 people.

The population living in the Kathmandu Valley, where the nation's capital is located, exceeds 3 million people. In 1934 an earthquake in the same area killed 20,000 people when 25 percent of the buildings collapsed. Unfortunately, not much has changed since 1934 except that the population density increased in the same area. The article continues to discuss actions by the

United Nations to reinforce schools, hospitals, and public buildings. If an earthquake does strike the region, which is isolated, relief efforts are expected to become difficult. Worthy of mention is that Mr. Robert Piper, the head of the United Nations' humanitarian effort in Nepal, has been working hard to coordinate building reinforcement programs. However, there are 30,000 schools in the country and only 200 had been reinforced as of March 2010.

Interestingly, the Nepalese Red Cross Society (NRCS) created a contingency plan for use if an earthquake occurs.[17] Its 82 pages contain information for planning for "coordination of relief efforts, continuity of operations, protection, safety, and security, information management, communications, and reporting, rescue, emergency medical assistance, and health services, relief, food and nutrition, shelter, water, sanitation, and hygiene, logistics and transport, IT and telecommunications and finance and administration."[18] But if an earthquake occurs it is likely many schools, public buildings, and hospitals will collapse, negating the assumptions of available resources on which the plan is based. It's a good plan, but the best option is to prevent the collapse of buildings and infrastructure in the first place.

In contrast, the 2010 Chilean earthquake had more than 500 times the energy of the 2010 Haitian earthquake, but only a few hundred people died from the event because buildings were constructed using reinforced concrete and strict building codes.[19] An interesting quotation from this same information source is that Chile has more earthquake seismologists and engineers experienced with preventive measures on a per capita basis than any other country in the world. Chile has had a long history of violent earthquakes. This created an incentive for its citizens and government to be prepared for destructive forces certain to occur in the future, such as the 2010 earthquake. However, this preparation required many decades of careful planning.

Contingency planning must be discussed in a context of what's practical. It must also incorporate a long-term perspective. If assumptions about infrastructure or resource availability, on which a plan is based, do not materialize, then a contingency plan will fail in its purpose. Scenario planning is useful because it helps identify issues and risks as well as several potential outcomes including failures of infrastructure or resources. There are also different types of contingency plans. Our focus will be on those created to prevent or manage catastrophic events that injure and kill people or cause widespread property and environmental damage. At a basic level, contingency plans attempt to address three areas of concern. Figure 7.5 identifies these areas as outcomes and threats, coordination infrastructures, and emergency response capabilities.

Outcomes and threats are identified by analyzing information associated with historical events of similar nature. As an example, if the contingency

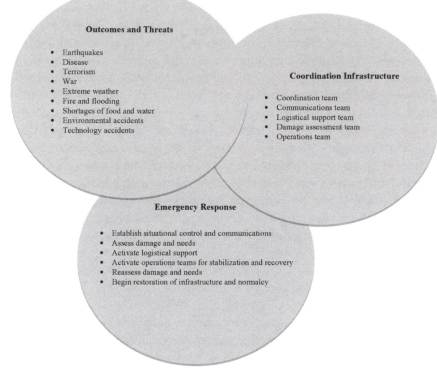

Outcomes and Threats

- Earthquakes
- Disease
- Terrorism
- War
- Extreme weather
- Fire and flooding
- Shortages of food and water
- Environmental accidents
- Technology accidents

Coordination Infrastructure

- Coordination team
- Communications team
- Logistical support team
- Damage assessment team
- Operations team

Emergency Response

- Establish situational control and communications
- Assess damage and needs
- Activate logistical support
- Activate operations teams for stabilization and recovery
- Reassess damage and needs
- Begin restoration of infrastructure and normalcy

Figure 7.5   Contingency planning and crisis management

planning is for earthquake events then an analysis of previous earthquake occurrences and subsequent relief efforts would be useful for creating future plans. If the plans were designed to prevent or manage the release of a dangerous chemical within highly populated areas, then an analysis of previous similar incidents would be very useful. There are also professional exerts who can help create specific types of contingency plans. Scenario planning is particularly useful for helping identify events that did not occur in the past or whose damage was minimal. In the latter situations, previous effects can be magnified by orders of magnitude and analyzed for potential outcomes (e.g., significant quantities of deaths, injuries, or property and environmental damage). Many of the catastrophic events discussed in this book are these types of events (e.g., earthquakes, disease and epidemics, acts of terrorism, wars and conflicts, conditions of extreme weather, and technological accidents).

A coordination infrastructure must also be created to manage relief efforts as well as the many supporting activities. Coordination infrastructure includes an executive committee, communication, logistical support, and damage assessment and operations teams. Each of these teams has unique roles and responsibilities if a catastrophic event occurs. An executive committee coordinates people and resources both prior to and during a relief response. Its responsibilities specifically include coordination of infrastructure teams and activities such as communication, logistical support, damage assessment, and operations teams. Communication activities include coordination of incoming information into and out of a disaster site including requests for resources, logistical support, and damage assessments. Logistical support brings tools, equipment, materials, and people to a disaster site to provide relief. The goal is prevention of injuries, deaths, and future damage. Damage assessment teams communicate with control centers to help prioritize relief efforts. After a disaster site has been stabilized these teams continue making site assessments to determine short, intermediate, and longer-term needs.

The third component of a contingency plan focuses on the emergency response activities after a catastrophic event occurs. These activities include activating teams that are part of the coordination infrastructure. Typical activities include establishing situational control and securing communications, assessing damage and needs, activating logistical support systems, activating operational teams for stabilization and recovery, and reassessing damage and needs after a few days of an event to determine if resource allocation is efficient. Longer-term activities include restoration of the area's infrastructure to return to normalcy over the weeks and months after an event.

The public's perception of potentially catastrophic events varies depending on how messages are communicated. Asking people if they think that a one in a thousand chance of an earthquake killing 100,000 people this year is worse than the certainty of 200 people killed in traffic accidents and they will likely say the earthquake is worse. This is despite the fact that 100 people are expected to be killed from an earthquake, constituting 100 deaths or 50 percent of those from traffic accidents. In this situation, it has been shown, the potential magnitude or effect horrifies people. They see 100,000 potential deaths as a certainty rather than a one in one thousand likelihood occurrence. However, if the question is reframed to something like, "Is it better to save 200 or 100 people with the same effort?" people will usually say save the 200 people. It matters how information is framed and communicated to people who may be impacted by a future event.

Prior experience also influences a person's attitudes regarding a best course of action. As an example, people have difficulty simultaneously considering a very large impact and a small occurrence probability. Their natural tendency is to avoid negative thoughts associated with the occurrence of large numbers of deaths and injuries and destruction of property. People also do not easily comprehend small occurrence probabilities. If you tell them the likelihood of a high-magnitude earthquake occurring is once every 250 years, most likely you will not get their attention. However, if the statement is in reference to the likelihood of a major earthquake hitting any one of these 25 cities in the next 10 years, almost certainly their attention is increased, although perhaps not enough to take immediate action. This cognitive effect also influences public perceptions and behavior.

Depending how information is framed and communicated relative to its occurrence likelihood and magnitude, actions may or may not be taken. This is one of the reasons, both before and after major catastrophic events, that people lose interest in taking preventive actions. They believe another event is very unlikely. However, this is always untrue from the perspective that although future events may not occur in the same location for many years, similar events will occur somewhere in the same region or in the world. Individuals, organizations, and governments should always be planning for such events by continually tightening building codes, creating internationally cooperative logistical systems, and developing the necessary contingency plans. A good question is, "What information, if any, do people and organizations need if the likelihood of a catastrophic event is not zero and its potential impact is severe?"

Across the United States, thousands of facilities produce chemicals to create products we use every day. Many of these chemicals are precursors, which are combined with other chemicals to create materials such as plastics, oil and gasoline, pharmaceuticals, and similar products. What people do not often think of as they go about daily activities is that some of these chemical facilities can become very dangerous in certain circumstances when error conditions align with each other. As an example, some of these facilities are located in heavily populated areas. If an accident occurred in these areas, hundreds, thousands, even millions of people could be quickly killed or injured.

In 2004, Rebecca Leung made a report of these types of facilities.[20] The report's title was, "U.S. Plants: Open to Terrorists." An example was given of one facility located near New York City where more than 1,000 tons of chlorine gas were stored in a heavily populated area of 12 million people. These people could be exposed to deadly chlorine gas if it were accidently or intentionally released. In fact, there are more than 100 chemical facilities across the United States where an accident could affect more than a million people. A different report estimated there are 7,395 facilities within the United States where a worst-case event could impact more than a thousand people.[21]

Interestingly, legislation recently introduced by Representative Bennie Thompson, a Democrat from Mississippi, titled "H.R. 5577: Chemical Facility Anti-Terrorism Act of 2008," could not pass the United States Congress because of heavy lobbying by organizations representing chemical manufacturing interests. The cost of the bill would have been five dollars per American between the years 2010 and 2013.[22] Similar legislation has also been killed. These include a previous bill titled, "S. 2145: Chemical Facility Anti-Terrorism Act of 2006," sponsored by Senator Susan Collin, a Republican Senator from Maine. It was a bill to enhance security against potential terrorist attacks at chemical facilities. It would have cost less than two dollars per American over five years to implement.[23]

If there is a catastrophic chemical accident within the United States in the coming years impacting thousands of people, how can people claim it was not unexpected? Perhaps the probability is currently small, but given the catastrophic effects, more should be done to prevent these events. If such an event did occur, it would share, with previous catastrophic events, similar recurrence factors including regulatory laxness, dangerous equipment, dangerous application environments, complex systems, significant potential for financial loss or loss of life if failure occurs, political sensitivity, and so forth. It should be noted that the organizations are required to provide estimates of environmental impact. But they are free to communicate potential effects in obtuse terms people find difficult to understand. Recall, framing communications is important for understanding. Also missing are specific instructions people should take if there is an event as well as the warning signs before an event occurs. These communications are often conveniently missing. The public seldom knows what to do if a disaster occurs. Unfortunately, a Bhopal-type disaster could also happen in the United States and with similar effects because responsibility is usually diffused across many organizations and individuals. The effective result is: no one is responsible.

Despite known risks, organizations are reluctant to share or communicate worst-case scenarios with others and especially potential victims, for a variety of reasons. These reasons are seldom based on fact or even common sense. One of the most common excuses organizations provide for the lack of effective communication is people will become alarmed, panic, or take extreme actions in response to perceived threats. But, with contradictory reasoning, the same organization withholding important information will most likely expect public cooperation if a catastrophic event occurs. If people have not been warned or told where and how an event is likely to unfold or their expected behaviors, how can they be expected to behave in ways that help prevent deaths and injury or help relief efforts?

Perhaps one of the worst effects of hiding important information is that organizations become lazy and inwardly focused, complacent to the point where attitudes reflect a culture of denial that a catastrophic event will even occur. In these cultures, good contingency planning is almost impossible. Scenario planning can help eliminate this complacency. It promotes collaboration by encouraging creation and analyses of very unlikely events. Hurricane Katrina comes to mind. Recall, people died because they were not told what to do if water from damaged levees flooded the city. If the scenario planning had been used to analyze possible outcomes and contingency plans created to manage these outcomes, relief efforts would most likely have been more effective. People say hindsight is 20–20; but the effects from Hurricane Katrina were not impossible to predict in advance of its devastating damage. In fact, some of them still exist. Organizations may become uncomfortable with the types of information; scenario planning may produce, and then attempt to suppress it. But they do so to their disadvantage.

Arriving from a recent trip to Singapore in April, 2010, I remember exiting the flight with United Airlines at Washington Dulles Airport to transfer to a domestic connecting flight to Boston, Massachusetts. At the same time, people were rushing off other international flights after retrieving luggage from passport security. The group converged as a hoard where it was met by additional customs agents who did a second identification screening. Once past the second checkpoint we were forced into a line where our baggage would eventually be scanned and identifications rechecked. The time slowly passed as the waiting line tortuously meandered toward the final screening checkpoints. The connection time for the next flight was approaching quickly.

Next to the waiting line were process improvement experts who handed us cards with time stamps so they could monitor our movement toward the final checkpoint, which we could not see because of partitions. I wanted to tell them to consult basic textbooks regarding queuing theory and how to design systems so people do not have to wait very long for service. But the one suggestion that continually came to mind was they should have been providing us with timely information regarding waiting time to reduce the stress of waiting for the security check. I wondered how much longer it would be to the final screening. Was it to be 5 minutes, 10 minutes, or perhaps 60 minutes? The lack of information was stressful. In addition to collecting time-stamped information, the process improvement experts should have been interviewing people waiting in the line and security agents to gather information useful for improving the process.

Remember the Union Carbide Chemical plant explosion that occurred in Bhopal, India? If the local residents knew of the potential dangers from an explosion at the facility and its poor safety practices, would maintenance perhaps would have been better? People should be informed of potentially dangerous situations for their protection to hold organizations accountable for their actions. A failure to do so creates unnecessary risks for communities around the world as well as the United States. Organizations should also be forced to create contingency plans prior to an event and share the information publically. People need to be kept aware of what's happening around them to be able to plan their actions and correctly behave. They are much easier to work with when well informed. In summary, scenarios should be explored, contingency plans created, and people informed. This makes a difference between having a well-informed public behaving correctly verses one ill-equipped if a catastrophic event occurs. It also creates a more proactive public that holds organizations, politicians, and others accountable.

Many months ago, as I began writing this book, my goal was to discuss technology failures as well as failures of construction works such as bridges, dams, buildings, and structures. The technology failures were focused on failures of machines and dangerous processes. But, as the research expanded, I saw an advantage for discussing failures in general, across diverse industries, products, and services as well as catastrophic failures affecting many people. In time, I began looking for common themes to tie the different events together and identify ways to predict or mitigate the enormous amounts of destructive damage occurring each year around the world. The result was an expansion of perspective to include the combined effects of cognitive and organizational factors as well as technological ones for creating error conditions that contribute to mistakes.

It is obvious, technology failures alone cannot explain most catastrophic events. This is especially true when logistical systems and relief efforts are major contributors to failure. Individual and organizational attitudes and behaviors also greatly influence the effects of catastrophic events and are often major contributors to deaths, injuries, and property damage. The focus of this book has become one of identifying tools and methods to help people work through many of the cognitive and organizational barriers to change.

In the newspaper today, there was an article describing a new policy by the United States and other developed countries toward poorer countries that need economic aid.[24] The new message is the United States wants to help countries become independent rather than just throwing them money. This may be a step in the right direction. Historically, developed countries have thrown economic aid over the fence at underdeveloped countries. The result has been decades of economic dependency. Partnerships are beneficial if countries cooperate to mutual benefit.

This concept has applicability for managing catastrophic events. Cooperation is very much needed to avoid the chronic problems associated with relief efforts. The sooner cooperative relief efforts are preplanned, and activated when natural disasters or major catastrophic events occur, the better. Imagine a world wherein, regardless of political, religious, or cultural boundaries, cooperative networks exist to help people in time of need to reduce loss of life. Countries do not need to politically agree with neighboring countries to work with them to help others.

Immediately after Hurricane Katrina devastated New Orleans, the country of Cuba offered the United States hospital ships to help the injured. However, the offer was rebuffed for political rather than humanitarian reasons. If Cuba was devastated, wouldn't the United States help it? This is an example of the type of mutual regional dependency that is necessary in the future because catastrophic events will certainly increase, if only because of higher population densities in disaster-prone regions around the world. In the absence of effective disaster planning, things will only get worse.

It is interesting that the effects of unexpected catastrophic events can sometimes be mitigated through an analysis of interrelationships of drivers, that is, major causes, relevant conditions, and outcomes. These analyses help create and effectively execute contingency plans if failure events occur. Rethinking unexpected consequences shows that technology failures contribute little to catastrophic events, even though technology failures, such as people dying in aircraft accidents, people being cut and crushed by machines, and similar incidents are dramatic and horrific. The fact is that more people die every year through preventable causes or mismanagement of logistical and relief efforts. Unfortunately, we remain poorly prepared for anything but the most minor failure events. It doesn't have to remain this way.

It is true that some events will always be more catastrophic than others. A major information technology mishap may cost hundreds of millions of dollars to repair, but in comparison to a major earthquake or environmental disaster, the effects are minor. Also, some industries are inherently more dangerous than others. Examples include oil and gas as well as process-focused focused organizations operating in dangerous conditions. Naturally, BP comes to mind in this regard. But an analysis of the more than 40 catastrophic events discussed in this book shows that deficiencies of cognition and organizational culture often lead to unexpected failures.

All risks cannot be eliminated from the world, but they can be better managed across diverse types of systems and organizations. However, they can often be better managed through the efficient design of products, services, and logistical systems that integrate cognitive and organizational culture influences into a framework for creating solutions. In this context, it is important to openly share information.

Table 7.2
Risk recurrence analysis: future hypothetical corrective actions

Risk Recurrence Factor	2010 Toyota Recall	Anderson SAP ERP issues for Fox-Meyer	2009 Continental Flight 3407 Near Buffalo	2010 Haiti Earth-quake	2005 Hurricane Katrina	2009 SEC Failures	2010 Deepwater Horizon GoM Oil Spill
1. Organizational cultural issues resulted in significant previous failures	N	N	N	N	N	N	N
2. A lack of risk analysis and contingency planning	N	N	N	N	N	N	N
3. Regulatory laxness	N	N	N	N	N	N	N
4. Dangerous equipment	Y	N	Y	N	N	N	Y
5. Dangerous application environment	Y	N	Y	Y	Y	N	Y
6. Complex systems	N	Y	Y	Y	Y	Y	Y
7. People-dependent or cognition issues	N	N	N	N	N	Y	N
8. Significant potential financial loss or loss of life if failure occurs	Y	Y	Y	Y	Y	Y	Y
9. Would impact many people across large geography	Y	Y	N	Y	Y	Y	Y
10. Politically sensitive	Y	N	N	Y	Y	Y	Y
11. Application technology ahead of control technology	N	N	N	N	N	Y	N
12. Dependent on complicated logistical systems and resources for failure mitigation	N	N	N	Y	Y	Y	Y
13. Poor root cause analysis and mitigation	N	N	N	N	N	N	N
Score (0–13)	5	3	4	6	6	6	7
% Recurrence	38%	23%	31%	46%	46%	46%	54%
Recurrence likelihood	Med	Low	Low	Med	Med	Med	Med

Risk recurrence classification: 04 low (0%–37%); 5–8 medium (38%–68%); 9–13 high (69%–100%)

If we revise assumptions regarding recurrence risks shown in Table 6.5 to those shown in Table 7.2 we see they can be reduced for some of the original events. Let's examine the 2009 Continental Flight 3407 accident near Buffalo. Certain recurrence factors related to this accident cannot be eliminated. These include the fact that an airplane is a dangerous piece of equipment that operates in dangerous environments thousands of feet in the air. Also, it is a complex system that includes people, information, and technology. A mishap anywhere in the system such as in maintenance, repairs, servicing between takeoffs, air traffic control issues, or pilot errors can cause catastrophic failure and loss of life. However, some risk recurrence factors such as regulatory laxness and certain cognitive and organization factors can be better managed. Recall, in the aftermath of the accident, the investigation found pilot training could have been more effective (an organizational issue) and the pilots became distracted during the flight (a cognitive issue). The result was that wrong evasive actions were taken when the plane began to stall. Lax regulatory oversight may also have contributed to the accident because pilot training could have been more effective.

It is also interesting that a recurring theme is if regulations become lax and ineffective, failures often occur. The 2009 SEC failures and the 2010 Deepwater Horizon have been prominent in this year's news. Weak regulatory oversight was in part to blame for these events. However, if these and other recurrence factors associated with the events are changed, the likelihood of future failures decreases. As an example, the recurrence risk (as defined in this book) of an event similar to the Deepwater Horizon decreases from 92 percent to 54 percent. This does not imply a similar event will not reoccur, but only that if organizational and cultural issues at the companies involved including BP are addressed, regulations are enforced, more effective risk analyses and contingency plans created, control technologies designed and deployed, and cognitive issues more effectively addressed, then recurrence risks will decrease.

Ineffective or delayed responses also contribute to or magnify the effects of catastrophic events. Examples include the frequent poor planning and breakdowns of logistical systems associated with relief efforts. These contribute to delayed responses. Finally, there are limits to how far we can mitigate risk. Some industries are just inherently complex and dangerous. The risk will always be higher in these industries. To the extent organizations within these industries work continuously to reduce risk, aside from new technological developments, much more can always be done. However, organizations seldom do everything possible to reduce risk because there are few incentives to do so. The economic consequences are many years away if an event actually occurs. Also, if people are killed or seriously injured, people in the organization are seldom held accountable. This is why risky behavior is so prevalent. It usually makes economic sense to take risk rather than avoid it.

SUMMARY

Rethinking unexpected consequences requires analyzing diverse events for commonality of causal factors and the effectiveness of solutions. Once similar events are placed into common categories it is easier to see why things fail. First, human error is always lurking in the background. It's very difficult to completely eliminate its effects. Although good design, production, and other work practices help reduce risks, errors of perception and attitudes influence the judgments of people and their interactions within groups are prevalent. People within groups also influence each other for good or bad depending on circumstances. Overlaid on these interpersonal interactions, organizational culture often complicates group decision making. Dysfunctional behaviors such as departures from best practice standards increase the likelihood of failure. This is especially true if management systems are not well designed to begin with, not transparent, or not adhered to by everyone including executives. These are some of the reasons why things fail. As we know from earlier chapters, there are many others.

Even if a product, service, or logistical system has been well designed, perceptions of use may cloud judgments by users, the general public, and others regarding its intended functions and features. In fact, even well-designed products, services, and logistical systems are sometimes perceived as defective although they are not. Cognitive and group influences are often at play in these situations by influencing expectations and perceptions of performance. In some of the most serious events discussed in earlier chapters, functions and features of even well-designed safety systems were actually dismantled by individuals and groups for convenience. The result was catastrophic failure. Chernobyl comes to mind. Good design practices and management systems are necessary, but not sufficient for the prevention of failures. In fact, they are of limited usefulness if they can be ignored, modified, or shut down.

Only a few executives or key stakeholders are needed to derail well-designed systems. As an example, projects and organizational priorities can be changed, resources diverted, and monies withheld from design, production, and other work activities including safety and maintenance. It happens frequently, but usually causes only minor failures. There is seldom personal accountability for making wrong decisions, whether through ignorance or direct action caused by conflicts of interest. Organizations need to create internal and to an extent external transparency around decisions made in regard to design, production, and other work activities. If failures occur, standardized methods should also be used for investigating causal factors based on industry best practices. However, even if organizations take these precautions, they cannot completely prevent failures if their industry or organization has certain types of recurrence risks.

Some organizations operate in very dangerous working environments. The oil and gas industry is a good example. People love to blame it for high profits and for failures. Of course they should be blamed if guilty, but the reality is that they operate very large, complicated, and dangerous equipment within harsh environments such as deep under the ocean or in the frigid winters on northern Alaskan coasts and other inhospitable locations. The infrastructure of oil and gas exploration equipment and refining facilities is concrete, steel, and other material subject to corrosion, fracture, and fatigue and deterioration. If not maintained there will be failures. Oil and gas infrastructure, as well as that of other industries, must be continually inspected and kept in good working condition. Mistakes in judgment by management, employees, contractors, or others regarding design or maintenance requirements will under extreme conditions cause catastrophic failures.

Unfortunately, effects of poor judgments accumulate slowly, such as corrosion of pipelines. It is not until a major event occurs that they become obvious. The Bhopal disaster comes to mind. Oil and gas workers in remote production facilities work two weeks on a job site. When at the job site they often work 12 hours each day and continuously for 14 days. Fatigue in these conditions is always a potential causal factor for failures. Each industry has its own issues regarding risk recurrence factors.

As an example, oil and gas, chemical production, or the automotive industries are quite frequently involved in high profile failure events. However, failure alone is not enough for an event to be considered catastrophic. The long list of recurrence risks includes effects on large numbers of people, impact over a widespread geographical area, and political sensitivity. Reviewing this list of recurrence risks shown in Table 7.2 suggests catastrophic events are not as unexpected as they first appear. However, this is small comfort to people adversely affected by them. It should also be noted that the list of recurrence risks is not meant to be exhaustive. Others will most likely be added in the future. But it is certainly a good place to begin to look for reasons why catastrophic events occur and repeatedly within some industries and organizations.

What can an organization do to reduce its risk? Especially those organizations that operate within high-risk industries? The easy answer would be to say everything must be done well, from design to production. But a more definitive answer is expected. An organization must acknowledge it is subject to several recurrence risks. It must incorporate these concepts into its health and safety systems. It must always work from a design perspective to design out cognitive influences. Its culture must also be transparent, at least internally and to neutral parties. Unfortunately, few organizations have truly transparent cultures. In the most secretive ones, key stakeholders are egotistical, self-serving, or arrogant. Design, production, distribution, and health and safety decisions are based on biases, little new information, or dysfunctions.

Truly independent third parties should also be retained for advice, audits, and analyses. These third parties should not have conflicts of interest. There should also be checks and balances and internal accountability based on roles and responsibilities. Finally, scenario planning is one of several critical methods for creating what-if and devil's advocate scenarios that test an organization's conventional wisdom. An integral part of such scenarios should be an economic analysis to show management the wisdom of effectively planning for unexpected events that have potentially catastrophic consequences.

NOTES

1. "Rescue Crews Pull 2 More from Haitian Market: 3 Others Were Rescued Earlier There; U.N. Staffer, Hotel Co-Owner Also Saved," MSNBC.com, January 17, 2010, http://www.msnbc.msn.com/id/34829978/ns/world_news-haiti_earthquake.

2. Roger Bilham, "Killer Quakes on Rise with Cities on Fault Lines," *Bloomberg BusinessWeek,* April 15, 2010.

3. International Strategy for Disaster Reduction (ISDR), "Earthquakes Caused the Deadliest Disasters in the Past Decade," news brief, January 28, 2010, http://www.unisdr.org/news/v.php?id=12470.

4. Joel Achenbach, "Under the World's Greatest Cities, Deadly Plates," *Washington Post,* February 23, 2010.

5. World Health Organization, "The World Health Report 2004: Changing History." Copies of this publication can be ordered from: Bookorders@who.int, http://www.who.int/whr/2004/en/.

6. Douglas W. Hubbard, *How to Measure Anything: Finding the Value of Intangibles in Business* (Hoboken, NJ: Wiley, 2007).

7. Ian Wylie, "There Is No Alternative to . . ." *Fast Company,* June 30, 2002.

8. Fritz Zwicky, "Morphologie and Policy Analysis," presented at the 16th EURO Conference on Operational Analysis, Brussels, 1998.

9. Charles B. Reynolds, "What Really Happened on September 18, 2008?" www.associtaedcontent.com, accessed September 6, 2010; David M. Herszenhorn, "Congressional Leaders Stunned by Warnings," *New York Times,* September 19, 2008.

10. Michael Schrange, *Serious Play: How the World's Best Companies Simulate to Innovate* (Boston: Harvard Business School Press, 2000).

11. James William Martin, *Operational Excellence: Translating Customer Value through Global Supply Chains* (Boca Raton, FL: Taylor and Francis, 2008).

12. "California Pipeline Blast Raises Safety Questions," CNN, September 11, 2010, www.CNN.com.

13. "Death Toll in Calif. Blast hits 7, Police Say," MSNBC, September 12, 2010, www.msnbc.com.

14. Andrew Restuccia, "Given Natural Gas's Dangers, Worries about Pipeline Regulation and Oversight Abound," *Washington Independent,* August 10, 2010, www.washingtonindependnt.com.

15. Kim Landers and Craig McMurtie, "Aid Struggling to Reach Haitians," Australia Network News; ABC News, Friday, January 15, 2010, http://www.abc.net./au/news.

16. "Haiti Earthquake Response," 6-Month Report, July 14, 2010, Inter Agency Standing Committee (IASC), Report of the Response to Humanitarian Crisis in Haiti, http://www.humanitarianinfo.org/iasc/pageloader.aspx?page=content-news-newsdetails&newsid=143.

17. "Catastrophic Earthquakes: Will Nepal Be Next?" *Huffington Post,* March 22, 2010, http://www.huffingtonpost.com/2010/03/22/catastrophic-earthquakes_n_508937.html.

18. *Earthquake Contingency Plan 2008,* Nepalese Red Cross Society (NRCS), National Headquarters, Kathmandu, http://reliefweb.int/node/288236.

19. Frank Bajak, "Chile Earthquake 2010: Why The Haiti Earthquake Wasn't as Strong, but Far More Devastating," *Huffington Post,* February 27, 2010, http://www.huffingtonpost.com/2010/02/28/chile-haiti-earthquake-2010-comparison_n_480153.html.

20. Rebecca Leung, "U.S. Plants: Open To Terrorists, *60 Minutes* Finds Lax Security at Many U.S. Chemical Facilities," June 13, 2004, http://www.cbsnews.com/stories/2003/11/13/60minutes/main583528.shtml.

21. Dana A. Shea, "RMP Facilities in the US as of February 2008," Congressional Research Service, March 4, 2008, Sourcewatch Organization, http://www.sourcewatch.org/index.php?title=Chemical_security_legislation_(U.S.).

22. H.R. 5577: Chemical Facility Anti-Terrorism Act of 2008, http://www.govtrack.us/congress/bill.xpd?bill=h110-5577.

23. S. 2145: Chemical Facility Anti-Terrorism Act of 2006, http://www.govtrack.us/congress/bill.xpd?bill=s109-2145.

24. "Obama: U.S. Changing Battle Plan on Poverty, World Leaders Make New Financial Pledges to Help Women and Children," MSNBC.com News Services, updated September 22, 2010, 6:01:59 P.M. ET, http://www.msnbc.msn.com/id/39311362/ns/world_news.

CONCLUSION

How often have I said to you that when you have eliminated the impossible, whatever remains, however improbable, must be the truth? (Sherlock Holmes)

—Arthur Conan Doyle

People are surprised when an earthquake or other catastrophic events cause extensive destruction and death. These events were certain to occur sometime, but people did not prepare. As an example, earthquakes cause most damage because buildings are not reinforced and relief responses are ad hoc, so millions of people die each year for lack of medicines, food, water, and shelter. There are actions we could take to save millions of lives and prevent injuries. Property and environmental damage could also be mitigated to varying degrees. Perhaps it's time to admit that poor preparation and coordination as well as cognitive, group, and organizational behaviors are important contributors to tragedy. According to Albert Einstein, "Insanity is doing the same thing over and over, but expecting different results." We need to do things differently.

Mr. Jared Diamond wrote a book titled *Guns, Germs and Steel: The Fates of Human Societies.*[1] It describes why some societies dominated others over the past several thousand years. Reasons for dominant societies include moderate environments to grow grains and cultivated foods, and domestication of animals providing food, work, and transportation. As population densities increased, infectious diseases eventually conferred immunity. These factors increased high population densities to create advanced cultures and technologies. This enabled one culture to eventually dominate another.

In Mr. Diamond's second book, titled *Collapse: How Societies Choose to Fail or Succeed,* he describes how societies fail and the resulting group behaviors.[2] When societies grew too fast and outstripped their resources, there was usually an eventual collapse and societal breakdown, which contributed to pestilence, war, and even cannibalism between competing groups in the same region. In contrast to worldwide logistical systems that more easily match resources to demand, many of the failed societies were isolated (e.g., islands within a deteriorating environment).

The world's population is increasing. Forecasts are it will grow from six to nine billion people by 2050. It may be possible to feed three billion more people, but only if radical changes are enacted in consumption habits and allocation of food amounts. However, if the past is an indication for the future, it is very unlikely that three billion more people will be properly fed in the future.[3] Scenarios similar to those described by Mr. Jared Diamond are most likely: wars and conflict. Stronger nations and cultures will most likely dominate weaker ones. The future becomes even more uncertain when considering future catastrophic events. These usually dislocate many people and damage critical infrastructure.

Technical failures are difficult to predict because several error conditions align to cause a failure. An example is the crash of Alaskan Airlines Flight 261 on January 31, 2000, in the Pacific Ocean near Point Mugu, California.[4] The plane crashed because of excessive wear of its jackscrew assembly's acme nut threads, which actuated the rear stabilizers. According to the government report, "The excessive and accelerated wear of the accident jackscrew assembly acme nut threads was the result of insufficient lubrication, which was directly causal to the Alaska Airlines flight 261 accident. . . . Alaska Airlines extensions of its lubrication interval for its McDonnell Douglas MD-80 horizontal stabilizer components and the Federal Aviation Administrations approval of these extensions, the last of which was based on Boeing's extension of the recommended lubrication interval, increased the likelihood that a missed or inadequate lubrication would result in excessive wear of jackscrew assembly acme nut threads and, therefore, was a direct cause of the excessive wear and contributed to the Alaska Airlines flight 261 accident." Steel threads can be worn down if subjected to excessive force and heat. The result is a smooth surface that cannot retain its mating component.

I recall working on a trash compactor for a friend several years ago. The compactor went through its normal cycle, but would not compress the trash. After the cycle, I examined the screw that slowly turns to move the compactor foot. Its threads were stripped, so it became a smooth metal rod without threads. Worse, the compactor's foot, a flat plate, was bent into the shape of a V rather than flat. Obviously it had been compacting hard objects, which were likely metal cans. These hard objects placed too much force on the threads of the compactor screw and stripped its threads and bent its foot.

If a mechanical system is stressed beyond its yield point, failure is sudden and sometimes catastrophic. So it was also with the airplane's jack-screw acme nuts: they could not move the rear horizontal stabilizer of the airplane up and own for pitch control. It was later found the thread failure was caused by excessive wear of the threads because of insufficient lubrication. Lubrication helps lower the temperature of mating components when they are under stress of an applied force. It was found insufficient lubrication was the result of reduced maintenance intervals. This type of accident is difficult to predict unless correct lubrication intervals had been recommended in advance.

Isolated events caused by a combination of error conditions (e.g., technical failures or behaviors contrary to policy and procedures) cannot be easily predicted in advance. In these situations error conditions are weak signals. But once a failure occurs, then error conditions are identified and eliminated. Then different types of failures caused by an alignment of new error conditions will occur because there are no previous patterns to analyze and prevent.

Sudden and horrific accidents are sometimes caused by small changes that are unnoticed because they are weak signals. Only in hindsight does a pattern emerge showing a slow buildup of error conditions events that finally led to catastrophic failure. However, it is usually easy to identify causes for failures, and especially isolated technical ones, after they cause damage.

This book presented a different perspective for failure analysis. The discussion has included many different types of failures. The conclusion is that the effects of many catastrophic events are predictable. There are early warning signs which, if understood, provide strong rather than weak signals. But social psychological and organizational causal factors as well as technical ones must be considered.

In earlier chapters, we discussed the role of design teams for creating useful products and services. In a creative process, project structure must be used to ensure simplification, standardization, and mistake proofing of work activities. Simplification reduces complexity of products, services, and systems. Less complexity implies fewer things will be in error. Standardization ensures things are done the same way each time. It also reduces confusion and error conditions. Mistake proofing eliminates the effects of human error and helps manage error conditions or failures if they occur.

There are many ways to effectively mistake proof products, services, and systems. People will always make cognitive errors. Designing out the potential for error is a powerful strategy for preventing failures.

It is also important to review a team's progress with customers and key stakeholders as a product or service moves toward commercialization. A balance should be achieved for all stakeholders including customers, the organization, and the general public. However, mistakes can and do occur when designing and commercializing products and services for many reason with the results that the performance of some products and services is less than it should have been. There are often several reasons. There could be unnecessary complexity with respect to functions and features. Perhaps best-in-class design methods were not used? Or customers and key stakeholders were not consulted to provide prioritization? There may be necessary functions, but features may vary by market segment. A successful design in one market segment may be a failure in another one. There are often many other reasons.

There is a long list of very successful products and services. When the original iPod appeared on the market in 2001, the consensus was its design was exceptional. Time has affirmed the product's ability to meet its design intent over the past 10 years. In fact, the product line has been extended to include the iPod Nano, the iPod Shuffle, and the iPod Touch, as well as the iPod Classic. Cognitive influences permeate its design features and functions. Its success also depends on production and distribution as well as related commercialization activities. What would have happened if this product had not been manufactured or distributed with the same forethought and care it was designed? The result may have been commercial failure enabling competitors to more easily compete.

In addition, correct tools and methods are required to translate customer requirements, create design alternatives, and test them to ensure they work as expected. Good designs must also be easy to use because of human limitations, be easy to maintain and repair, and be easy to dispose of at the end of their useful lives. Much needs to be considered when designing products and services. As an example, some software updates are easy and economical for maintenance. One example is when Microsoft software prompts for permission to download updates or upload information to diagnose software performance problems. In fact, automatic software updates often work so well that the likelihood of error conditions and mistakes is reduced to almost zero. Designers must also anticipate how products and services will be misused and modify them accordingly because some failures ascribed to technology are in fact caused by human error.

Social psychologists know the importance of cognition as well as group and organizational behaviors on design activities and within organizations. In addition to information filtering and similar issues, cognitive dissonance is a particularly troubling phenomenon for contributing to errors. Recall that cognitive dissonance is an uncomfortable feeling when a person has two opposing thoughts or behaviors in contradiction. The phenomenon becomes an issue if people engage in destructive behaviors to reduce dissonance (e.g., distorting facts intentionally or unintentionally). There are several other relevant cognitive effects. Most of the catastrophic events discussed in this book were caused by human errors that had as their root cause a cognitive influence. Also, it isn't only group dynamics that must be considered, but also individual attitudes, behaviors, and how they coalesce into a team's beliefs and behaviors. Group errors occur with environments influenced by organizational norms and values, that is, culture. Experts know that human and other types of errors align to cause catastrophic failures (e.g., James Reason's Swiss cheese model). However, recognizing combinations of causal factors is not an easy task, especially in the face of weak signals, but once the signals are identified, design modifications can be made to reduce the likelihood an error condition will reoccur.

Numerous stakeholders affect the decisions made by design teams, including important functions and features. Cost is an example. Designers have costing targets that, if exceeded, make a design a commercial failure. This requires them to design within cost constraints, that is, be profitable. The design or production processes become prone to error if constraints are haphazardly forced on a team. The list is long on ways in which organizational and major stakeholders can derail a design process. Sometimes the results are deadly.

As we move outside the boundaries of human control, failure prevention becomes more elusive. Examples include major catastrophic events where error conditions align in unusual ways to result in disasters that suddenly cause shock and damage. Different strategies need to be employed to mitigate the effects of these catastrophic events. Fewer people will be killed if buildings are reinforced, like the ones in Chile, rather than those in Haiti. Relief efforts can also be better coordinated. Ideally, once a catastrophic event occurs, people should execute according to a contingency plan based on scenario planning.

Attitudes and behaviors are significant influencers for the design of products and services and how they are used. Recall, that people misinterpret design intent or fail to read instructions. Sometimes there is direct sabotage of products and systems. The effects may be minor or severe. Attitudes also affect groups or teams in different ways. Sometimes they are very well managed, informed, and able to execute work activities at very high standards. However, other groups and teams become dysfunctional.

How do we ensure people and groups within organizations will perform well? Design must be considered the basis on which to create safe products and services. This is in part the basis for a safety culture. The process must also be transparent to everyone to avoid or detect errors of judgment and unethical conduct. Organizations must provide resources to do the necessary work, that is, they should not be stretched so thin as to be ineffective. There should be well-managed work practices including production, testing, and audits. If issues are found, corrective actions systems should be activated to resolve them. Red flag conditions must be eliminated. Recall that red flag conditions cause error conditions. In turn, error conditions cause mistakes or failures. Red flag conditions include poor training, ineffective procedures, poor environmental conditions (e.g. lighting, noise, and others), and complicated work systems, to name a few.

Organizational structure and culture also influence the likelihood for failures. It is difficult enough to manage the behaviors of individuals and groups within an organization. If the organization itself does not aspire to higher standards, there is not much individuals and groups can do to compensate. Organizations may appear to have transparency. However, it requires only a few unethical employees, stakeholders, suppliers, or customers to create havoc even in otherwise well-managed organizations. Transparency and trust are important, but personal accountability rigorously enforced is also an effective strategy for ensuring people comply with organizational policies.

A review of some of the catastrophic events discussed in earlier chapters supports this belief. As an example, Table 4.1 provided several examples of ethical issues commonly affecting many organizations. In fact, anyone within an organization can behave unethically. Complicating the situation is the way in which people find logical arguments for convincing themselves that behaviors are ethical. Powerful internal stakeholders can also be problematic. Several catastrophic events were caused by powerful stakeholders who overrode opinions of employees with less influence. Organizations struggle to find ways for preventing these issues because at their basis, all policies and procedures are people-dependent. They can be easily ignored.

It is interesting that punishments from unethical behavior are usually minor. Personal accountability is seldom assigned to poor behavior. This is why it frequently occurs. It also becomes insidious when not punished. In the context of failure, behaviors should be considered unethical if they promote higher risk by violating safety and compliance policies. Individual, group, or key stakeholder behaviors are particularly troubling when substituted for officially sanctioned and vetted policies and procedures. Ethical behavior is important for preventing failures. The list of major organizations destroyed because of unethical behaviors is long. In an uncertain, complex world, both the number and magnitude of failures is likely to increase. This is why understanding good design principles, cognitive factors, ethical behaviors and organizational influence is more important than ever. Although a design team and others within an organization may compensate for organizational shortcomings, there are limits. And sometimes limits are stretched too far.

Assuming there is a well-organized infrastructure that protects an organization from errant employees, groups, and key stakeholders, a next step is to create systems for hazard identification and risk assessment. This requires creating an inventory of equipment, processes, and other sources for hazards. This information is used to identify primary as well as secondary or specific effects of hazardous conditions. A risk assessment is made of the likelihood of each secondary hazard occurring, its effect, and current controls. Prioritization is made to eliminate or manage these conditions and secondary effects. Analyses should also be made for hazards of products, services, and manmade or natural disasters. Relief agencies are to be concerned with the latter hazards.

Supporting systems for hazard identification include those activated if failures occur. It is important a thorough root cause investigation occur. These investigations are focused directly on failures of products or services or major man-made and natural events as well as logistical systems supporting relief efforts. An examination of the events discussed in this book shows root cause investigations were done differently for isolated as opposed to man-made and major natural disasters. In situations where political influences were strong, sometimes effective root cause analyses were not done at all and solutions remained unidentified long after the event. In some situations there remains a severe potential for damage. Particularly disturbing are chronic failures of medical and relief systems—failures that contribute to millions of deaths. More can be done, but priorities are vague.

When traveling through the southeastern United States, you see systems to protect people from tornados. Tornados cause serious damage across the United States. Sirens sound alarms, organizations routinely train their people to seek shelter if a tornado moves in to the area, and tornado shelters are widespread to prevent deaths and injuries. I recall visiting a client in Jackson, Tennessee, a few years ago. Jackson is located between Nashville and Memphis. Over the previous 15 years, I visited the city several times. Earlier in the evening as I flew from Boston to Memphis, lighting strikes could be seen in the clouds below over a large area. I knew there were likely to be tornado warnings for the area when I landed. In fact, the weather in Memphis was lousy: dark and rainy when I landed. I later found there were several tornados moving across the area. Somehow as I drove to Jackson I had missed them. When I pulled into Jackson, the town had been moderately damaged, sirens screamed, and traffic lights blinked on and off at random in the traffic intersections.

The next morning at the client's manufacturing facility, on the way into the main security gate, I saw a massive mound of earth. The security guard said it was a protective cover for the facilities tornado shelter. I admired how well it was built. Soon after entering the main lobby of the manufacturing facility, the plant manager met me and said several people who were to attend the seminar could not come because either their homes or relatives' homes had been damaged by a tornado. The news became worse when I was told a young man working at the facility and his family had been killed after a tornado destroyed their home. As part of the following conversation, I was also told 37 people had been killed by tornados in the region within the past five years. We wondered if the frequency and severity of the storms was getting worse.

This was a tragic event, but not unexpected given the recent history of tornado activity in the region. If home tornado shelters are not built or homes are built on slabs or people live in trailers, loss of life should be expected no matter how unlikely a tornado. In other words, although we cannot predict a specific tornado or earthquake with certainty, we know one will occur in a region. Building structurally sound homes, schools, hospitals, and other structures including tornado shelters makes sense. How we prepare for natural disasters is in our control. Relief efforts are also controllable to varying degrees. Although, they are too often confused and poorly coordinated, at least in their early stages. This is especially true if the underlying root causes are politically influenced. In summary, losses can be reduced through proper action.

Congressman Barney Frank is a fierce advocate for his constituents in Southeastern Massachusetts. Recently, he blasted the U.S. Commerce Department's refusal to increase fishing limits. Many of Congressman Frank's constituents are fisherman. Frank stated, "Commerce Secretary Locke's adamant refusal to consider the scientific evidence regarding fish stocks, and the callous and dismissive tone of National Oceanic and Atmospheric Administration (NOAA) Assistant Administrator Schwaab's refusal to acknowledge the economic crisis facing fishermen were unworthy of their responsibilities as federal officials. . . . There is a sad contrast between what they told us they were prepared to do last October and what they blatantly refused to do in January. I had hoped that bringing our concerns to the level of the Secretary of Commerce would mean a fairer result for the fishing industry. It is now clear that the secretary is unwilling to exercise independent judgment and that an anti-fishing attitude prevails in the National

Marine Fisheries Service. . . . This is unacceptable. I have worked with the Obama administration on a number of important issues since the president came to office, and I will continue to be supportive of our common public policy goals. But the president must understand that if the administration persists in such a serious assault on the livelihood of the working men and women of the fishing industry, it will make it difficult for me and others to maintain this degree of cooperation."[5]

What is the answer? The information can be confusing. The fishing industry has seen its days at sea reduced by more than 50 percent in the past 10 years. The fishermen have called for help restocking and managing ground fish in the region. In other words, they believe government should be working to manage and increase fishing stocks rather than rely on an enforcement strategy. A recent NOAA fishing stock assessment showed mixed results. Cod were nearing a sustainable rate and Haddock stocks were increasing.[6] One conclusion is that an integrated solution must be implemented, and right now the most effective management strategy is reducing fishing days. It appears to have been working over the past several years.

Politics affects many of the decisions to take or not take actions for preventing man-made and natural disasters. Arguments concerning fishing and other special interests affect the ability of a country to take actions based on fact and not opinion. Fishing is no different. Other examples are the rush to explore and produce oil and gas in the Gulf of Mexico. The control technology has been shown to be limited in effectiveness. Building houses in marginal or even dangerous areas such as New Orleans and the coastal regions of the United States and other countries is hazardous. Implementing security systems based on political expediency rather than fact works poorly. There are many more examples.

Catastrophic disasters will become worse because more people will inhabit marginal living areas near flood plains, earthquake-prone cities, and areas historically experiencing destructive events. Technology may mitigate some of the effects, but if history is a guide, not their magnitude. People living in poorer regions of the world have few choices where to live. Worse, they are often subject to cultural, religious, political, and economic constraints. This implies the effects will only become worse. However, on a positive note, according to a World Bank report, some progress is being made: "The proportion of the developing world's population living in extreme economic poverty—defined as living on less than $1.25 per day (at 2005 prices, adjusted to account for the most recent differences in purchasing power across countries)—has fallen from 52 percent in 1981 to 26 percent in 2005."[7] But, how far can Third World economic progress be pushed? More can and should be done to help these people. But, the choices are few.

An interesting statistic recently provided by the United Nations Population Fund (the UNFPA) was that, "For the first time in history, more than half its human population, 3.3 billion people, will be living in urban areas. By 2030, this is expected to swell to almost 5 billion. Many of the new urbanites will be poor. Their future, the future of cities in developing countries, the future of humanity itself, all depends very much on decisions made now in preparation for this growth. . . . . The next few decades will see an unprecedented scale of urban growth in the developing world. This will be particularly notable in Africa and Asia where the urban population will double between 2000 and 2030: That is, the accumulated urban growth of these two regions during the whole span of history will be duplicated in a single generation. . . . By 2030, the towns and cities of the developing world will make up 81 per cent of urban humanity."[8] Recall, many of the building structures in these poorer cities quickly collapse when earthquakes and natural disasters occur.

Based on these predictions and the history of catastrophic failures deaths, injuries and damage from natural disasters are almost certain to be higher. Other negative effects such as political instability, poverty, and disease outbreaks will also increase as urban population densities soar across the poorer and richer regions of the world. A recent example was the outbreak of avian influenza similar to the recent H1N1 virus. Recently, an article stated, "But speaking to reporters on the sidelines of an influenza conference in Hong Kong, researcher Robert Webster warned against complacency. 'We may think we can relax and influenza is no longer a problem. I want to assure you that that is not the case,' said Webster, chairman of the virology and molecular biology department at St. Jude Children's Research Hospital in Memphis, Tennessee. Webster predicted that the next pandemic could be sparked by a virus that spreads from water fowl to pigs and then on to humans such as the H5N1 strain of bird flu, which has killed 300 people over the past seven years. He noted that after several years of decline, the number of bird flu cases in humans increased in 2009, lifted by an uptick of cases in Egypt. 'H5N1 can kill 61 percent of humans infected, but it doesn't know how to spread from human to human. But don't trust it because it could acquire that capacity. So we must stay vigilant.'"[9]

The news is full of similar stories regarding the likelihood of future pandemic events. The only unknown is when they will occur. Recall, people have a tendency to ignore events having a low likelihood even if their impact is expected to be severe. Complicating the situation is that countries have few choices in regard to where their people live. Many of their cities have existed for hundreds or thousands of years in their current locations. But a willful disregard for technology and weak governmental laws and regulations will contribute to future catastrophic damage through pandemics, natural disasters, or other causes.

Similar comments can be made for preventing environmental disasters. There were two news stories on *USA Today* website today.[10] The first was titled, "U.S. Issues Deep-Water Oil Drilling Rules; Moratorium Stands,"[11] and the second, "BP's New CEO Bob Dudley Creates Unit to Enforce Safety Practices."[12] Recently, Mr. Mark Bly, head of BP's team investigating the Deepwater Horizon Gulf of Mexico disaster, reported the results of his team's investigation to the National Academy of Engineering committee. BP blamed the accident on itself, Transocean (the owner of the rig), and Halliburton (who did the cementing work). In response, a committee member named Mr. Najmedin Meshkati, a professor at the Viterbi School of Engineering at the University of Southern California, asked BP why it left out critical elements describing shift duration and worker fatigue. He also asked, "How could you call this great work accident investigation. . . (without) addressing human performance issues and organizational issues and decision-making issues?"[13] Given the importance of cognitive and organizational influences for failure, we now know just how correct Mr. Meshkati was in his criticism of BP's report. How many more people will die or be injured, and how much more environmental damage will occur in the future? Judge for yourself the likelihood of future failures.

In 2010, a very destructive computer worm was unleashed across the world. It attacks industrial equipment. It is believed the focus of the attack was Iran and its nuclear program. Infected computers were found in Iran, Pakistan, and India as well as in the United States, the United Kingdom, Germany, and other countries. It is common knowledge that Iran has been a politically controversial country. In early 1978 demonstrations began there against the shah and worsened over the year, forcing the shah to leave the country in January 1979. In the ensuing political vacuum, Ayatollah Khomeini, a Muslim cleric, returned to Iran and assumed political and religious power after government troops were defeated by rebels. After the defeat, Iran became an Islamic Republic on April 1, 1979. The revolution was in part a protest against Westernizing influences within the country over several decades. After a few years of infighting between various power groups, Iran emerged a fundamentalist Islamic republic and Ayatollah Khomeini became its supreme leader.

Around the same time, Saddam Hussein became president of Iraq, replacing Ahmad Hasan Bakr. Over the next year, opposition groups were eliminated and Saddam Hussein consolidated power. At that time a pro-Iranian group, the Da'wa party, attempted to assassinate Tariq Aziz, the Iraqi deputy prime minister. In response Iraq ordered the expulsion of 40,000 Iranian-born born Shi'is as well as execution of people thought responsible for the attempted assignation. During this time Iran incited the Kurdish rebels in Khuzestan to rebel against Iraq. In September 1980, Iraq invaded Iran and a period of conflict continued until August 20, 1988. Earlier in the conflict, Iraq also began work on a nuclear facility that was later destroyed by Israel on June 7, 1981. But the conflict escalated when Iraq invaded its neighbor, Kuwait, on August 2, 1990. UN Resolution 660 ordered Iraq to withdraw from Kuwait. On January 17, 1991, allied forces led by the United States launched Operation Desert Storm, which ended the war on February 28, 1991. Eventually, Saddam Hussein was overthrown by allied forces in a war begun on March 19, 2003, and ended on May 1, 2003. This war created a political vacuum in the region that Iran continued to exploit until the formation of an Iraqi government.

Over the years since the Iranian revolution and the wars with Iraq, the Iranian Islamic Republic began building nuclear facilities of various types around the country. The Bushehr nuclear power facility was built in 2000 and there are several other facilities. International suspicion that Iran was attempting to build nuclear weapons had begun in the mid-1990s. During this time, the United Nations demanded inspections, which were allowed by Iran to varying levels; but sites under construction do not have to be reported based on the terms of Iran's safeguards agreement with the United Nations. One facility in particular has been troubling to many nations, including Israel and the United States. This is Natanz. The facility is a uranium enrichment plant, with several thousand centrifuges producing uranium enriched to a low level. The facility is well protected with reinforced concrete to approximately 24 feet underground, and is covered with 6-foot concrete barriers and more than 60 feet of soil. It is also heavily protected by security forces.

This infrastructure positioned Iran to become a future nuclear power. In combination with its advanced missile technology and hatred of Israel, many nations think Iran is a danger to peace in the region. But the alternatives for mitigating its nuclear threat have been few: invasion or a strike against its nuclear facilities. Unknown to all but a few people, a computer worm was created to cause industrial equipment to malfunction. It was found in July 2010 by a security firm, VirusBlokAda, located in the Republic of Balrus between Russia and the Ukraine. The computer worm was named Stuxnet. It attacks supervisory control and data acquisition systems of programmable logic controllers (PLC) in industrial equipment. It is targeted toward industrial equipment having variable frequency drives. It is very complex and its source code is approximately one-half megabyte. It attacks at three levels: the Windows operating system, industrial software application, and a Siemen's programmable logic controller (PLC). Also interesting is that the work only activates with variable frequency drives manufactured by Vacon, a Finland company, and Fararo Paya, based in Iran. The Stuxnet worm modifies the frequency over a wide range and damages motors.

In an article in *The Telegraph*, it was reported the Russians warned the attack by the Stuxnet worm or virus could cause major damage of Iran's Bushehr similar to the Chernobyl accident. Recall, the Russians built this nuclear facility.[14] Consensus is the worm was created in Israel with help from other Western nations. Its target was Iran and the centrifuges located at the Natanz facility, which apparently was upgraded to manufacture military-grade uranium. In a recent article in the *Jerusalem Post*, it was reported that the attack has set the Iranian military nuclear program back several years.[15]

In the many catastrophic events discussed in this book, a common theme is that things often go very wrong and when least expected. A successful cyber-attack on Iran today causing extensive collateral damage across the world portends a future in which extremist groups can launch similar attacks against industrial equipment in many countries. The industries and processes within those industries would be vulnerable to extensive damage. An article published by Fox Business reported computer networks within the United States are attacked thousands of times each day.[16] It went on to state that at risk were America's energy infrastructure, financial systems, and other industries. Worm or virus attacks on equipment and machines make the future situation even more dangerous because the potential for catastrophic failure reaches new proportions. Also, not only are threats from software sent over the Internet an issue, but hardware inserted into computers and other electronic equipment can be programmed to launch attacks in the United States. Defenses have been good so far, but threats continual to increase. We live in a brave new world where, because of the complexities, competition and technology advances will ensure that catastrophic events will continue to threaten us. Only time will tell us if we can effectively prevent their occurrence and consequences.

The discussions of the past seven chapters led to the identification of risk recurrence factors. These factors help identify the likelihood of major catastrophic events occurring either during an event or in its aftermath. A greater number of risk recurrence factors or higher levels imply an organization has a higher likelihood of failure. It is a fact that some organizations have inherently riskier work operations than others, so a potential for failure is always lurking. The practical solution is that organizations must be vigilant. The potential for error is always present because red flag conditions, poor design practices, cognition, and group and organizational dynamics often exacerbate already dangerous conditions.

Examples include the many failures of products, services, and logistical systems across very diverse industries. These failures were analyzed to identify causes for failure and also solutions. The events included prominent events related to construction, electromechanical products, information technology (IT) systems, health care organizations, regulatory agencies, and security failures. Construction failures included the recent collapse of the I-35W Mississippi River Bridge in Minnesota, the 2005 Hurricane Katrina in New Orleans, and the Chernobyl disaster. Electromechanical failures included Air France Flight 447 and Continental Connection Flight 3407 near Buffalo. Information technology failures included the Mariner I Space Probe, the National Cancer Institute, the Panama City miscalculation of radiation dosage, and similar incidents. Health care failures included the 2003 SARS outbreak in Asia and recent production problems with the H1N1 swine flu virus vaccine. Regulatory failures included the 2008 SEC regulatory issues, Fannie and Freddie failures, and health and safety issues such as food contamination. Security failures included the release of software viruses and ineffective profiling of suspected terrorists. The goal has been to demonstrate that failure prevention is feasible, ethical, and economically beneficial.

As a final story, two recent news articles had these ominous titles: "Plans Being Drawn Up to Let States Declare Bankruptcy" and "State Bankruptcy Bill Imminent, Gingrich Says."[17] My grandfather often said, "There is always someone trying to scare you into doing what they want you to do." He was discussing religion, but politicians try to scare people too. In the United States, states are sovereign entities that cannot go bankrupt. However, there are groups advocating this strategy as the best ways to balance state budgets. It is an interesting argument. If states are forced to honor the many obligations and debts incurred over the past several decades, the federal government will need to pay expenses.

Laws and regulations are created, in part, by societies to ensure high standards of conduct and to facilitate commercial activities. To the extent they do these things well, economies benefit to varying degrees. Laws and regulations are also sometimes created to favor one group over another. In extreme situations they unfairly make rich people poor and poor people rich. They can do much good or harm. To the extent they harm people, economic activities are adversely affected and everyone has less on a per capita basis. If people incur debt, they have options: reduce expenses, increase income, or do both. The logic behind this simple arithmetic is often lost on politicians who promise their constituents jobs, pensions, and other benefits, while maintaining or reducing taxes. Everyone knows these promises cannot be true, but people continue to believe in a fallacy. In ancient Rome, citizens gave their votes to wealthy politicians for bread, oil, wine, and circuses. In addition to circuses, Romans also enjoyed amphitheaters, theaters, public baths, and other forms of entertainment. Modern societies are not much different from Roman society. Populaces can become lazy when societies mature and grow rich. This is not an argument that increasing expenses or reducing taxes would be bad, but rather that doing both leads to financial collapse over time unless there are mitigating circumstances (e.g., lower taxes result in high employment resulting in high total tax income to compensate for expenses).

But can a state declare bankruptcy although it can raise income through taxes while it refuses to reduce expenditures? There have been several recent municipal bankruptcies based on Chapter 9 of the Federal Bankruptcy law.[18] An example is Orange County, California. But municipalities must volunteer for bankruptcy. Opinion is that state bankruptcies would also be legal if state sovereignty is not infringed, but Congress would need to ensure this. Current law enables municipalities to force bondholders to accept unfavorable terms of payment. It also enables them to renegotiate union contracts. Pensioners would also most likely lose. Taking a short-term approach will unfairly harm some groups and effective solutions will likely not be implemented. Behaviors would not change and root causes for the crises would also remain. Most likely there would be unexpected consequences using this expiate approach for controlling mounting debt. The fact is, the root causes have not been fully examined, additional complexity is being created, and the issue is politically charged.

States are able to tax their citizens in several ways to raise money to pay for expenses. But in the past several decades, as of July 2005, the financial burden on states was estimated as $1.85 trillion.[19] This is a large amount of money, but if placed in perspective, it is a small percentage of state gross domestic product, based on 2007 information, which estimates the percentages between 2 percent and 20 percent.[20] Only a few states have debt percentages exceeding 10 percent. These include Alaska, Connecticut, Maine, Massachusetts, Montana, New Hampshire, New Jersey, New York, Rhode Island, Virginia, and Vermont. Recall that states are sovereign entities and can tax their citizens. What is interesting is that a report of 2008 per capita tax collections by state shows little correlation between a state's debt as a percentage of gross product and per capita state and local taxes.[21] States could raise taxes, but some groups want an easy and quick solution.

California is held as poster child for a state government out of fiscal control. However, its debt of gross product is only 6.45 percent. It also ranked only 39th in per capita taxes at local and state levels. Several New England states are much worse financially, having higher debt-to-gross-product levels, that is, greater expenses and higher per capita taxes as shown in the top 10 states in per capita taxes. In a 2010 Reuters news article it was reported that California's debt was approximately $63.9 billion.[22] California's state tax revenues were approximately $400 billion in 2010. This is hardly a situation where bankruptcy is required. The real issue is that people, special interest groups, and politicians do not want to make difficult choices to reduce spending and increase taxes. This is a recurring theme for catastrophic events, a failure to consider facts and take necessary action. Instead, the proposed actions are likely to make a poor situation worse. Hysteria, political maneuvering, and shifting consequences for poor financial decisions to others who did the right things increase the likelihood for failure. Difficult and fair choices must be made. These are examples of major man-made crises that can be effectively solved, but not with old behaviors.

The Dreamliner 787 is designed to carry between 200 and 300 passengers and crew. Its nautical range is approximately 8,000 miles at airspeed of 560 miles per hour. But a recent news article reported it was three years behind schedule.[23] According to the article, experts think cost containment efforts partly delayed its scheduled commercial release. However, based on the information discussed in the past seven chapters, we know there are likely other reasons, that is, one or more recurrence factors.

Recall, in the first chapter, we discussed the Boeing 787 Dreamliner airplane, in the context of design and project management. It was originally promised to be commercially available in May 2008; but as of 2009 it was late and $2 billion over its development budget. This forced Boeing to write-off $2.5 billion. Issues occurred, in part, because of leading-edge technology and logistical complexity. As an example, major components and systems of the aircraft (engines, fuselage, and control systems) are manufactured in Japan, South Korea, several locations in the United States, France, Sweden, Italy, and possibly others, and transported for final assembly.

The airplane is 20 percent more fuel-efficient than comparable aircraft such as Boeing's 767. To reduce its weight, it relies on extensive use of composite materials. Composite materials have limitations. In fact, there were structural issues with the airplane's fuselage. Recently, there have also been electrical fires. According to the Federal Aviation Administration (FAA), another potential issue is that the aircraft's onboard flight control system may be vulnerable because it permits passengers to use the same computer system as the aircraft's on-board flight control systems, but with software safeguards.[24] Boeing disputes the accusation and intends to demonstrate to the FAA that its computer security is effective and adequately protects the aircraft's flight control systems. Although Boeing has been working on the issue, there are no independent verifications of an effective solution. It is easy to hack computers and software systems controlling electromechanically designed systems (e.g., Stuxnet worm). Some experts believe only if the flight control systems are completely isolated will the aircraft be safe. Unfortunately the project has demonstrated there are several risk recurrence factors operative.

The first recurrence factor is "organizational cultural issues which resulted in significant previous failures." A 2005 news article in *BusinessWeek* had the title, "Why Boeing's Culture Breeds Turmoil."[25] Up to 2005 Boeing had been involved in several scandals because of ethical lapses. These included bid rigging, illegal employment negotiations, and excessive late-night drinking by executives. There were also numerous internal rivalries between and within business units. The article also related a story where the CEO position was up for grabs by Mr. James McNerney, a former General Electric executive, and an insider, Mr. Alan R. Mulally. Mr. McNerney won the CEO positions and Mr. Mulally became the CEO of Ford Motor Company. But the relevant question is, "Has the Boeing culture improved?" A recent article in *Bloomberg* reported Boeing hired consultants to help reshape its culture because of the 787 delays.[26] However, experts know it takes many years to successfully change an organization's culture.

Other relevant recurrence risks include a lack of risk analysis and contingency planning, regulatory laxness, dangerous equipment, dangerous application environments, complex systems, people-dependency, cognition issues, significant potential financial loss or loss of life if failure occurs, the potential to impact many people across large geographical areas, politically sensitive fact-finding investigations, application technology ahead of control technology, dependency on complicated logistical systems and resources for failure mitigation, and poor root cause analysis and mitigation. The Dreamliner project has several of these risk recurrence factors. It is important, to all of us who fly, that Boeing reduce their number in the future.

People bring creativity, knowledge, and enthusiasm when designing products, services, and logistical systems. They also bring biases and personal prejudices that cause them to be fooled, with tragic consequences— cognitive research shows this is true. It may be difficult to accept the fact that our minds routinely distort facts, conveniently forget them, or modify them to fit with previous expectations and experiences, either consciously or subconsciously. Everyone is influenced. Informal and formal groups also have significant power of member's attitudes and behaviors for good or bad. Organizational culture and ethics also influence people, groups, and work teams. It is a rare person that can stand up to group pressure to conform to its beliefs and behaviors regardless if they are good or bad. It will become increasingly important to begin using this knowledge to prevent or mitigate the effects of future catastrophic events.

The decision to write this book was not difficult. I have wanted to learn how the things around us are designed and how they fail. The planned approach for writing was straightforward. However, I was sidetracked. I began to research cognitive factors and their relationship to human errors; it became obvious that many failures are not necessarily caused by technology. Design (functions and features incorporated into products and services) is certainly an important influence on failure. Social psychological influences are particularly relevant: cognition, individual, and group behaviors, as well as organizational culture and ethics. But by now you should understand that the occurrence and consequences from catastrophic events are not unexpected.

> Writing a book is an adventure. To begin with, it is a toy and an amusement; then it becomes a mistress, and then it becomes a master, and then a tyrant. The last phase is that just as you are about to be reconciled to your servitude, you kill the monster, and fling him out to the public.

—Winston Churchill

NOTES

1. Jared Diamond, *Guns, Germs and Steel: The Fates of Human Societies* (New York: Norton, 1997).

2. Jared Diamond, *Collapse: How Societies Choose to Fail or Succeed* (New York: Viking Press, 2005).

3. Bradford Plumer, "Is There Enough Food Out There For Nine Billion People?" *The New Republic,* February 3, 2010.

4. National Transportation Safety Board, *Aircraft Accident Report: Loss of Control and Impact with Pacific Ocean Alaska Airlines Flight 261, McDonnell Douglas MD-83, N963AS, January 31, 2000,* NTSB Number AAR-02/01, NTIS Number PB2002-910402, http://www.ntsb.gov/publictn/2002/AAR0201.htm.

5. Steve Urbon, "Barney Frank Barks at Obama Administration over Fishing," *Boston Herald,* January 13, 2011, http://news.bostonherald.com/news/politics/view/20110113barney_frank_barks_at_obama_administration_over_fishing.

6. *An Independent Lens,* "A Fish Story," Public Broadcasting Service, posted December 8, 2006, http://www.pbs.org/independentlens/fishstory/fishmanagement.html.

7. The World Bank, *Overview: Understanding, Measuring and Overcoming Poverty,* 2010, http://web.worldbank.org/WBSITE/EXTERNAL/TOPICS/EXTPOVERTY/0,,menuPK:336998~pagePK:149018~piPK:149093~theSitePK:336992,00.html.

8. United Nations Population Fund, *The State of World Population 2007: Unleashing the Potential for Urban Growth,* 2010, http://www.unfpa.org/swp/2007/english/introduction.html.

9. Min Lee, "Expert Warns of Complacency after Swine Flu Fizzle," Associated Press, September 5, 2010, http://www.msnbc.msn.com/id/39014647/ns/health.

10. "Oil Spill in the Gulf: One Year Later: Impact on the Gulf Shores," *USA Today,* October 2, 2010, http://www.usatoday.com/news/nation/story/environmental%20impacts%20of%20oil%20on%20the%20Gulf/38887184/1.

11. Julie Schmit, "U.S. Issues Deep-Water Oil Drilling Rules; Moratorium Stands," *USA Today,* October 2, 2010, http://www.usatoday.com/money/industries/energy/2010-10-01-oildrilling01_ST_N.htm?csp=34money&utm_source=feed

burner&utm_medium=feed&utm_campaign=Feed%3A+UsatodaycomMoney-TopStories+%28Money+-+Top+Stories%29.

12. Robert Barr, "BP's New CEO Bob Dudley Creates Unit to Enforce Safety Practices," Associated Press, September 29, 2010, http://www.usatoday.com/money/industries/energy/2010-09-29-bp-creates-safety-unit_N.htm?csp=34 money&utm_source=feedburner&utm_medium=feed&utm_campaign=Feed%3 A+UsatodaycomMoney-TopStories+%28Money+-+Top+Stories%29.

13. Dina Cappiello, "Mark Bly, BP Oil Spill Lead Investigator, Admits Limitations with Internal Probe," September 26, 2010, *Huffington Post,* http://www.huff ingtonpost.com/2010/09/27/mark-bly-bp-oil-spill-inv_n_740050.html.

14. Con Coughlin, "Stuxnet Virus Attack: Russia Warns of 'Iranian Chernobyl,'" *The Telegraph,* January 16, 2011, http://www.telegraph.co.uk/news/worldnews/eu rope/russia/8262853/Stuxnet-virus-attack-Russia-warns-of-Iranian-Chernobyl. html.

15. Yaakov Katz, "Israel Tests Stuxnet Virus at Dimona Reactor," *Jerusalem Post,* January 17, 2011, http://www.jpost.com/Defense/Article.aspx?id=203895.

16. Jay Bavisi and Joseph M. Grimm, "Biggest National Security Threat: Cyber Attack," *Fox Business News,* July 26, 2010, http://www.foxbusiness.com/personal-finance/2010/07/26/biggest-national-security-threat-cyber-attack.

17. Mary Williams Walsh, "Plans Being Drawn Up to Let States Declare Bankruptcy," *The New York Times,* on MSNBC.com, January 21, 2011, http://www.msnbc.msn.com/id/41188877; Lisa Lambert, "State Bankruptcy Bill Imminent, Gingrich Says," Reuters, January 21, 2011, http://www.reuters.com/article/idUSTRE70K6PI20110121.

18. David Skeel, "Give States a Way to Go Bankrupt: It's the Best Option for Avoiding a Massive Federal Bailout," *The Weekly Standard,* 16, no. 11 (November 29, 2010), http://www.weeklystandard.com/print/articles/give-states-way-go-bankrupt_518378.html?page=3.

19. Chris Edwards, "State and Local Government Debt Is Soaring," Cato Institute, June 8, 2006, http://www.cato.org/pubs/tbb/tbb_0706-37.pdf.

20. "State Debt Per Capita, Fiscal Year 2007," The Tax Foundation, February 19, 2009, http://www.taxfoundation.org/research/printer/268.html.

21. Gerald Prante, "State-Local Tax Burdens Dip as Income Growth Outpaces Tax Growth, New Jersey's Citizens Pay the Most, Alaska's Least," a table from the Tax Foundation's Special Report No.163, published in August 2008, http://www.taxfoundation.org/files/sr163.pdf.

22. Jim Christie and Peter Henderson, "California Debt Rating Cut as Cash Crunch Looms," January 13, 2010, http://www.reuters.com/article/idUSTRE60 C5Z620100114.

23. W. J. Hennigan, "Dreamliner Has Been a Nightmare for Boeing," *Los Angeles Times,* January 21, 2011, http://www.startribune.com/business/114399974.html ?elr=KArks:DCiU1OiP:DiiUiD3aPc:_Yyc:aULPQL7PQLanchO7DiU.

24. Kim Zetter, "FAA: Boeing's New 787 May Be Vulnerable to Hacker Attack," *Wired,* January 4, 2008, http://www.wired.com/politics/security/news/2008/01/dreamliner_security.

25. "Commentary: Why Boeing's Culture Breeds Turmoil: The Sacking of Stonecipher Won't Fix a Company Marked by Excess and Infighting," March 21, 2005, http://www.businessweek.com/magazine/content/05_12/b3925039_mz011. htm.

26. Susanna Ray, "Boeing Adviser Will Reshape Culture amid 787 Delays," *Bloomberg*, August 25, 2010, http://www.bloomberg.com/news/2010-08-25/boe ing-hires-adviser-to-reshape-seattle-culture-amid-787-dreamliner-delays.html.

GLOSSARY

Analytical hierarchy process (AHP)   A method that allows paired comparisons between alternatives.

As-is map   A graphical depiction of a process that is usually quantified and created by verifying how each operation in a process is performed.

Assessment   A methodology for evaluation process performance.

Attitudes   Expressions of approval or disapproval.

Autocratic   Making decisions and supervising performance of others.

Basic need   One of the three types of Kano needs. Customers expect basic needs to be met by all suppliers.

Bureaucratic   High interaction of leaders with employees with persuasion to do specific work tasks.

Capacity risk   Not having sufficient production resources to meet demand.

Cause and effect diagrams (C&E)   A graphical tool that shows qualitative relationships between causes (X's) and their effect (Y).

Cause and effect matrix (or C&E matrix)   A matrix used to prioritize several inputs (X's) for data collection across several outputs or Y's.

Chemical stress   A degradation of performance caused by chemicals.

Cognition effects   Attitudes, persuasion, social cognition, self-concept, and cognitive dissonance; social influence and group dynamics as well as interpersonal relationships and attraction.

Cognitive dissonance   Inconsistencies between personal actions and beliefs.

Collaborative   Delegation of decisions and work by leaders to others.

Computer-aided design (CAD)   A software system that allows models of a product to be created on a computer.

Computer-aided manufacturing (CAM)   A software system that uses CAD models of a product to manufacture the actual product using machines.

Concept phase The first phase of the Automotive Industry Action Group (AIAG) system, in which the product or service design is defined.

Concept review and approval Create cross-functional teams, define customer requirements, identify key design requirements and goals, preliminary process flow charts and basic sequence of production or construction, draft of quality assurance plan.

Concurrent engineering (CE) A project management system in which organizational functions work together to design products or services.

Confidential information leaking Knowingly making available confidential information to third parties not authorized to possess the information e.g. causing confusion by

Conflicts of interest Favoring suppliers, customers, or stakeholders to the detriment of the team and organization (e.g., receiving money or other benefits to influence attitudes or behavior).

Continuous improvement Process improvement activities that are deployed over an extended time.

Corrective maintenance A set of tools and methods that attempt to prevent unexpected equipment failures.

Cost risk Exceeding a project's budget.

Cultural change A situation in which an organization begins to practice one or more new behaviors.

Current controls The current tools, methods, and systems available to prevent the occurrence of a potential failure cause.

Customer value Cost, time, function, utility, and importance of a product or service as perceived by a customer.

Defect A nonconformance relative to a specific customer requirement.

Dependent variable The variable that is explained by one or more other variables that are independent.

Design failure modes and effects analysis (DFMEA) A risk analysis method showing relationships between failure types or modes, their effects, and causes, as well as likelihood ratings of each and current controls.

Design for manufacturing (DFM) A design methodology that uses several rules and techniques and attempts to simplify and modularize designs.

Design methods complexity reduction, technology application, mistake proofing, redundancy.

Design standards Information used to ensure designs meet minimum accepted standards related to fit, form, and function.

Detection likelihood The ability to know if a failure cause exists, measured between 1 and 10.

Disruptive behavior Verbal statements or behavior that cause deterioration in goodwill between customers and key stakeholders, and that reduces team cohesiveness.

Diverse team A group of people brought together to work a project and having diverse viewpoints, skills, or demographics.

Effectiveness A situation in which the right things are being done.

Error conditions A situation that may cause a mistake.

Excitement need One of the three types of Kano needs in which customers are delighted by a design characteristic.

Failure mode The type of failure.

Failure modes and effects analysis (FMEA) An analytical tool showing the relationship of failure modes to causes and evaluating their risk levels.

FDA Federal Drug Administration

5-Why analysis Methods for doing a simple root cause analysis.

Forming stage The first stage in a team maturation process.

Group dynamics Rules, norms, and relationships that people within a group use to influence each other and to differentiate themselves from other groups.

Groupthink A situation in which team members consistently agree with each other even if their decision is incorrect.

Interpersonal attraction Factors that influence the desire of people to associate.

Interpersonal relationships The ways in which people interact with each other, both positively and negatively.

Issue An event that is certain to occur and needs to be addressed by a team.

Judgmental forecasting A set of qualitative forecasting methods that rely on nonquantitative information to predict future events; telling customers or key stakeholders of team issues yet to be resolved prior to scheduled briefings, or telling suppliers sourcing information such as cost or competitive performance.

Kano A theory that describes customer satisfaction in terms of basic, performance, and excitement needs.

Legal risk New laws that, if enacted, may negatively impact a project.

Lying and false statements Knowingly presenting information that does not accurately reflect the truth about requirements, project status, testing results, and similar information.

Market demand risk Demand assumptions (e.g., sales and quantities) are not realized.

Market penetration A calculation of the potential number of buyers of a product or service.

Market segment Potential buyers of a product or service who have been stratified using stratification rules.

Matrix organization Sharing decision making and collaborating on work.

Mental models Individual perceptions of how the world works.

Misrepresenting intellectual rights Claiming ownership or special rights to trademarks, patents, or proprietary information that knowingly or unknowingly belongs to third parties.

Mistake proofing A set of concepts, tools, and methods designed to identify and eliminate error conditions or detect and eliminate mistakes and defects.

Mistakes Errors that result in a failure.

Norming stage The third stage of team maturation in which team members begin to agree on team objectives.

Occurrence likelihood The likelihood of a potential cause occurring measured between 1 and 10.

Performance need A Kano need that helps differentiate one supplier from another.

Performance risk Not achieving customer requirements relative to functions and features.

Performing stage The fourth stage in a team maturation process in which a team works toward common goals and objectives. Also: Competent team members efficiently execute work tasks without conflict. Differences of opinion are successfully facilitated and resolved in the team's mutual interest.

Persuasion Methods used to influence adoption of an attitude.

Physical creep A degradation of performance caused by a mechanical force that deforms a physical object over time.

Physical impact A degradation of performance caused by mechanical force.

Pilot and commercialization Trial runs of new design, initial capability analyses, measurement systems analysis, manufacturing control plan, and approval of quality plan.

Plan Do Check Act Deming cycle used for problem solving.

Potential causes The likely cause(s) for a failure mode.

Potential failure effect The type of effect of a failure mode on a customer.

Preventive maintenance A system of tools, methods, and concepts designed to ensure systems are available for use.

Problem statement A verbal description of the operational problem that must be solved by the project.

Process batch A system that transfers materials or information to subsequent operations when all units have been processed.

Process capability A method used to compare process performance against customer specifications.

Process design Packaging standards, product/ process quality systems review, process flow chart, floor plan layout, process failure mode and effects analysis (PFMEA), prelaunch control plan, process instructions, measurements systems analysis, preliminary process capability study plan, packaging specifications.

Process failure mode and effects analysis (PFMEA) A method that analyzes how a process can fail to correctly build a product or provide a service.

Process mapping A method used to show the movement of materials and information through the system.

Product group A collection of products having similar characteristics.

Productivity A year-over-year measure of outputs divided by inputs and usually expressed in financial terms.

Product life cycle The demand phases a product goes through over time including its introduction, growth, maturity, and decline.

Project charter A document in either electronic or paper format that provides justification for the project.

Project evaluation and review technique (PERT) A project probabilistic scheduling methodology used to find a network's critical path.

Project identification A process of identifying projects to increase organizational productivity or stakeholder satisfaction.

Project management A set of tools and techniques used to manage project deployment.

Project metric An operational metric that is used to measure project success and correlates to financial and business metrics.

Project milestone A major set of project activities that is used to monitor project schedule completion.

Project objective A section of the project charter that states the specific business benefit of the project.

Project plan A combination of work tasks, budgets, schedules, and resources brought together to complete a project.

Project planning The process of scheduling the various work tasks and elements necessary to complete the project.

Project resources Materials, labor, money, and information necessary to complete the project.

Project selection The process of identifying work to benefit the business and customer according to strategic goals and objectives.

Pugh matrix A tool that enables several alternatives to be compared against a baseline scenario.

Radiation stress A degradation of performance caused by radiation.

Red flag conditions Conditions signaling failure ahead, including complexity, poor design, inability to measure performance, poor documentation and procedures, tools, and methods, little training, poor environmental conditions, stressful working conditions between people and groups, and utilizing capacity beyond stable level.

Regulatory risk Current laws or regulations that may negatively impact a project.

Response variable The dependent variable, which is also called a key

Risk Probability of occurrence

Risk prioritization number (RPN) The multiplicand of the severity, occurrence, and detections ratings measured between 1 and 1,000.

Scheduling risk Not achieving a project's schedule.

Self-concept Comparisons to others or standards that contribute to self-esteem.

Severity The magnitude of a failure mode's effect on an external customer, measured between 1 and 10.

Should-be map A graphical depiction of a process with non–value-adding operations removed.

SIPOC Acronym for supplier, input boundary, process, output boundary. and customer. Also, a high-level map showing suppliers, inputs, the process, outputs, and the customer.

Social cognition Perception formation of others or patterns including filtering of environmental stimuli.

Social influence Influence of group size, beliefs, and status on individual behavior.

Standard operating procedures (SOPs) Procedures that are determined to be the best way to do a job.

Statistical risk Stating the null hypothesis is false when it is true (type I error) or stating it is true when false (type II error).

Stealing property Taking intellectual or other property that belongs to a third party, illegally or without the owner's permission (e.g., taking trade secrets or other proprietary and confidential information from customers or suppliers).

Storming stage The second stage of the team maturation process, in which a team disagrees on a project's goals and objectives. During this stage, competition is present between team members for power and influence. Interpersonal conflicts may occur.

Supply risk Unable to receive needed materials, labor, information, or other resources for a project.

SWOT analysis Strengths, weaknesses, opportunities, and threats.

Target costing Determining the price at which a product or service will sell and subtracting out the desired profit margin.

Technology risk Being unable to use a new technology.

Testing and evaluation Procedures for reliable design: laboratory and field testing of prototypes, reliability testing and modeling, tolerance design, design capability analysis, updated design FMEA.

Thermal stress A degradation of performance caused by heat.

Threatening others Engaging in abusive verbal or physical behavior to control another person's statements or behavior (e.g., threatening loss of employment, group status, or physical and emotional safety).

Tolerating incompetence Allowing other team members to make repeated mistakes of judgment or action because of a lack of experience, education, or interest (e.g., tolerating ineffective team leaders, inexperienced designers, or poor sourcing strategies).

Universal principles for design Methods contained within general topics of cognition, best-in-class design methods, learning theory, and organizational structure and culture.

Value-adding operations (VA) Operations that a customer desires in a product or service.

Value elements These consist of time, price, utility, function, and relative importance to a customer.

Value stream mapping (VSM) A process of mapping material and information flows through a process.

Vibration stress A degradation of performance caused by vibration.

Violations of law Allowing others to make statements, provide information, or behave in ways that subvert team or organizational strategic and tactical goals.

Voice of customer (VOC) Customer needs and values translated into requirements.

Voice of the business (VOB) Financial and operational goals; an objective that must be considered in process improvements.

Voice of the process (VOP) Characteristic-by-characteristic central location and dispersion (variation) measured within a process.

INDEX

ABOUT THE AUTHOR

JAMES WILLIAM MARTIN is a management consultant and the author of several books focused on product and process design. He has coached thousands of people across Japan, China, Korea, Singapore, Malaysia, Thailand, Australia, and North America to use fact-based methods to improve their products and services. As a management consultant and teacher for more than 20 years, he also served as an instructor at the Providence College Graduate School of Business, where he instructed courses in decision analysis and related courses, and counseled graduate students from government organizations and leading corporations in the greater Boston/Providence area. His interests include environmentally friendly design as well as personal and organizational ethics, productivity, and change management. He was also formally in charge of materials development, testing, and failure analysis at Honeywell's Automotive Aftermarket Division, where he managed laboratories for materials engineering and coordinated research and testing with outside universities and laboratories. He holds a master of science in mechanical engineering, Northeastern University; master of business administration, Providence College; and bachelor of science degrees in industrial engineering and biology from the University of Rhode Island.